THE
PHILOSOPHER

THE PHILOSOPHER

A HISTORY IN SIX TYPES

JUSTIN E. H. SMITH

PRINCETON UNIVERSITY PRESS
PRINCETON AND OXFORD

press.princeton.edu

Jacket art, from the top: **Fig. 1:** Margaret Lucas Cavendish, Duchess of
Newcastle. Print Collection, Miriam and Ira D. Wallach Division of Art,
Prints, and Photographs. The New York Public Library. Astor, Lenox, and
Tilden Foundations, **Fig. 2.** Buddha Sakyamuni, courtesy of Carlton
Rochell, **Fig. 3.** *The Death of Socrates*, 1787, oil on canvas, by Jacques-Louis
David, **Fig. 4.** Baruch de Spinoza, oil painting, c. 1665; in the Herzog-
August Bibliothek, Wolfenbuttel, **Fig. 5.** *Portrait of a Chinese Mandarin*, oil
on canvas, c. 1825–1852, by George Chinnery. Bequeathed by Claude D.
Rotch, **Fig. 6.** *The Money Changer and his Wife*, 1539, oil on panel, by
Marinus van Reymerswaele, Museo del Prado, Madrid

Library of Congress Cataloging-in-Publication Data

Names: Smith, Justin E. H.
Title: The philosopher : a history in six types / Justin E. H. Smith.
Description: Princeton, NJ : Princeton University Press, 2016. |
Includes bibliographical references and index.
Identifiers: LCCN 2015034074 |
ISBN 978-0-691-16327-7 (hardcover : alk. paper)
Subjects: LCSH: Philosophy. | Philosophers.
Classification: LCC BD21 .S57 2016 | DDC 100—dc23
LC record available at http://lccn.loc.gov/2015034074

British Library Cataloging-in-Publication Data is available

This book has been composed in Linux Libertine O

Printed on acid-free paper. ∞

Printed in the United States of America

10 9 8 7 6 5 4 3 2 1

This book is dedicated to the memory of
BUD KORG (1938–2015)

Now he who wonders and is perplexed feels that he is ignorant (thus the myth-lover is in a sense a philosopher, since myths are composed of wonders).

—ARISTOTLE, *Metaphysics*, BOOK I

Let the fish philosophise the ice away from the Rivers in winter time.

—JOHN KEATS, *Letters* (1819)

… these unwholsome vapours, that distempered the Aer, to the very raising of Storms and tempests; upon which a Philosopher might amply discourse.

—JOHN EVELYN,
Fumifugium; or, the Inconveniencie of the Aer and Smoak of London Dissipated (1661)

CONTENTS

ACKNOWLEDGMENTS

Undoubtedly the greatest portion of gratitude must go to my editor at Princeton University Press, Rob Tempio, who has had the vision to first recommend this project to me. In matching me with this task, and this new way of engaging with philosophy, he saw more clearly than I an inclination that existed only *in potentia*, and its coming to actuality is entirely the result of his willingness to cultivate it. Throughout the process he has given expert and nuanced advice on the form the book should take, making intuitive suggestions that consistently show the mind of a real lover of books at work. I have also received invaluable intellectual guidance and input throughout the writing process from Stephen Menn, as well as from D. Graham Burnett, James Delbourgo, Jonardon Ganeri, Aaron Garrett, Patrick Lee Miller, Steve Nadler, Dalia Nassar, Anne-Lise Rey, Adina Ruiu, Lisa Shapiro, John Sutton, Anand Vaidya, Stéphane Van Damme, and Charles T. Wolfe. I have been fortunate to have early drafts of the manuscript, or portions thereof, read and commented on by Jerry Dworkin, Zoli Filotas, and Susanna Forrest. I have moreover benefited greatly from the opportunity to present portions of this work in venues at which I was able to receive feedback from such sharp minds as Ray Brassier, Karine Chemla, Tsuyoshi Matsuda, and

Paul Yachnin, in Beirut, Cambridge, Kyoto, Paris, Sydney, and many other places besides. I am surely forgetting many other people, who will likely find my cryptomnesia at work in the following pages; the secret signs of their influence, I hope, can count in their own way as acknowledgments.

THE
PHILOSOPHER

INTRODUCTION

This book, an essay in the proper Montaignean sense, seeks to answer that most fundamental of philosophical questions: What is philosophy? It does so, however, in an unusual way: by refraining from proclamations about what philosophy, ideally, ought to be, and by asking instead what philosophy has been, what it is that people have been doing under the banner of philosophy in different times and places. In what follows we will survey the history of the various self-conceptions of philosophers in different historical eras and contexts. We will seek to uncover the different "job descriptions" attached to the social role of the philosopher in different times and places. Through historical case studies, autobiographical interjections, and parafictional excursuses, it will be our aim to enrich the current understanding of what the project of philosophy is, or could be, by uncovering and critically examining lost, forgotten, or undervalued conceptions of the project from philosophy's distinguished past.

This approach could easily seem not just unusual but also misguided, since philosophy is generally conceived as an a priori discipline concerned with conceptual analysis rather than with the collection of particular facts about past practice. As a result of this widespread conception, most commonly, when philosophers set about answering the question as to the nature of their discipline, they end up generating answers that reflect the values and preoccupations of their local philosophical culture. Thus Gilles Deleuze and Félix Guattari answer the question, in their 1991 book *What Is Philosophy?*,[1] by arguing that it is the activity of conceptual innovation, the generating of new concepts, and thus of new ways of looking at the world. But this is a conception of philosophy that would be utterly unfamiliar to, say, Ludwig Wittgenstein, who suggested that philosophy is the practice of "shewing the fly the way out of the bottle,"[2] or, alternatively, that it is "a battle against the bewitchment of our intelligence by means of language,"[3] and it would be more unfamiliar still to the natural philosopher of the seventeenth century, who studied meteorological phenomena in order to discern the regularities at work in the world around us, and had no particular interest in devising new concepts for discerning these regularities. Thus when Deleuze and Guattari argue that philosophy is the activity of concept coining, they should really be saying that this is what they would like philosophy to be.

Philosophy has in fact been many things in the 2,500 years or so since the term was first used, and here we will be interested in charting its transformations. We will be equally interested in exploring the question whether the activity of philosophy is coextensive with the term, that is, whether it is *only* those activities that have been explicitly carried out under the banner of *philosophia* that are to be considered philosophy, or whether there are also analogical practices in cultures that have evolved independently of the culture of ancient Greece that can also be called by the name "philosophy." I will be arguing that they can and should be, but even if we restrict our understanding of philosophy to those cultural traditions that bear some historical and genealogical relationship to the practice in ancient Greece that was first called by this name, we still discover a great variety of divergent conceptions of what the activity in question is. Let us, in any case, in what follows, use the term "Philosophia," with a capital "P," when we wish to explicitly mark out the genealogical connection between authors, arguments, and texts throughout the broader Greek, Roman, Islamic, and Christian world, while using "philosophy" to designate cultural practices, wherever they may occur, that bear some plausible affinity to those cultural practices that fall under the heading of "Philosophia," which, again, signals a particular historical tradition and thus, strictly speaking, a proper noun.

The sociologist Randall Collins, author of an extensive and very wide-scoped study of the development of schools of philosophy throughout history and at a global scale, identifies as philosophers those people, anywhere in the world, who treat "problems of the reality of the world, of universals, of other minds, of meaning."[4] Collins does not discern any particular difficulty in picking out clear-cut examples of philosophical schools in different regions and centuries, and the problems he lists are not of particular or sustained interest to him as a sociologist. Yet there have been many self-identified philosophers who have not been interested in the problems in this list and have instead been interested in other, very different problems (for example, explaining "unwholesome vapours"). There are, moreover, many thinkers who have been interested in these problems but who have not belonged to the sort of schools of interest to Collins; they have had the right interests, but have lacked the sociological embedding to be able to come forward, socially, as philosophers.

Typically, where there is such a sociological context, philosophers have expended considerable effort to identify those activities or projects that philosophy is *not*. Some of these are mutually exclusive in relation to at least some others. Philosophy, to begin with a classic distinction, is not sophistry. This contrast in turn breaks down into two further defining features of the activity. First of all, philosophy is concerned with finding the truth, whatever the truth may be, unlike sophistry, which is concerned, to use the well-known phrase, with "making the weaker argument the stronger." Second, philosophy is practiced by people who are not interested in worldly gain. Philosophers do not accept money in exchange for their truth-revealing arguments, while it is principally for the sake of money that Sophists engage in argumentation. Philosophy moreover is the activity that deploys the laws of logic, or the rules of proper reasoning, in order to provide true accounts of reality. Here philosophy contrasts with traditions that we today think of as "religion" and "myth," to the extent that these tend not to take inexpressibility or logical contradictoriness as weaknesses in attempted accounts of reality. On the contrary, it is often argued that logical contradiction, expressed in the form of "mysteries," plays an important role in the success and durability of religions. Christianity, for example, endures not *in spite of* its inability to answer the question of how exactly three persons can be one and the same person, but rather *because of* the impossibility of answering this question. Philosophy has seldom been able to rely on mystery in the same way, even though it has often been called in to support mysterian traditions using tools that are largely external to these traditions.

Philosophy, to continue, is often held to be the activity that is concerned with universal truths, to be discovered by a priori reflection, rather than with particular truths, which are to be discovered by empirical means. One way of putting this point is in terms of a contrast with an archaic sense of history, where this latter practice has both civic and natural subdomains, both of which are concerned with *res singulares*, or particular things. This sense of history also contrasts with poetry: Aristotle distinguishes in the *Poetics* between history and poetry on the grounds that the former tells only about actuality, while the latter is concerned with all possibilities, whether they in fact happen, or fail to happen. He writes that "it is not the function of the poet to relate what has happened, but what may happen: what is possible according to the law of probability or necessity." For Aristotle, philosophy is not concerned with particular things as intrinsically of interest, and therefore sees poetry and philosophy as more like each other than either of these is like history. "The poet and the historian," he explains,

> differ not by writing in verse or in prose. The work of Herodotus might be put into verse, and it would still be a species of history, with meter no less than without it. The true difference is that one relates what has happened, the other what may happen. Poetry, therefore, is a more philosophical and a higher thing than history: for poetry tends to express the universal, history the particular.[5]

The scope of poetry is wider than that of history, but poetry is also often contrasted with philosophy to the extent that the poets see no need to speak of the possibilities over which their thought ranges. Thus philosophy is like poetry and unlike history, on this old distinction, to the extent that it ranges beyond the actual, while it is like history and unlike poetry to the extent that its claims must not violate any appropriate rules of inference. As we will see, however, this division of the various endeavors that goes back to Aristotle, while a common one, is by no means universally accepted: from Heraclitus to Francis Bacon, G. W. Leibniz, and many others, the focus on the actual, and indeed on the particular, has been seen as a crucial component of the philosophical project.

Where, now, is "science" in these distinctions? What we mean by "science" is generally closest to what was formerly called "natural history": the methodical collection of particular facts in order to gain further knowledge about the actual world. There is also "natural philosophy," which was long understood as the speculative project that parallels the natural-historical project of collection of particular facts. Seen as the joint endeavor of natural history and natural philosophy, science was long constitutive of philosophy, and the circumstances and consequences of its separation are among the questions to which we will be returning frequently here.

Philosophy, then, is not history, myth, poetry, religious mystery, or sophistical argumentation, and it is not, any longer, science. It is an intellectual activity that bumps up against these other intellectual activities, perhaps overlapping with them, or coming to their aid, while also remaining quite distinct from them. Or so we often think.

In truth the activity of philosophy is often more muddled. To invoke a geological metaphor, philosophy generally only occurs in ores, and the process of extracting it to obtain it in its pure form is generally very costly, and often damaging to the sought-after element. As a reflection of its muddled character, in its earliest usages "philosophy" is generally deployed pejoratively, to describe an activity of people who are confused, who fail to understand the precise nature of their undertaking. This is particularly clear when we turn from "philosophy" to the agentive form of that noun, to the person who enacts or participates in or does philosophy: the philosopher.

Interestingly, while "philosophy" is only sometimes pejorative, variations on this word almost always are. From its first appearances in English in the late sixteenth century, the verb "to philosophize" has been almost without exception used to describe a pompous, posturing, or spurious sort of reasoning and has often been contrasted with true love of wisdom. Thus, for example, Henry More writes in the *Antidote against Atheism* of 1662, "My intent is not to Philosophize concerning the nature of Spirits, but onely to prove their Existence."[6] This declaration is somewhat analogous to the bumper sticker sometimes found in the United States declaring: "I'm not religious, I just love the Lord!" That is, the speaker is conscious of the negative connotations surrounding the *type* of person associated with the activity in which he or she is engaged, and so insists that he or she is *only* doing the activity, without belonging to the type. The verb "to philosophize" is also often used to describe a sort of pointless and ineffectual expenditure of intellectual energy that changes nothing in the world; thus Keats's imploring of the fish to do what he knows they cannot do, to philosophize away the ice on the rivers in wintertime.[7] In recent decades Anglo-American philosophers have adopted the phrase "to do philosophy." It is common now to take philosophy as a clearly defined activity, as something that one "does" in the same way that one might do physical exercise. We also see a retrojection of this locution back into the distant past, as a translation of the Greek verb *philosophein*. To find Aristotle speaking of "philosophizing" sounds archaic and somewhat degraded, while to find him reflecting on what it means "to do philosophy" seems up to date and respectable.[8] Interestingly, the apparent disappearance of negative connotations to the agentive form of "philosophy," "philosopher," seems to parallel the shift in the verbal form from "to philosophize" to "to do philosophy."

Evidently, the shift in both the verb and the agentive noun has much to do with the professionalization of philosophy, with the transformation of philosophy from something with which one might engage—whether pompously or humbly, fraudulently or honestly—as part of a way of life, to something that one is enabled to do only with the appropriate accreditation within a particular institutional setting. While professional philosophers in the developed world today might not wish to acknowledge that when they speak of "doing philosophy" they are speaking of a particular professional activity akin to practicing law or doing hospital rounds as a physician, it is unlikely that many of them would admit that philosophy is something that can be "done" in Tibetan monasteries or the winter encampments of the Inuit. Although the word is avoided, most professional philosophers today probably suspect that what Inuit are doing as they pass the long dark hours of winter speculating on the nature of time or the origin of the world is something closer to "philosophizing," in the somewhat degraded sense of needless or fanciful intellectual expenditure.

On both sides of the shift we've identified, from questionable philosophizing to professional doing of philosophy, the term "philosophy" has generally been free of negative associations, standing, like some transcendent idea, above the shabby efforts of would-be philosophers to realize it in their own thought and work: somewhat in the same way "poetry" stands to both "poet" and "poem." Philosophy and the self-identified philosophers who aspire to "do" it have a very different relation between them than, say, that between medicine and the physician, where the relationship appears to be something of reciprocal ennoblement. Medicine is a noble art because of the work of its practitioners, and physicians are noble because medicine is in its nature a high calling. In contrast, self-proclaimed philosophers must always be ready to defend against the accusation that they are not living up to the calling of philosophy, and are therefore philosophers only in name. In other words, philosophy is not necessarily present wherever there are self-described philosophers. Thus Thomas Hobbes writes of the ancient Greeks in the *De corpore* of 1655:

> But what? were there no philosophers natural nor civil among the ancient Greeks? There were men so called; witness Lucian, by whom they are derided; witness divers cities, from which they have been often by public edicts banished. But it follows not that there was philosophy.[9]

These days, though you might get hit with a lawsuit for telling someone with a professional degree in philosophy that he is "not a philosopher,"[10] as Hobbes reminds us the simple presence of philosophers is not enough to guarantee the presence of philosophy.

The present history cannot be written in a conventional chronological order, since straightforward chronology, from past to present, from them to us, inevitably implies some sort of commitment to the march of progress, whereas part of our purpose here is to show that philosophy's motion throughout history from one self-conception to the next has been at best a sort of random stumbling, and at worst a retreat from an earlier more capacious understanding of the endeavor. What therefore must be avoided is the sort of historiography in which past thought is construed as preliminary or propaedeutic to what would eventually emerge as mature philosophy. This approach is sometimes disparaged as "the royal road to me," and it characterizes many of the most influential general surveys of the history of philosophy, notably Bertrand Russell's famous *History of Western Philosophy* of 1945.[11] The idea of progress in historical processes has come under severe criticism by historians over the past several decades. Historical narratives that presume a gradual advance through stages, from a rudimentary or primitive stage in a process to a more advanced and perfected one, and that identify the agents of change as a select number of great people, mostly men, have been deemed methodologically "Whiggish," and have largely been replaced by historical narratives that emphasize the limits of individual human agency and the adaptive sense of change within any given process. That is, change now tends to be conceived not teleologically, as change for the better, but simply as change that makes sense within a given context and a given local rationality. Thus, for example, the Industrial Revolution is not the result of the inventiveness and determination of a few clever European men but rather a gradual process of adaptation to new economic exigencies by players who could never have seen anything close to the full picture and that involved the incorporation of new technologies that had mostly been developed outside the European sphere. Similarly with military history: out with the brave and clever generals, in with an analysis of geographical and demographic advantages that favor one side, for a time, without ever ensuring the inexorable and unending ascendancy of one particular group over the others, as the star and the focus of history.

Significantly, Whiggish teleology has been largely left behind in the study of technology and science—fields where one *could* plausibly make a case that there is such a thing as real progress, and therefore that the history of the domain is, appropriately and accurately, a history of progress or ascendancy. Machines just keep getting better and faster, which is what technologists want them to be doing. How then could the history of technology not reflect this happy collusion between human will and reality? We can set this complicated question aside for now in order to turn to a related question that is more central to our present interests. Most philosophers, whether they wish to hold on to some idea of philosophical progress or not, will agree that philosophical progress is not exactly like technological progress. Philosophical arguments do not get "faster" or "more powerful" in the way that machines do. What is more, there is often thought to be an "eternal" dimension to the activity of philosophy, which renders progress impossible to the extent that past representatives of the tradition are conceptualized as our contemporaries, engaged with us in an "eternal conversation" that unites the living and the dead in a single activity, in which we are all potentially equal regardless of the century in which we are born. Almost no one would wish to say that Aristotle had all the resources available to him to be as advanced in physics as Einstein was, while very many people would, by contrast, be prepared to argue that Aristotle was as advanced in his contributions to, say, moral philosophy, as has been anyone who came after him.

It is not hard to see how conceptualizing philosophy as an eternal conversation with its past representatives could, though superficially transhistorical and even atemporal, nonetheless support a teleological or progress-based conception of the history of philosophy. In taking the dead as our contemporaries, who are in no position to speak any more for themselves or to demand clarification or precision in our representation of their views, inevitably past philosophers get construed in our own image. But how can this be permitted to happen, when other disciplines with historical components, not least history itself, have become so sensitive in recent decades to the need for rigorous methodological reflection on historiography? The answer could well have to do with a simple lack of interest in the question of historical methodology *as* a philosophical question. That is, while philosophers, or at least the majority of philosophers in the English-speaking world, might be interested in the metaphysical problem of how we can know the past, they do not seem to be particularly interested in the problem of how we can know the past of philosophy itself, of how we can know that our characterizations of the aims and arguments of past philosophers are the correct ones. They are not interested in thinking about the way in which we deploy standards of evidence when considering textual sources, or secondary testimony, or other such philological matters. To take an interest in these questions would be to acknowledge that philosophy *has* a philological component, and therefore cannot be, simply, an unmediated, eternal conversation. And so, often, in the general refusal to consider the discipline as in part a philological endeavor, past figures come to be treated as mascots for positions that are deemed important today, whether these positions played an important part in the self-conception of the past philosopher or in the community in which he or she thrived. We tell stories about the past, and call it "history."

"History" and "story" have the same etymology, indeed are the very same word in many languages, and there are some who argue forcefully that storytelling is the most we can ever do in our efforts to reconstruct the past; after all, even if all the things we report about the past are factually true, they are still selected by us, and are favored over infinitely many equally true facts that did not make the cut. Ironically, then, while the Whiggish historian who tells us how *a* led to *b* led to *c* led to *me* is probably going to insist on her loyalty to the truth, she is telling stories like the rest of us; she is making history turn out a certain way by selecting a series of facts deemed salient enough to constitute history.

And yet there may be a way, even in acknowledging these difficult issues, to do it better, to give a more adequate account of the past, not because it gets more of the facts from the past right, but because it picks out and strings together those facts from the past that, together, cause us to believe that we now understand more clearly what some historical process has really been about. This belief need not be definitive, nor need it last forever. A compelling account of the past is not like a scientific discovery.

A story needs characters, and in the history of philosophy we observe the recurrence, in a number of different times and places, of a few basic types of thinker, all of whom have been held to be "philosophers," notwithstanding the great differences between them.

There is, to begin, the Curiosus, the great forgotten model of the philosophical life. A principal concern of this book is to solve the mystery of his disappearance. He is the philosopher who expatiates on storms and tempests, on magnetic variation, on the fine-grained details of the wings of a flea. The Curiosus is often a Curiosa: many of the adepts of early modern experimental philosophy were women.

Curiosae and Curiosi believe that there is nothing shameful about knowledge of *res singulares*: singular things. These too can reveal the order of nature as a whole, and it is eminently the task of the philosopher, on their view, to discover this order. The paradigm statement of this approach to philosophy may well be found in Aristotle's defense of the worthiness of marine biology against unnamed critics: looking into the viscera of some sea cucumber or cephalopod, he proclaims, citing Heraclitus, who was caught by distinguished visitors lounging naked on a stove: "Here too dwell gods." This dictum was invoked in Aristotle's explicit defense of the philosophical value of the study of zoology. The Curiosus, a familiar figure of the seventeenth century, just prior to the emergence of the figure of the scientist, seems to have been the last of the philosophers to see the gods, so to speak, in the particular things of nature.

Second, there is the Sage. This is likely the oldest social role of the philosopher and predates by dozens of millennia the first occurrence of the word *philosophos*. The label here is to be understood in a broad sense, to include any socially revered figure who is held forth as a mediator between the immanent and transcendent realms, who is held to be able to speak for the gods or interpret what is going on beyond the realm of human experience. It includes, for example, the Brahminic commentators on the sacred scriptures of India, who have provided us with the textual basis of classical Indian philosophy. This social role is also surely continuous with that of shamans and like figures in nontextual cultures, even if it only starts to look to us like a philosophical or quasi-philosophical endeavor at the point in history when the mediating role of the priests is laid down in texts that display some concern for conceptual clarity and valid inference. It is a role occupied by women and men alike, even if women in this role have often been deprived of institutional or broad social recognition. Tellingly, the French term for a midwife, a role long held to involve wisdom relating to the human body and its place in nature, is *sage-femme*: a "wise woman" or "woman sage."

Third, there is the Gadfly, who understands the social role of the philosopher not as mediating between the social and the divine, nor as renouncing the social, but rather as correcting, to the extent possible, the myopic views and misunderstandings of the members of his own society, to the extent possible. Socrates is a special case of the Gadfly, since he does not have a positive program to replace the various ill-conceived beliefs and plans of his contemporaries, in contrast with the various social critics or *philosophes engagés* who follow in this venerable and still vital vein.

Fourth, there is the Ascetic, who appears in what Karl Jaspers helpfully calls "the Axial Age,"[12] the age in which Buddhism and Christianity come onto the world stage, both positioning themselves as explicit rejections of the authority of the priests in their ornate temples. Cynics, Jainists (known to the Greeks as "gymnosophists" or "nude Sophists"), early Christians, and other world renouncers provide a template for a conception of philosophy as first and foremost a conformation of the way one lives variously to nature, or to divine law, or to something beyond the illusory authority of society, the state, or the temple. The Ascetic continues to be a familiar figure in philosophy throughout the Middle Ages, though now mostly confined within the walls of the monastery, and still has late echoes in secular modernity in figures such as Friedrich Nietzsche. Nietzsche is generally seen as a peculiar individual, but this may have something to do with the fact that there was by the late nineteenth century no longer an obvious social role for him to play. Asceticism as a style of philosophy had gone out of fashion.

Fifth, there is the Mandarin. This is a pejorative term, though unlike "Courtier" (as we will soon see) it describes an entire class of people rather than exceptional individuals who may emerge from that class. The term comes from the examination system that produced the elite class of bureaucrats in Imperial China, and may be easily extended to the modern French system that produces *normaliens*, and also with only a bit more stretching to the system of elite education in the Anglo-American sphere out of which the great majority of successful careers in philosophy take shape. Mandarins have a vested interest in maintaining what Thomas Kuhn called "normal science" and are typically jealous guardians of disciplinary boundaries, wherever these happen to be found in the era of their own professional activity. Like Courtiers, Mandarins often have wealthy benefactors (now corporate rather than royal), and they stay close to centers of power (top schools in philosophy today tend to be found within a short drive or train ride from the world's major metropolitan concentrations of capital). But unlike Courtiers, they are able to pursue their careers more or less as if money were not an issue, and indeed are the ones quickest to denounce the Courtiers for their unseemly conduct. It is the Mandarins whose fate is most uncertain in the postuniversity landscape into which we may now be entering.

A well-known and much despised social role for the philosopher, the sixth and final type, is the Courtier. A recent popular book set up Baruch Spinoza as the noble Ascetic against the unscrupulous Leibniz, who was ready to sell his philosophical services to whichever European sovereign was willing to pay the highest salary.[13] We were meant to understand, from this narrative opposition between their two social roles, that Spinoza was *eo ipso* the better philosopher. It is as if we believe that one cannot be simultaneously ambitious and wise, simultaneously a worldly striver and a deep thinker. It is with the Courtier, too, for the first time in our list, that money makes its explicit appearance (though it was surely there in some of the temples of the priestly Sages as well). The more recent incarnation of the Courtier is the "sell-out," or, to put it in somewhat more euphemistic terms, the "public intellectual," who unlike the Gadfly is out there in society, not in order to change it, but in order to advance himself and his own glory. (The gendered pronoun here is intentional, and for the most part accurate.) But there is a problem in determining who fits this description and who does not; all philosophers need support, and few have the fortitude to retreat into pure asceticism. Those who get cast as Courtiers seem to be the ones who take earthly wealth and glory as the end in itself, rather than at most as a by-product of their pure love of wisdom. Or at least they are the ones who do a particularly bad job of concealing the fact that it is wealth and glory they are after. Whether, however, these desiderata are strictly incompatible with profound thought is an important question. Leibniz would seem to provide a counterexample to the claim that they are incompatible, but an interesting question remains, and indeed a question whose answer could tell us much about the nature of the philosophical project, as to why "Courtier" continues to function as such a potent ad hominem against the integrity of a philosopher.

This list, unlike Kant's list of the categories of the understanding, is not exhaustive, and it is not obtained by rigorous deduction. It could be amended and revised without end. One might also add the Charlatan, for example, the self-help guru who promises to explain everything you need to know. But what we will find is that our six types, and various hybrids between them, give us enough to make sense of the life work and the social impact of more or less everyone who has been called a "philosopher" over the past few millennia.

Six chapters follow, and each chapter will be visited by at least one of the six types just listed, speaking in his or her own voice. Each chapter will to a greater or lesser degree circle around some of the philosophical problems of interest to a representative of a given type. But each chapter will do more than that, too; each will, namely, seek to elucidate a particular opposition that has been brought into service by philosophers seeking to define what is and what is not philosophy. The position of the featured philosophical type with respect to the opposition explored in any given chapter will not always be perfectly transparent, and where this is the case the reader is invited to make the implicit connections on his or her own.

In chapter one we will focus in particular on the idea that philosophy is principally an endeavor that deals with universal truths as opposed to particular facts, and we will see significant evidence that such a conception of philosophy occludes from view a large portion of what people have been doing under the banner of philosophy for the past few millennia. Chapter one's plaidoyer for the philosophical importance of singular things will return again and again throughout the book, and may be seen as a leitmotif, even as we move on to focus on other oppositions. In chapter two we will focus on the conceit that "philosophy" is a sort of proper noun, describing a particular tradition that descends from Greek antiquity, and we will contrast this idea with its opposites, which hold, variously, that philosophy is something that is practiced by specialists throughout the world in vastly different cultures, or even that philosophy is something that is entirely interwoven with culture and so is something in which all people participate qua culture-bound beings. In chapter three we will turn to questions of genre: the distinction between personalistic first-person writing and objective, treatise-like, third-person writing most of all, but also the distinction between literature and poetry on the one hand and philosophy-writing as a genre on the other. We will look at the ways in which these distinctions have served to bound philosophy off from neighboring endeavors, and we will question the legitimacy of this bounding. In the fourth chapter we will turn to the question of philosophy as an embodied activity, and we will consider the potential significance of the fact that in the history of Western philosophy there are in general very few instructions as to what we should be doing with our bodies while our minds are exploring the universal and the eternal. This point of difference between much Western philosophy and at least one familiar school of Eastern philosophy—familiar to the West, that is—will then convey us into a broader discussion of the problematic nature of the classification of philosophical traditions by reference to these familiar cardinal points of the compass. In chapter five we will turn to the distinction between "analytic" and "continental" philosophy, as well as to related provincialisms, in the aim of discerning what more significant divisions between approaches to philosophy these may be concealing from our view, and we will return, once again, to lessons drawn from both chapters one and two: the importance to philosophy of attention to singular things, and, among these, the singular beliefs of people who belong to intellectual cultures other than our own. In the sixth and final chapter, we will turn to the difficult question of the relationship between philosophy and money: whether the two are incompatible, and, if not, what risks we run when we permit the two to join forces.

1

SINGULAR THINGS
AND TIMELESS
TRUTHS

Featuring the Curiosa

One of the very earliest occurrences of the agentive term "philosopher" is found in a fragment of Heraclitus, in which, evidently, he is mocking the school of the Pythagoreans with this term. In fragment 35, the Greek philosopher writes that "men who are *philosophoi* must be inquirers into many things indeed."[1] The author, whom we now think of as one of the founders of the tradition of philosophy, expresses uncertainty and bemusement as he attempts to understand who exactly the philosophers are. Our own confusion will only be heightened when we learn that the term translated here as "inquirers" is, in the original, *historas*, which might also be translated as "historians," in the sense of people who are interested in singular things, and in telling "stories," or giving accounts that range over the actual, rather than over the possible, thus in contrast to both poetry and philosophy in Aristotle's later understanding.

Heraclitus is writing long before Aristotle would offer us his definition of "history" in contrast with poetry, already considered in the introduction. We might see Heraclitus's uncertainty about the scope of the term "philosopher" as a simple consequence of the unsurprising imprecision of a term that has just come into existence and has no established patterns of usage. But in fact something very much like an assimilation of "philosopher" to "historian," where a historian is understood simply as the person who inquires into many things, or the person with an appetite for singular facts about nature or society, continues beyond the archaic era and well into the golden age of Greek philosophy. Most of us are familiar, for example, with the accusations leveled against Socrates by his peers at the Athens court, that he sought to make the weaker argument the stronger, and that he had corrupted the youth of the city and denied its gods. But there is another accusation, corollary to the denial of the gods, that is often passed over without comment but that might be the most significant of all of them—namely, that Socrates has an excessive interest in the physical causes of phenomena that happen in the heavens above and in the earth below. In other words, the great philosopher is accused of being what would later be called a "natural historian." He is too curious about particulars and believes that by their investigation we can understand the workings of nature. It is in this connection that Aristophanes will lampoon the character of Socrates as holding, for example, that thunderclouds in the heavens function no differently than flatulence in human beings.[2]

Certainly, Socrates's accusers are wrong about him: he is no more a curious investigator of nature than he is a Sophist, and he does not appear to care much about what goes on in the heavens or below the earth. Yet while we are all familiar with the defenses of Socrates against the accusation of sophistry, the accusation of supporting natural-scientific inquiry passes under our radar, for we no longer even understand why such an accusation would be in any way damaging. But the historical record could not be clearer: until well into the early modern period, the people who were called "philosophers" were regularly accused of the transgression of looking into the workings of the heavens and of earth no less often than they were accused of making the weaker argument the stronger. Particularly when the term "philosopher" was used pejoratively (and we may say with confidence that the majority of its occurrences throughout history have been at least moderately pejorative), it was understood to suggest the activity of a "curiosus naturae," someone who is curious about the particular workings of nature, about the formation of clouds and icicles and will-o'-the-wisps. Consider, for example, Laurent Lange's 1735 description of the disposition of the "curious" practitioners of natural philosophy in their study of mammoth remains in Siberia:

> They say that [the mammoth] has a great horn in front, of which it makes use for pushing the earth in front of it and carving a path, and that the bones of which we have just spoken are nothing other than this horn, which has much in common with the tooth of the elephant that is found in Siberia. Some curious practitioners of natural philosophy [*Des curieux dans la Philosophie naturelle*] maintain that this Mammoth is the Behemoth mentioned in chapter 40 of [the Book of] Job, and whose description agrees so well with this beast: for its jaws are

of a substance that appears externally to be false copper, and as hard as a stone.[3]

Lange, following an established convention, intends a slightly mocking sense of "natural philosophy," as straying too far from the very concrete matter of describing paleontological remains in order to speculate on matters of biblical exegesis. But still, he also takes for granted that mammoth bones are within the normal purview of the natural philosopher, and that it is the virtue of curiosity that drives the natural philosopher to study them. By contrast the negative connotation of "philosopher" today is more often one of pure windbaggery, speculation detached from a concrete referent in the real world, the capacity to blow hot air about meaningless abstractions, to invent words that no one, including their inventor, could possibly understand, and so on. It is not a connotation of excessive curiosity. The reason for this shift has very much to do with the rise of modern science.

Philosophy seems to have effectively distanced itself fairly early on from sophistry (bracketing, for now, the compromising fact that professional philosophers continue to accept remuneration), and its relations with the institutions of religious faith have generally been too unstable for these two to be confused for very long. But the shared ancestry of philosophy and what would eventually be called "science" is a good deal more complicated, and in many respects the effort to understand the overlap between these two human endeavors continues to define what philosophy is. We might venture in a preliminary way that philosophy, or at least the tradition that descends from Philosophia, consists in the tension between Socratic disengagement from the world in search of adequate knowledge of fixed and unchanging concepts, on the one hand, and, on the other, the curious inquirer's investigation of what goes on in the heavens above and the earth below. If we leave this latter half out, if we pass too quickly over this part of the accusation against Socrates (whether it was justified or not), we will misunderstand much of what philosophy has been all along. In so doing, we will fail to understand what philosophy is.

One of the most significant developments in philosophy since the eighteenth century, to which we have already alluded, is that it has gradually lost its institutional connection with science, and so also its self-understanding as not just being interested in science or "pro-science," but as *including* science. Nietzsche intriguingly observes that science first emerges when people are no longer able to "think the gods well" (*Wissenschaft … entsteht, wenn die Götter nicht gut gedacht werden*). His meaning here is somewhat cryptic, but one plausible interpretation is that Nietzsche understands "science" in the sense in which this term was beginning to be understood during his lifetime, as a practical, fact-oriented matter independent of philosophy.[4] Science arises, on this reading, when the profound philosophical questions, about the first causes or ultimate principles of nature, come to be seen as irrelevant to the matter of measuring, classifying, and harnessing the powers of the things of the natural world.

There are many good arguments for reaffirming the union of science and philosophy, not least that doing so could well be one of the best hopes for the continued thriving of philosophy within the university and within the broader culture. We have seen, recently, some promising steps in this direction, notably the movement that has called itself "experimental philosophy."[5] But it is a testament to the partial character of the turn for which the new experimental philosophy is pushing that most of its advocates do not even know, or really appreciate, that they are recycling a label, that there were self-described experimental philosophers some centuries before them, who had a conception of philosophy that was rather more fully thought out and complete than that of many of our contemporaries. A more thorough reunification, one that is closer to the spirit of early modern experimental philosophy, would be one that does not simply adopt the methods of one branch of empirical science—psychology in the case of recent experimental philosophy—nor would it, as analytic philosophy has often done, position itself as a clarifier or analyst of the logic and methodology deployed by scientists in the making of their contentful claims. Rather, it would see the making of contentful claims about the world as *themselves* fully and unproblematically philosophical.

Such an approach seems to have been characteristic of most European philosophers until at least the mid-eighteenth century. Interestingly, vestiges of it remain in the life sciences even into the twentieth century. Thus, for example, D'Arcy Wentworth Thompson writes in his monumental 1917 work, *On Growth and Form*, of Kant's short-sightedness in supposing that the growth and development of living beings could never be accounted for in quantitative terms, yet the work, which is a demonstration of just this possibility is also precisely and explicitly a continuation of the tradition of philosophical reflection, from Aristotle through Kant, on the limits of mechanism and the value of teleological explanation. Like "warp and woof," the author comments, "mechanism and teleology are interwoven together, and we must not cleave to the one nor despise the other: for their union is rooted in the very nature of totality." It is, moreover, for Thompson, philosophy that "bids us hearken and obey the lessons both of mechanical and of teleological interpretation."[6] His work is a response to, and a continuation of, the philosophical tradition, and it is also, eminently, a work of science. One is in fact consistently surprised by the level of interest among biologists, writing just a century ago, in questions such as the value of Aristotelian teleology in accounting for the mechanisms of Darwinian natural selection. Biologists continued to think about the content of their discipline by reference to authors and texts that have over the course of just the last several decades been cordoned off as "philosophy" in an era in which other sciences, notably physics and chemistry, had become relatively more independent of their philosophical sources.

There has been tremendous progress in the life sciences since the beginning of the twentieth century, and there is a familiar argument that identifies the source of this progress in the specialization of its practitioners, in the freeing of them from the old weight of speculative tradition, instead allowing them do the hard laboratory-based and quantitative work necessary to make real discoveries about how living nature actually works. This is no doubt correct, but what it leaves out is that a capacity for self-understanding, cultivated through reflection on the natural world, and for engagement with age-old questions, might be among the legitimate desiderata, alongside "progress" in the narrowest sense, of what is now called "scientific" inquiry. In the early seventeenth century Francis Bacon had implored his contemporaries to "lay their notions by," in order to go about the urgent task of collecting empirical data.[7] He did not, however, think that notions should be lain by forever, that is, that people should altogether stop reflecting or speculating on the significance of the accumulated data. He simply thought that it was urgent, in the name of what we today would call "scientific" progress, to reform the institutions of data collection. By now, however, the institutions have been reformed, and the progress that has been made since Bacon has been astounding. If Bacon were to be resuscitated, and to be given a tour of nuclear power plants, to be shown how microprocessors work, and so on, he would likely declare that he is most impressed, but also that it is perhaps time, now, to bring our notions *back*.

What is more, at the moment he made the call Bacon did not think of the laying by of notions as a suspension of philosophy; he thought of it as a particular approach to philosophy, one among others that had been inherited from antiquity. This inheritance is one that has been largely forgotten, and that makes John Evelyn's epigrammatic allusion above to the discourses of the philosopher upon the quality of the air seem so foreign. It is not a marginal or subterranean current in the history of philosophy, either, but one of the prevailing visions throughout history of what philosophy is or ought to be. Again, in one of the very first occurrences of the term "philosopher," there is an explicit description, however critical, of this character as someone who is "interested in many things indeed." And this is similarly the understanding of philosophy in the title of the *Philosophical Transactions*, the journal of the Royal Society of London that began appearing in 1666 and that may be seen as a sort of realization of many of the hopes for the organization of natural-philosophical inquiry that Bacon had spelled out some decades earlier.

It is also the understanding of philosophy that we find among some of the major thinkers of early modern philosophy, whom we would later retroactively transform into philosophers in the etiolated sense that better suits our own sensibilities. Leibniz offers a revealing case in point. The perception that Leibniz was more at home when engaged in a priori speculations than when investigating particulars seems to have hounded him even during his own lifetime. Thus he complains to his friend, the Swedish linguist J. G. Sparwenfeld, in a letter of 1698, that "people ... tell me I am wrong to abandon solid and eternal truths in order to study the changing and perishable things that are found in history and its laws."[8] Later, in a 1708 draft of a proposal to Peter the Great for the classificatory system to be used in the eventual library of the Saint Petersburg Academy of Sciences, Leibniz identifies history—recall, again, Heraclitus's description of the *philosophoi* as *historas*—as one of the three "Realien" or distinct domains of science, alongside mathematics and physics. It is, namely, the one that "involves the explanation of times and places, and thus of singular things [*res singulares*]."[9]

The Curiosus or Curiosa is a figure who has some characteristics in common with the "philosopher of science" and with the current incarnation of the "experimental philosopher," but who differs from these in his or her understanding of the relationship between the content of science and the project of philosophy. It is through the figure of the Curiosus/a that we might hope to regain, for philosophy, a forgotten way of understanding the interest and value of singular things.

For most of the history of the term "scientia" and its equivalents in the various national languages of Europe, such as "science," "wetenskap," or "Wissenschaft," designated any systematic body of knowledge, including those we would recognize today as science, but including also such evidently unscientific endeavors as theology. In German universities today—institutions traditional enough to retain some of the taxonomy of the disciplines that preceded the reshuffling that occurred in the Enlightenment—one may still study *theologische Wissenschaft*: theological science. In general, this broader meaning of "science" remains more salient in continental Europe than in the English-speaking world: in France one may still study "the human sciences," in Germany the "sciences of spirit," and these include, not least, the academic discipline of philosophy. In any case, here, when we speak of the intricate relationship between philosophy and science, we do not mean by the latter one of the fields that has been designated by *scientia* or by any of its cognates, but rather the sort of inquiry into the workings of nature, in the heavens above and the earth below, for which Socrates was accused by the court at Athens, and which has in other times and places been called "natural history," "natural philosophy," or, simply, "philosophy." Scholars both within and outside of the academic discipline of philosophy today often comment on the vestigial use of "philosophy" in the "PhD" degree that is given out to new doctors in, for example, biology or chemistry. It is noted with passing curiosity that everything used to be philosophy. But the full significance of this observation is seldom appreciated. What it really means, among other things, is that if we are going to write a history of philosophy that takes actors' categories seriously, it will be a history of metallurgy and distillation as much as it will be a history of metaphysics or logic.

But beyond this, there is another very important reason to pay attention to all the varieties of "philosophy" that would bequeath to us the "Ph" in "PhD." While there were often clear attempts to articulate the various respects in which philosophy was not law, history, poetry, and so on, the endeavors we would later come to call "science" seemed simply too close to the heart of philosophy to positively disown them. Socrates was able to do so, to deny that the Athens court's accusation was just, because he was an exceptional sort of philosopher who rejected positive doctrines in general and preferred a conception of philosophy as a dialectical method that generally yielded only aporetic results. But Socrates may also be seen as the exception that proves the rule. Thales, Aristotle, Albertus Magnus, Descartes, Leibniz: all were philosophers who investigated the workings of the natural world not as side projects, not as hobbies, but because they believed that these investigations were intrinsic to the projects in virtue of which we, today, think of them as philosophers.

It is this sort of investigation that has been understood under the name "philosophy" in most cases where this word, or the agentive "philosopher," is used in a pejorative or derogatory way. Socrates may not have looked into the workings of the heavens above or the earth below, but a "philosopher" is someone who does look into such things. We see this connotation already in Heraclitus's allusion to the *philosophoi* as *historas*. And we see it millennia later in François Bernier's 1671 *History of the Late Revolution of the Empire of the Great Mogol*, where the French materialist in Moghul India contrasts the person who "plays the philosopher" in observing the use of saltpeter for cooling water before a long voyage under the Indian sun, with the person who wastes no time in such reflection and simply continues on in preparation for departure. For the space of "half a quarter of an hour," he relates, "this Flaggon is stirr'd in water, into which hath been cast three or four handfuls of Salt-peeter; this maketh the water very cold, neither it is unwholesome, as I did apprehend, but only that sometimes it causeth gripings at first when one is not accustomed to it." Bernier quickly interrupts these reflections, as if embarrassed: "But to what purpose, to play so much the Philosopher, when we should think to depart, and to endure the Sun, which at all seasons is incommodious in the Indies."[10]

What is a philosopher? If we agree with Bernier, it is someone who stops and reflects on how refrigeration works when there are more pressing matters to be seen to.

We are, again, familiar with the story of the exact sciences splitting off from philosophy over the course of the seventeenth and eighteenth centuries, and with the corollary idea that philosophy since that time is simply what is left over after, so to speak, the children have left home. But what this narrative leaves out, as correct as it may be in itself, is that during the period before the separation, it is not just that the sciences were housed within philosophy, but that they were constitutive of philosophy, and it was precisely the constitution of the activity of philosophy by people who were intent on looking into the heavens above and the earth below that made philosophy a contested and controversial activity.

I, being sick of an Ague, have come out to Country for a change of Air. But in truth I am not so sick at all, and I embrace this circumstance with whole heart, for it enables me to pursue, as is my true vocation, my observations touching upon divers questions of Natural Philosophy.

The Marquis, when he comes galloping through England between diplomatic missions to Vienna and Constantinople, makes light of my inquiries, and says mockingly how good it is that Philosophy now includes matters suitable for Ladies too. There was no room for the feminine sex in the Schools and their endless debates about the *Quiddity* of this and the *Thisness* of that, he laughs, but how fitting for a

Marquise, with leisure to spare, to look with her magnifying Lens at the industry of Silkworms, at the fine detail of the leg of a Flea, or to place two such Lenses together within a Tube, and to look out at the Heavens, to chart the Eclipse of the Moon or to follow the path of a shooting Star.

But the Marquis cannot see past his own Nose, I tell him, for in truth such matters were always of great concern to the Philosopher. For did Aristotle himself not wade in the Tides, searching for ever new forms of Corral, of Medusae and Polypi? Did he not describe the formation of Clouds and other Meteors, and the fatty exhalations of earth that we call Comets? No, 'tis the Schools that shrank Philosophy down to the mere quarrel over Words, distorting the legacy of the great Aristotle, while neglecting altogether the work of Hippocrates, the Elder Pliny, Isidore of Seville. As if these too were not Philosophers! What these men possess, and the discoursers upon *Quiddity* lack, I believe, is Curiosity. Those discoursers suffer from Wind, they do not hunger for the World, nor have they Appetite for the astounding and infinite diversity of its Particulars.

When I arrived at the Estate yesterday I was delighted to learn that the servant child Tom had, with his parents' encouragement, kept strong our Experiment in the culture and production of Silk since I helped him with it Summer last. My own Mother suffered not her servants to speak or play in her presence, nor in any way to show their fellow Humanity. Yet from the earliest age I could not help but take an interest in the knowledge they pass down from one generation to the next, which differs from the Learning of the natural Philosophers principally in this, that it be communicated not in books but in speech and in practice. The cures Tom's Mother offers for the Bee-Sting, for example, or even for a condition as mundane as the *hic*-Cough: is this not just as much a part of the totality of Learning, as are the observations made upon the elliptical Orbit of the Planets?

Meanwhile Tom's Father turns up stones with mysterious unknown Writing upon them, during his long walks through the forest, and he has even shewn me his collection of Bones turned to Stone, among them monstrous horned Carapaces, and what look like the thigh bones of Oxen, but are far too large to belong to any known Beast of the Land. If we are ever to amass that great store of Observations, of which Lord Bacon only dreamt, that will help us to make truly sound Generalisations and to apply these efficaciously for the improvement of all Mankind, we will have to rely not just upon the Observations made by men of Learning—nay, for there are not nearly enough such Men—, but by everyone in a position to make 'em, regardless of Sex or Station.

Now that I am here in the Country I will have time to return to my Correspondence, yea, to reestablish my lapsed Citizenship in the Republic of Letters, which has no Territory but in the Minds of Men. I am everywhere addicted to Contemplation, but it is only in quiet retreat that I have that much-needed Peace that enables me to turn my Thoughts into Words.

I will begin, this morning, with a brief report to Mr. Oldenburg on the Effluvia of the Loadstone, which I have been studying ever since I met that Irish impostor Valentine Greatrakes, who claimed for himself the Power to cure Illnesses by the bare Laying on of his Hands, but in fact was relying upon the hidden virtues of the Magnet. These virtues, I have now shewn, are no different from any other in Nature: they are to be explained not by hidden Affinities betwixt the Things of nature, nor by I-know-not-what action at a distance, but by the Emission of invisible Corpuscles that act directly upon surrounding Bodies, just as a heavy hammer acts directly upon the anvil that receives its Blows. Ah, but the absence of Mystery reveals in turn the greatest Mystery of all: the Order and Perfection of Nature itself! Who needs posit Ghosts and Sprites *derrière les coulisses*, when the Machine of this unending Natural Theatre is already wondrous enough!

My next letter will be to Godfrey William von Leibnitz, of Hanover, who is surely my most faithful Correspondent of all, since our first meeting in the year 1676 following his entry into the Royal Society. I was in London at the time tending to some of the Marquis' debts, incurred by rash investments in the West Indies Sugar manufactory, while he meanwhile was waiting out a spell of inclement Weather for his transit home from Calais. Of course, as a woman I was not permitted to attend the closed Events of the day, but Leibnitz had wished to speak to me, I learned, about my Methods for the Production of Silk, so it was arranged that we would meet to walk through Hyde Park that very afternoon.

He confided in me his grand Plan to pay for many great projects—the establishment of learnèd academies in far-away Russia, the Illumination of the streets of Vienna by means of artificial Light— all with Revenues derived from a system for Sericulture so intensive it would rival, in the city of Berlin alone, all the Silk of China. He was a *rêveur*, that young man, and I happily told him everything I know, for I do not consider Knowledge a secret to be jealously guarded, and in any case I do not consider my own Technique for Breeding the Worms so as to yield perfect consistency in the quality of their threads any great Secret: I learnt it from Tom!

We spoke of many other things besides, of course. What a perfect Harmony of Minds I discovered with that man! I have never shunned the Company of his sex, but I have also never been infected with the disease of amorous Love. The Love however that is often called Platonick, it must be understood, is not devoid of Desire, but is rather a true and fitting Realisation of a Person's deepest and truest Desire: to know lasting Union with another, lasting because it does not depend upon the fleeting states and vicissitudes of the Body.

So, as I've said, I must write to Leibnitz. But I hear Tom coming up the stairs just now. I expect he will wish to show me this Stove he has been building, which regulates its own Heat, so he says. He calls it his own perpetual motion Machine! Truly, that boy has some ideas. I should like to see him a member of the Royal Society too someday. And afterward there is that tiresome Query from the Manx Physician, what's-his-name, who wishes to solicit my opinion concerning the two-headed Calf lately turned up on that Island. And of course there are always more of the Marquis' affairs to tend to: the Sugar debts; the Hounds he wants returned to the breeder, who it seems have no taste for hunting down helpless Foxes.

And then there is the fiction I am composing, though I daren't tell anyone yet, about a young Marquise who transits to the Moon by a clever use of Magnetism, and there conducts all manner of Observations. This Fiction, like all Fictions, engages the fancy, so that the reader might be more readily led to the use of Reason. If only more of the writing of Philosophy could proceed in this wise, truly I believe we would see a great Increase in the numbers of Philosophers. I have just added this morning a new turn of events in the story, where the Heroine encounters a sort of Moon-Gnome who represents the figure of Mister Des-Cartes. I must write it out quickly before it sinks back down into the dark Morass of unfertilised Ideas. I am beginning to fear that the Letter to Leibnitz will have to wait until tomorrow.

I have no proper Learning in any subject, but I make do as best I can, through Correspondence and Communication with others, and by Force of my own Determination, in those subjects for which I have a natural Inclination. I lack such an Inclination in Mathematics, and in general in those fields of Learning that are concerned with Universal and Eternal things. My Mind's Eye focuses as if spontaneously upon the variety of Things that come into being and pass away, the Manifold of mortal, corruptible, astonishing Things. 'Tis my most basic belief that these Things, too, are a veridical Reflection of the Wisdom of God, and that one may just as easily turn to them in order to discover the Divine Truths that do not change, as to the fixity of numbers and the relations between them. Here too, I say, is Philosophy.

The figure of the philosopher is fairly rigidly gendered throughout most of the history of philosophy—to wit, as a man—and this legacy almost certainly plays a greater role in the current issues the discipline is facing surrounding gender equity, at least in the English-speaking world, than its nonhistorian participants are able to see. That is, philosophy is likely weighed down by aspects of its earlier self-definition that no longer come out explicitly, but that still play a role in defining who may count as a philosopher, even as the explicit gender dimensions of these aspects no longer remain easily visible.

Take, for example, the apocryphal story of Phyllis riding Aristotle, which recalls for us a period in the history of culture in which philosophy, and philosophers, were implicated not just in elite disputation, but also in popular lore and moral instruction. The tale of Phyllis and Aristotle is an exemplum, that is, a stock lesson telling you—and here, "you" are not a subtle follower of philosophical arguments, but a common fellow influenced by memorable stories accompanied by vivid images—what you ought not to do. The fact that it was the greatest philosopher in Western history who provided the exemplum is worthy of pause, but we will get back to that in a moment.

Phyllis was the preferred consort, perhaps the wife, of Alexander the Great, who in his turn was a disciple of the great philosopher. This much is historical fact. A legend arose over the course of the late Middle Ages according to which Aristotle grew enamored of Alexander's spouse or lover, who for her part consented to give the philosopher what he wanted, but only as his dominatrix. In particular, she wished to ride on his back, with the philosopher down on his hands and knees like a beast.

An anonymous Latin text relates that Aristotle had initially instructed his disciple Alexander to abstain from amorous relations with his own wife, since this diverted him from the manly projects in which he was engaged (empire building, philosophy, and such). Phyllis was therefore spurned, and to get revenge she decided to seduce not her own husband, but the old philosopher who had drawn her husband away from her. This proved not so difficult after all, and soon enough Aristotle began to solicit her carnally, to which Phyllis responded:

> This I will certainly not do, unless I see a sign of love, lest you be testing me. Therefore, come to my chamber crawling on hand and foot, in order to carry me like a horse. Then I'll know that you aren't deluding me.[11]

Hans Baldung's 1503 pen-and-ink drawing (image 1), as well as his 1513 woodcut (image 2), are some of the most vivid representations of the ensuing ride. A still more striking rendering of this subject is the fourteenth-century French bronze aquamanile that shows Phyllis plainly slapping Aristotle's rear, just like she might a horse, in full three-dimensional splendor (image 3).

What exactly is going on here? It should be pointed out that there is a long tradition associating Aristotle with the bawdy, going back at least to the mid-sixteenth-century Latin translation, by Theodor Gaza, of the Greek author's biological works treating, most relevantly, the reproduction of animals, and therefore also the cosmic significance of sexual difference, copulation, and such. From this association there arose the countless editions of works bearing the title *Aristotle's Masterpiece*, which were essentially manuals of advice for midwives, plus a diverse selection of "secrets" about the feminine sex. One could still purchase late editions of the *Masterpiece* in London sex shops into the 1920s.[12] Even before the Gaza edition, Aristotle's name would have been loosely associated with the topic of animals via Albertus Magnus, the thirteenth-century teacher of Thomas Aquinas who wrote, among many other works, a treatise *De animalibus*. Although it might be hard for us to see today, to the extent that animals owe their very existence to copulation, from a certain medieval point of view there is already something bawdy in the very study of zoology.

It seems quite likely that in addition to Aristotle the advisor of midwives, another aspect of his legacy that could be playing a role in this legend is that of Aristotle the happily married father and family man. We know in fact that Aristotle went to Macedonia as Alexander's tutor shortly after the death of his wife, Pythias, with whom he had had a daughter. He would later have another female lover who would bear him a son, Nicomachus, for whom he would eventually write one of his two major works on ethics. It is also likely that he had a male

1

2

3

IMAGE 1. Hans Baldung Grien, *Phyllis and Aristotle*, 1503. Pen and ink. Prints and Drawings Collection, Musée de Louvre, Paris © RMN–Grand Palais. Image courtesy of Art Resource. IMAGE 2. Lucas van Leyden, *Phyllis and Aristotle*, 1512. (Print from *A History of Wood Engraving*, by Douglas Percy Bliss, Spring Books, London, 1964). Image courtesy of Art Resource. IMAGE 3. Aquamanile in the form of Aristotle and Phyllis, late 14th or early 15th century, bronze. Image courtesy of Metropolitan Museum of Art, New York. Image courtesy of Art Resource.

lover, but whether he did or not, it remains the case that Aristotle was far more active in social reproduction through opposite-gender pairing than great philosophers have typically been held to be. Nietzsche observed that all the great philosophers have been unmarried and nonreproductive—except for Socrates, who was however married to a "shrew" or a "nag," as if to demonstrate precisely the lesson that philosophers ought not to marry. He writes in *The Genealogy of Morality* of 1887:

> Heraclitus, Plato, Descartes, Spinoza, Leibniz, Kant, Schopenhauer—they were not married, and, further, one cannot **imagine** them as married. A married philosopher belongs to **comedy**, that is my rule.[13]

Strangely, Nietzsche does not even mention Aristotle in this connection, but if he had he would have had to acknowledge that the Stagirite is both an exception to the rule as well as an exception to Socrates's exception that supposedly proves the rule.

The figure of Phyllis riding Aristotle begins to appear at the moment when Aristotle is beginning his slow decline as the preeminent representative of philosophy, as "the Philosopher." Several more centuries would follow in which celibacy would function as the norm and implicit ideal among philosophers. Many of the problems that philosophy as an academic discipline is currently having in the matter of gender equity could, again, have to do not just with its legacy of macho grandstanding, the old-boys'-club sense of entitlement that so many of its cocky male practitioners have, but also, at least in part, with the fact that the discipline has its deep historical roots in something akin to monasticism, where the boys' club is constituted not on the basis of a shared commitment to prowling, lecherous domination of women, but rather to an ideal of separateness.

Nietzsche was a raving and sorry case who failed to implement philosophy as a practice of the good life. But his historical point could nonetheless help us to bring into relief the exceptional situation of current academic philosophy. The life of the philosopher, in many times and places, and particularly in the tradition with which Nietzsche identified and which was the focus of his critique, was for many throughout the tradition something akin to life in a monastic order. It placed an extremely high demand on its initiates and forced them to choose between different and competing fundamental goods. Aristotle betrayed philosophy, on the understanding we are reconstructing, by allowing it to get mixed up with the sensual, corporeal realm. The exemplum thus works at two levels at once, for the initiates and the masses alike. Keep your wits by staying away from temptresses, it tells the male masses, while to the male philosophers, it says: maintain the standard of pure rationality by not getting mixed up with the natural world and its cycles of generation and corruption.

One might speculate that the demographic problem philosophy faces today, in which women students and faculty are systematically disadvantaged, discouraged from continuing, and made to feel less than at home in the milieus of professional philosophy, flows directly and inescapably from the way philosophy continues to define itself as an intellectual project. This is not to say that reason is "masculine" and the senses are "feminine," but only that centuries-old associations have a way of insinuating themselves into our speech and action far more than most people, and certainly most nonhistorians, like to think. Within the supposedly intellectually grounded defense of philosophy as a largely a priori discipline separate from the natural and cultural worlds, there is an echo of that old exemplum about staying pure and free of temptation.

If we are willing to dwell among the antiquated concepts of a gendered cosmos a while longer, of the sort that made the legend of Aristotle and Phyllis make sense, we might note that in the actors' categories of the Renaissance and early modern worlds, the trait of curiosity, of the sort on exhibit in *Aristotle's Masterpiece*, was conceptualized as feminine, and that in this respect the predominant conception of philosophy in the sixteenth and seventeenth centuries was one that made room for the feminine, and occasionally for actual women too, within philosophy. Consider, for example, Johannes Kepler's 1630 *Somnium*, a sort of ecstatic vision recounting the voyage of a hero, a certain Duracotus, to the moon with the aid of Icelandic spirits conjured by his mother, a witch by the name of Fiolxhilde.[14] This text vividly revives some of the tropes of ancient lunar fiction, such as the fantastical *True History* of Lucian of Samosata, and does so in the service of the new anti-geocentric cosmology. Kepler, most famous for defending the Copernican system and for establishing the elliptical orbit of planets, begins his *Somnium* (sometimes subtitled *A Posthumous Work on Lunar Astronomy*) as follows:

> My name is Duracotus. My country is Iceland, which the ancients called Thule. My mother was Fiolxhilde. Her recent death freed me to write, as I had long wished to do. While she lived, she carefully kept me from writing. For, she said, the arts are loathed by many vicious people who malign what their dull minds fail to understand, and make laws harmful to mankind. Condemned by these laws, not a few persons have perished in the chasms of Hekla.[15]

The narrator goes on to describe his mother's commercial undertakings in what might be euphemistically called "folk medicine," or, slightly more bluntly, "natural magic":

> In the earliest years of my boyhood my mother, leading me by the hand and sometimes hoisting me up on her shoulders, often used to take me up to the lower slopes of Mt. Hekla. These excursions were made especially around St. John's Day, when the sun is visible all twenty-four hours, and there is no night. Gathering some herbs with many rites, she cooked them at home. She made little bags out of goatskin, which she filled and carried to a nearby port to sell to the ship captains. This is how she earned her living.[16]

That Kepler decides to preface what turns out to be a serious work of lunar astronomy—to be precise, a theoretical reflection upon the features of the still-unobserved dark side of the moon—with this narrative setup is peculiar, not least because we know, and his contemporaries knew, that it reflects Kepler's own life in significant ways. Kepler's mother, Katharina Kepler, née Guldenmann (1546–1622), was in the years leading up to the *Somnium*'s composition being held in prison in Stuttgart on suspicion of witchcraft, under threat of imminent torture and execution. Her son fought for years for his mother's release, and eventually won it, but much of their life was spent in the frenetic uncertainty of the *Hexenjagd*. Kepler was interested in witchcraft, then, not only as a source of fanciful characters for his thin fictions.

The *Somnium* is two things at once: an apologia for folk-scientific practices of the sort Kepler's mother presumably excelled in, perhaps, to return to that revealing phrase, as a *sage-femme*, and, in the second half, it is a defense of the Copernican system on the basis of the relativity of observed orbits, as established by a lunocentric astronomy. The Icelandic protagonist of the *Somnium* is trained in proper astronomy in Denmark, and is impressed there by the similarity between his new learning and the traditions embodied by his mother: "I was delighted beyond measure by the astronomical activities" on the continent, he writes, "for Brahe and his students watched the moon and the stars all night with marvelous instruments. This practice reminded me of my mother, because she, too, used to commune with the moon constantly."[17]

Duracotus eventually returns to Iceland and is reunited with Fiolxhilde. She initiates him into her secret arts, which include the power to summon a spirit that specializes in organizing trips to "the island of Levania," which lies "fifty thousand German miles up in the ether," and which, it turns out, is nothing other than the moon.[18] It transports Duracotus there, yet once on the moon, the magical theme recedes entirely, and Kepler turns to straightforward astronomy, describing a world in which it is the Earth, or what he calls Volva, that waxes and wanes, rather than the moon. The principal concern here is to establish that the Earth has no intrinsic features that make it the preferable site for the taking of astronomical observations.

There is certainly no need here to investigate the profound interpretative issues to which this fascinating text gives rise, in particular, the question as to why Kepler so thoroughly and abruptly abandons the theme of Icelandic natural magic once his protagonist arrives on the moon, and commences there with a straightforward astronomy that will last him, more or less, until the end of the work. What is important here is to note that, manifestly, Kepler is identifying different sources for the sort of natural philosophy he sees himself as practicing:

the one source official, institutional, book-based, mathematical, and masculine; the other secret, popular, orally transmitted, informal, and feminine. Evidently, he wishes to portray these two traditions as of a pair, and as equal components of his own approach to nature.

Interest in what had traditionally been considered "women's knowledge," as for example knowledge of the therapeutic effects of the different plants sold by elderly women at the local marketplace, would come to be part of the legitimate range of interests of early modern philosophers working broadly within the Baconian framework that valued comprehensive data gathering over abstract theorizing. And it is within this broad framework that the so-called experimental philosophy (in its early modern sense) would develop in the second half of the seventeenth century, attracting brilliant women such as Margaret Cavendish to its cause. It may be that what we see in Kepler is an explicit opening up of natural philosophy to a tradition of "women's knowledge" that had run parallel all along to the tradition we usually think of as philosophy, whose history is inscribed with the names of men and their supposedly immortal innovations. It may be that the new spirit of philosophy that prevailed in the early modern period, which valued probing into nature's "secrets" and did not rest content with inherited abstractions and hollow definitions, was one that had become "feminized."

Of course those are scare quotes around the final word of the previous sentence: no traits are rigidly feminine or masculine, least of all such widely distributed behavioral or personality traits such as curiosity. But as Kepler's work shows, there does seem to have been a trait that was conceived in the era *as* feminine, and that had come to be seen as a positive element of natural philosophical inquiry. If this is correct, plainly it complicates the facile account of the early modern period Carolyn Merchant offered a generation ago, according to which the well-known mechanization of the world picture that supposedly defined the intellectual landscape of early modern Europe is one that also witnessed "the death of nature" and therefore also, according to Merchant, the occlusion of the feminine.[19] Fiolxhilde would surely not agree, nor would any reader who saw her placed next to Tycho Brahe as one of the great sources of natural knowledge for a fictionalized version of one of that century's greatest natural philosophers.

As an undergraduate at the University of California at Davis in the early 1990s, I was required to attend the classes of a teaching assistant, a graduate student, who loved philosophy vehemently. Never was he so indignant as when he felt his students were not taking philosophy seriously enough. One beautiful spring day an undergraduate suggested, as undergraduates often do, that class be moved outside, onto the grass. The TA expressed his concern that we would be distracted by the abundant signs of life, by the flowers, the butterflies, the other students playing hacky sack. "But that's philosophy too," the eager undergraduate pleaded. "It's *all* philosophy!" The TA was predictably furious and proceeded to give us a lecture to the effect that it is not all, in fact, philosophy, that philosophy is a narrow and technical discipline, with established methods and clear boundaries, and so on.

We remained in our desks that day, for which I was grateful enough, but something about this TA's attempt at an authoritative definition of the activity in which we were engaged rang false to me. Philosophy, it was already becoming clear, is the discipline that insists upon the reality of its boundaries, because philosophy is the discipline that has no real cohesion

except through agreement, shared or coerced, about what is
not philosophy. You will not find sedimentologists routinely
denouncing neighboring endeavors (unless these are blatantly
pseudoscientific) as "not sedimentology." Part of what gener-
ates the perceived need to cordon off the nonphilosophical
is that it is not only neighboring endeavors that threaten to
spill in uninvited; rather, all human endeavors are of equal
standing as prospective intruders. As the undergraduate put
it: "It's all philosophy." This student, in his naive way, lacking
experience with philosophy as a professional and institutional
practice, was looking to cultivate his own "philosophy of life,"
was looking for a disposition to the world, a temperament
and a mode of reflection, that would be applicable to all his
experiences, including those he might have on a grassy university quad.

There is however another sense in which "it's all philosophy," whose relationship to the first sense perhaps warrants
some consideration. It's all philosophy, also, in that the discipline of philosophy, the one defended by the loyal TA, in fact
nourishes and sustains itself by taking an interest in the endeavors of people outside of philosophy: in science, art, religion, domestic life, and sport. In recent years this sustenance
is described in terms of the fixed formula "philosophy of x,"
but in truth philosophy was engaging with questions arising
in, say, art or religion long before anyone spoke of philosophy
of art or religion. The "philosophy of x" formula seems to
imply that there is a well-defined domain of inquiry that can
be variously applied to any other domain of inquiry and that
can be recognized so to speak in its pure form, in isolation
from these other domains. Yet most of us, upon reflection, are
compelled to admit that there is very little in the philosophy
that goes into the philosophy of art that is the same as the

philosophy that goes into the philosophy of physics. Both philosophy of art and philosophy of physics are however interested in getting at the "ultimate truth" of what art and physics, variously, are all about.

There are lively debates today about whether physicists are really equipped to provide whatever philosophy of their own discipline might be needed, and many people agree that many brilliant physicists are also incompetent as philosophers of physics.[20] Yet in principle there does not seem to be any reason why rigorous and deep investigation of the questions arising within physics that we deem philosophical could not be understood as constitutive of the practice of physics. Historically, in any case, the separation between natural science and philosophy was never clear. In Aristotle's biological research, for example, it is clear that he was asking fundamental philosophical questions, about the ontology of kinds, and it is just as clear that he was performing fundamental scientific research on biological taxonomy. While some scholars have argued that here Aristotle is bringing a philosophy of science to bear in a particular domain of science,[21] it seems more accurate to say that Aristotle thought of himself as engaged in a single, unified project: that of coming to know the order of nature and its various causes, both mediate and ultimate. Aristotle believed that "it's all philosophy," in the sense that what we consider philosophy *and* what we would consider to be *x* for any number of "philosophies of *x*" are for him part of a single project.

Leibniz, too, saw the investigation of singular things as being just as crucial to his own intellectual calling as was the contemplation of timeless or universal truths. The disdain for singular things, like the love of them, has deep roots in philosophy. Socrates, as we have seen, abjured not only sophistry but also natural philosophy. But such a search had in fact been the central preoccupation of most pre-Socratic philosophy, and it would soon be again in Aristotle, and even in Plato's own later dialogues such as the *Timaeus*. All sought to pry into nature and discover its first principles: water, for example, or air, or hylomorphic compounds. And wherever such prying occurred, we find a mixture of theoretical interest and concern for practical, and often overt economic, gain. Natural philosophy is not just interested in the first principles of nature, but also in its powers, and how to harness them. This is precisely the significance of Bacon's use of the motto "Knowledge is power," subsequently appropriated by DARPA, the research-and-development agency of the US Department of Defense.

Although Socrates provides a model already in antiquity of philosophy as unconcerned with what goes on under the earth and in the heavens, it is only very recently that the self-conception of philosophers has become entirely separate from that of those who are now called "scientists." Only toward the end of the eighteenth century did natural philosophy cease to be an integral, perhaps the most important, part of what it is that philosophers think of themselves as doing. Thus, again, we find John Evelyn lampooning the philosopher as someone who discourses upon the quality of the air of London. No one in the seventeenth century raised an eyebrow at the association of the "Philosopher" with this sort of curiosity. Philosophy remained at least as closely linked in the popular imagination and in the self-conception of its practitioners to meteorology as to, say, logic. Descartes continued to dissect the heads of animals passed to him by the local butcher. Leibniz spent many of his most fruitful years as a metaphysician almost singularly devoted to research on the medicinal properties of the Brazilian ipecacuanha root, which culminated in the 1696 treatise,

On the New American Anti-Dysenteric.[22] He seems to have been more pleased with this work than any other of his vast accomplishments. Again, long before there was "x-phi," there was experimental philosophy, as practiced by Robert Boyle, Margaret Cavendish, and many others, some of whom wrote lucidly on the theoretical reasons why philosophy is best conceived as fundamentally consisting in the project of hacking through nature's thorns, to speak with the poet James Merrill, and kissing awake new powers.[23]

As Merrill is aware, this is an endeavor that is fraught with danger, as the US military's adoption of Bacon's motto vividly illustrates. Science, as natural philosophy, was generally perceived as being driven by what William R. Newman has called "Promethean ambitions,"[24] the desire among human beings to progress further than they should by probing where they should not. Thus science as natural philosophy was also conceptually very close to natural magic. But the conceptual separation of science from philosophy certainly did not slow down the Promethean ambition, or stop the kissing awake of new powers—the discovery of most interest to Merrill are the "new formulae of megadeath," that is, the technologies that have made nuclear holocaust a real possibility. Rather, the conceptual separation has only made a clear awareness of the implicit aims and values of science that much harder to maintain in our society.

What changed? Immanuel Kant's own career seems to straddle a divide between two epochs.[25] In his early formation, doing what was expected of him as a philosopher in training, the young Kant wrote a Latin dissertation *On Fire*.[26] He would go on in his career to write extensively of cosmogony, anthropology, and physical geography. But by the time of his mature, critical work, as for example in the 1783 *Prolegomena to Any*

Future Metaphysics That May Come Forward as a Science, Kant is sharply aware of a growing gap between science and philosophy, or, again, between natural philosophy and fundamental philosophy: the former is making rapid and unprecedented progress, while the latter keeps cycling back around the same questions, and never seems to get anywhere. Kant thus gives voice in the *Prolegomena* to a well-known crisis in metaphysics, but what is less often noted is the shift in the conception of science; he wants fundamental philosophy to "come forward as a science" and believes that if it cannot, then it has no future. But this implies at the same time that science is something distinct from philosophy, which until very recently it had not been.

The full explanation for this split is complicated and has to do not just with internal developments in the self-conception of philosophers but also with social and institutional history. In particular, after some centuries in which the centers of philosophical activity were located outside the university—in royal courts, museums, scientific societies, and so on—by the end of the eighteenth century philosophy was again becoming principally an academic endeavor, academic in our contemporary sense of being housed in a university faculty or department and being focused on pedagogical instruction within the bounds of a clearly defined curriculum.

2

PHILOSOPHY AND
PHILOSOPHIA

Featuring the Sage

On a certain plausible—but ultimately unsatisfactory—definition, "philosophy" is simply a proper noun. It describes a particular tradition, just like the terms "ballet" and "butoh." Most would find odd the claim that there is an indigenous tradition of Polynesian ballet, not because anyone believes that Polynesians are inherently incapable of appreciating or mastering this sort of dance, but simply because, as a matter of contingent historical fact, ballet emerged in Europe. This is a contingent historical fact that subsequently becomes essential to the definition of ballet. Ballet is, by definition, European. If it later appears anywhere else in the world, it does so by diffusion or appropriation, and not by chance, or in virtue of some innate, universal human capacity.

One way to approach the difficult question as to the nature of philosophy is to ask: is philosophy a human activity more like ballet, or is it more like dance? That is, is it a particular cultural tradition, or is it a universal human activity with many distinct cultural inflections? On the conception of "philosophy" as a proper noun, as a particular cultural tradition, it may be established with certainty that philosophy is an invention of the Greeks, and that it is something that was later practiced by Romans, Muslims in the Arab world and beyond, Christian Europeans, and more or less secular Anglo-Americans and all the different groups under their cultural dominance. Let us, again, call this conception of philosophy "Philosophia," in acknowledgment of the heritage that is ostensibly inseparable from its identity conditions.

If philosophy just is Philosophia, there can be no Indian philosophy, for example, even if there are indeed undeniable attainments of an Indian intellectual tradition. The six orthodox schools of classical Indian thought would have developed, we may presume, even if the Greeks had never existed. Thus the various Indian *darśana*s or schools of thought are not philosophy, while the *falsafa* of the Arabic-speaking world is philosophy, because it derives directly from the translation and incorporation into Islamic tradition of the works of Aristotle and other Greek authors who were self-consciously members of the tradition of Philosophia.

Much can be learned from a consideration of nomenclature. Here we find that even within Europe there is a tension between what we might call the "indigenous" and the "cosmopolitan" conceptions of philosophy. Dutch is among a handful of northern European languages whose speakers have coined their own term for the word that in most neighboring countries derives from Greek. Yet we can be certain that when the philosophy of Spinoza is taught in a department of *wijsbegeerte* in the Netherlands today, this is an instance of Philosophia. The very term, "wijsbegeerte," is a conscious fabrication from the model of the Greek word for philosophy. It is not a cognate of "philosophia," but a calque. This lexical pattern is also fairly common in the Germanic and Celtic languages of northern Europe, such as Icelandic, Faroese, Welsh, and Breton, to find artificial terms for "philosophy" that draw on the internal resources of these languages, conveying something of the same spirit as "philosophia" without translating the Greek term morpheme by morpheme. The Icelandic and Faroese "heimspeki" is in fact a calque not of "philosophia" but rather of the German "Weltweisheit" or "world-wisdom," an archaic alternative term for "philosophy," almost always understood in the sense of "natural philosophy," employed in premodern and early modern German. This term is significant, as it reveals something about the perceived scope of philosophy in that period and region: there, it is a fundamentally worldly endeavor, and as such it is limited and, in the classical sense, profane. It is contrasted with the true wisdom that piety affords. Thus we find in a note written into the front cover of a 1618 book owned by the Scottish-Russian natural-magician and experimental philosopher Jacob Bruce (Iakov Brius) the observation: "Worldly wisdom without God is the greatest foolishness (Weltliche Weisheit ohne Gott ist die grösste Thorheit)"[1] (image 4). By rendering "philosophy" as "world-wisdom," it may be that in the various languages of northern Europe there was a recognition of the sort of caution Bruce expresses, indeed of the impiety of excessive confidence in the project of philosophy.

What happens, now, when we leave the European sphere? In many cases, we find similar calques as in Iceland and Holland, though with their own unique connotations. The Japanese word that usually translates "philosophy," "tetsugaku," presents an interesting case in point. It was coined by the scholar Nishi

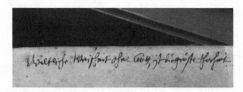

IMAGE 4. "Worldly wisdom without God is the greatest foolishness." Written in Jacob Bruce's copy of Valentin Weigel's *Philosophia Mystica* (1648). University of Helsinki Rare Books Collection. Photograph by the author.

Amane in 1873, following the Meiji Restoration, to designate Western philosophy in particular (Amane also coined the Chinese equivalent *zhexue*). It is composed of two semantic units, *tetsu*, meaning "wisdom," and *gaku*, meaning "learning." There is no mention of "love" here, yet this term may still be considered a neologistic partial calque, invented for the purpose of talking about an imported tradition. Later, in the early twentieth century with the rise of the Kyoto school of *tetsugaku*, the term would come to describe a hybrid tradition, incorporating elements of European philosophy as well as Buddhist and Shinto ones.

Tetsugaku, from its first appearance, designates a different domain of intellectual activity than either *rangaku*, on the one hand, which is the tradition of "Dutch" or European learning and is principally concerned with the importation of positive and applied knowledge of the natural sciences and technology, and, on the other hand, *kokugaku*, or Japanese philology, which is to say the study of national tradition.[2] The fact that earlier there had been no particular need for a term other than *rangaku* to describe Western learning has something to do with developments within Japan, but also with the growing separation between science and philosophy, *rangaku* and *tetsugaku*, in the West itself. "Dutch learning" was not understood in Japan as profane or impious, in the way that "world-wisdom" was often understood in Germany or Scandinavia. But it was, by definition, imported, and as such could at most only be one part, a carefully regulated and dosed part, of the intellectual life of Japan. The later appearance of *tetsugaku* in the nineteenth century, in turn, shows a clear conceptual distinction between the natural sciences on the one hand (which in Europe, again, had often been treated as "world-wisdom," and thus, on a certain understanding, as philosophy), and philosophy on the other, understood as abstract speculation on more or less "nonworldly" or transcendental matters. This is not surprising, given the broadly Buddhist, and therefore thoroughly transcendentalist, background of the coiners of "tetsugaku," and given their heightened receptivity to contemporary trends in European philosophy, particularly German Idealism and Romanticism, that made a sharp distinction between the sphere of interest of the natural scientist and that of the philosopher.

The great majority of words for "philosophy" throughout the world are, as in English, direct or indirect loans from the Greek "philosophia." Many if not most of these terms are the consequence of contact with the Arabic-Islamic world. To get a sense of this great diversity, languages that use some version of "philosophia" to describe the activity of philosophy include Albanian, French, Karakalpak, Mongolian, Tagalog, New Guinean Tok Pisin, and Haitian Creole. Rather than coming from recent European colonial impositions, in very many cases the Greek loan words in the languages of Africa and Asia, from Swahili to Uzbek to Yakut, come from direct or indirect contact with Islam, which spread the tradition of *falsafa* along with the Greek-derived vocabulary item.

In those cases where the word is not on loan from Greek, we often find neologisms designed to capture the spirit of "philosophia" and to signal that the activity in question comes from a different part of the world. We see a familiar pattern repeating itself from Japan to Mexico to the Andes. In Nahuatl, for example, there is no obvious premodern term that presents itself to do the work of "philosophy," but it is easy to create one from available roots. In his bilingual work, the *Historia general de las cosas de la Nueva España* (*General History of the Things of New Spain*), the sixteenth-century Franciscan missionary Bernardino de Sahagún simply borrows the Spanish phrase "filosofía natural" for the Nahuatl as well as the Spanish portion of the text (image 5).[3] More frequently, however, we find compound neologisms whose coiners strive to capture the meaning of "philosophy." In this way, one has the ability to stress indigenous tradition (as in *machiliztli*, "knowledge derived from tradition") or to speak of wisdom in general (as in *tlazohmatiliztli*, which is more plainly suited for referring to European traditions). However exactly they are composed, the sense of a need for such neologisms comes in recognition

IMAGE 5. Head of a Calmecac school addressing students, from the *Florentine Codex: General History of the Things of New Spain*, by Fray Bernardino de Sahagun, volume 1, del libro 2, fo. 128, figure 2) (1545–1590). Image courtesy of Biblioteca medicea Laurenziana. Reproduced with permission of MiBACT. Further reproduction by any means is prohibited.

of the fact that there is a word for a particular human activity that is used in other, globally dominant languages, and it is expedient to produce an equivalent term.[4]

Many examples of conventional terms for "philosophy" that cannot be categorized as loans, calques, or neologisms, but that have their own indigenous heritage and that mount a resistance to the incorporation of new terms, come from South Asia. Here one can avail oneself of the Sanskrit *tattvajānam*, which means literally "knowledge of truth" or "knowledge of the way things are," or one can invoke the notion of *darśana*, which literally means "vision" and which is also the term that traditionally designates the six *āstika* (orthodox) schools of Indian "philosophy": Nyāya, Yoga, Mīmāṃsā, and so on, as well, finally, as the unorthodox or *nāstika* schools such as Buddhism. "Darśana," in turn, is the most common term for "philosophy" in many of the modern Sanskrit-derived languages of South Asia, such as Hindi.

It has sometimes been noted that in classical Indian thought there is no single overarching activity of *darśana* in the Indian intellectual life-world that encompasses what goes on in each of the individual *darśanas*, in the way that, say, Philosophia was understood to encompass Platonism, Stoicism, Epicureanism, and so on. If we take any one of the *darśanas* separately, moreover, it does not seem to give us anything close to a perfect match with the range of activities encompassed, in various centuries and regions and traditions, under the heading of Philosophia. Mīmāṃsā is principally focused on exegesis of the sacred Vedas. Yoga involves a practical component of the sort that exists almost nowhere in the various schools of Philosophia. Nyāya, or the study of the rules of inference, looks very much like the logical tradition of Philosophia, but many practitioners of Philosophia would be hesitant to accept that logic by itself deserves to be called philosophy. For better or worse, *darśana* as a general term, used in the singular, does the work in modern Sanskrit that *tetsugaku* does in Japanese: it serves as a neutral term to pick out the shared activity of people whose activity bears an ancestral relation to Philosophia. I might attempt to describe myself as a *darśanapradhyāpakah*, a "professor of philosophy," but this sounds forced and would only ever be said for the purposes of intercultural communication. The plural *darśana*s, by contrast, do not exist to mediate between cultures.

The resistance of South Asia to the encroachment of loans and calques evidently has to do with the richness and depth of the indigenous intellectual traditions that most closely resemble Philosophia, and with the absence of a perceived need throughout much of the history of contact with Europe to learn philosophy from the foreigners. This in turn would seem to corroborate the oft-recited idea that philosophy is a human activity that has emerged independently only twice in human history: once in Greece, and once in India, with every other instance of philosophy being a radiation or diffusion of one of these. On such an understanding, Japanese and Chinese would have been more inclined to develop neologisms and loan words to describe the concepts and schools associated with Philosophia, and had already done something similar in the reception of Buddhism in its earlier radiation from India.

But to discern such a corroboration begs the question. To suppose that there are two separate and independent origins for philosophy, once as Greek love of wisdom and once as Indian vision, takes for granted that we have a clear understanding at the outset of what philosophy is, and that we have discovered the necessary and sufficient conditions of it exactly twice. Yet in discussions of this sort, one seldom finds these conditions explicitly spelled out, and when a demand is made that they be spelled out, the participants in the discussion flounder. They might specify that there must be an explicit set of rules of inference, or that there must be reflection not just on the content of knowledge but also on the grounds of knowledge, but for any such specification we can easily find traditions or schools in which these elements are absent, but that are nonetheless classified, traditionally and by wide agreement, as philosophy.

If in fact philosophy arose independently twice, then it could not possibly be comparable to ballet or some other distinct tradition of dance. But if it is not like ballet, then the most obvious alternative possibility is that it is like dance itself: a universal human activity that undergoes different inflections in different times and places. But if this is so, then we should not expect to find it in only two places, and instead should be able to take for granted that all human cultures everywhere, insofar as they are human, are going to be doing something homologous to the activity thought of by modern Europeans as philosophy.

The fact that the word for philosophy in so many places in the world is a word that derives from "philosophia" strongly indicates that with the circulation of knowledge in the Islamic and later in the European expansions, philosophy was conceptualized by the people who spread it as akin to ballet rather than to dance. Compare the words for "ballet" in various languages around the world: Arabic, *bāliye*; Hindi, *baile*; Tagalog, *ballet*, and so on. Correlatively, the word for the Japanese tradition of butoh dance theater is, in every language, "butoh" (or some close approximation of it). To attempt to describe butoh by a local name, borrowed from a familiar local tradition, would be to betray and misrepresent it. The term for philosophy has generally spread in the same way as "ballet" or "butoh," yet with some significant exceptions, which instead acknowledge the existence of local intellectual traditions. Are these latter cases betrayals of philosophy, or are they rather an acknowledgment that philosophy, again, is more like dance in general than it is like ballet?

Again, it would be nonsensical to ask why the Polynesians do not have ballet; they do not have it because it is a regional tradition (incidentally, this seems to be roughly the way Saul Bellow was thinking of the tradition of the novel in literature when he implied, to much dismay, that there is no Tolstoy among the Zulus[5]). Correlatively, it would be no less nonsensical to ask why the Nuer of southern Sudan ended up incorporating firearms into their society.[6] They did so because guns are useful for killing people, or for getting what you want from them by threat of force. To put it bluntly, guns have a place in every culture, in view of their immense usefulness in the advancement of what appears to be a universal human end. This is a usefulness, moreover, that it does not take previously unarmed cultures all that long to figure out. It does not matter what eventual ceremonies a given culture will build up around its guns (sergeants-at-arms, twenty-one-gun salutes, and such); the primary application of firepower will remain everywhere the same.

If philosophy were like gunpowder or guns, there would be no question as to its reach: everyone would share in it equally. If philosophy were like ballet, there would also be no question as to why everyone does not share in it equally. Still another comparison, one that keeps the example of military technology in view, would be to say that philosophy is not like the technology of war but more like a particular military tradition that grows up around the use of weapons and the preparation for war and involves the pinning of medals, the reference to great battles and strategies of the past, and so on. In the case of martial pageantry, it is clear what the more basic thing is around which the tradition springs up, just as in the case of ballet, there is also clearly a more basic thing, dance, which in turn appears to be something humans qua humans do.[7]

But what would that more basic thing be, in the case of philosophy? The sources are various. We have already considered how the strata of myth, ritual, law, and other elements of culture support the self-conscious activity of philosophers. No small part is also played, at least in some societies, by what we might call "bean counting," the tallying of exchanges (of cattle, grain, and such) by use of pebbles in bowls, of marks on clay tablets, and so on. Wherever we have traces of this sort of activity, we have concrete evidence of a sort of representational thinking (one pebble stands for one cow, and such) that we can rightly suppose to be just the small report of a more elaborate system of classifications, of setting up correspondences, and of seeking adequate definitions. Wherever you have people keeping track of things in this way, you most likely have people trying to come to terms with the nature of the things they are keeping track of. A charitable assessment of what the ancients were up to would have us suppose that wherever there is a trace of a society trying to keep track of the world for practical purposes (navigation, calendrical science, and so on), there is something like a theoretical elaboration of the grounds of the practice.

One might insist that this elaboration must, in addition and at a minimum, involve reflection on the grounds of knowledge of the given domain, rather than just on the domain itself, that it must, that is, centrally involve epistemology. But many of the early pre-Socratic philosophers, notably the Miletians, for example, do not worry about how they can know the claims they make are true. They just go ahead and make them. The expectation that philosophy must involve epistemology is very recent and makes demands on the term in question that few believed must be satisfied until at least the middle of the eighteenth century. It might thus seem odd to neglect the meaning of a term that has accrued over millennia for the sake of accommodating relatively recent trends; that is, trends that have really only come to dominate in the past few centuries. What is more, the possibility should not be excluded that even epistemology is rooted in the sort of processes I am describing. Recent work by Michael Friedman has made a convincing case, in more steps than I am able to recapitulate here, for tracing the Kantian theory of space and time as pure forms of intuition back to certain exigencies of medieval astronomy, which in the final analysis existed for the sake of calendrical science, which in turn had as its principal purpose the determination of the proper date of Easter.[8]

Plainly, though, the universal activity that relates to Philosophia in the same way that dance relates to ballet cannot *just* be what we have called "bean counting." First of all, systematic recording techniques for the inventory of different kinds of things that are possessed or exchanged only exist in certain societies, whereas what we are looking for must, like dance, be common to all societies. Many other activities present themselves as candidates here: storytelling, ritual, prayer, myth. But if these activities contain philosophy, this philosophy would be philosophy in the "ore" state: that is, again, it would be mixed with human cultural practices that need to be distinguished from philosophy lest philosophy simply become identical with all of human culture (though this possibility in turn deserves at least a respectful refutation).

How, we are seeking to determine, do we isolate the activity of philosophy? How do we distinguish it from other activities? One way of approaching these questions is to ask whether philosophy must exist as a *specialized* activity. Must it be practiced, that is, only at certain times by only certain members of a given society in order to be identifiable as philosophy? Paul Radin affirms this view in his curious work of 1928, *Primitive Man as Philosopher.*[9] For him, the philosophical temperament is equally distributed, and equally rare, throughout all human cultures. Just as not every twenty-first-century New Yorker will have the inclination to become a professor of philosophy, so in traditional Lakota society, not every person had the inclination to engage in the activity that Radin is prepared to identify as "primitive philosophy."[10]

Setting aside the obviously problematic character of the category of the "primitive," now, what is the activity that Radin has in mind? It is, above all, the concern to abstract away from isolated phenomena and toward the general regularities that make these phenomena happen the way they do. It is, relatedly, a concern to arrive at the reality behind the appearances. Not every member of every culture, Radin thinks, exhibits an interest in thinking about such things, but there will be at least some people in every culture who do exhibit such an interest. Effectively, what Radin wishes to do is to win for traditional non-European cultures the claim to being philosophical cultures by identifying a division of labor similar to the one analyzed by Aristotle in the *Politics*, where the Greek philosopher describes philosophers in general as a specialized and privileged elite within a broader society. Radin, unlike Aristotle, ignores the economic and material divisions that destine most members of a society to a life of labor and permit a few members to lead a life of contemplative leisure. He sees the division in society rather as flowing directly from a difference of temperaments—presumably, this would be the only way for him to explain the emergence of a specialized class of philosophers within a society, such as the Lakota, that is held to be egalitarian and classless.

Aristotle and Radin agree, in any case, that philosophy is a specialized activity characteristic of certain members of a society, and not a universal activity in which all members of a society take part insofar as they are members of that society. Radin's approach thus differs very sharply from that, for example, of Alexis Kagame and others who have attempted to extract philosophical traditions from the natural languages of linguistic communities. Thus in his *La philosophie Bantu comparée* of 1976,[11] Kagame begins by citing the Danish linguist Louis Hjelmslev's dictum that "there is no philosophy without linguistics." The Rwandan philosopher then goes on to construct a systematic philosophy of Bantu-speaking peoples, including, for example, an analysis of the Bantu concepts of God and the good. Kagame does not claim that there is a specialized class of members of Bantu-speaking societies consciously engaged in an activity that may be called "philosophy," but only that the natural languages of all members of Bantu societies contain, so to speak, a latent philosophy, to which everyone in these societies has immediate access simply in virtue of their mastery of the language. A similar approach, if less attached to formal linguistics, is taken by the Ghanaian philosopher J. B. Danquah in his 1944 work, *The Akan Doctrine of God: A Fragment of Gold Coast Ethics and Religion.*[12] For him, ethical and theological commitments are not the specialized products of a minority activity called "philosophy" within a given society. Rather, the philosophy is a sort of general feature of the culture, just like cuisine or folklore or ornamentation, and it can be discerned and systematized by anyone familiar with the culture and with the crystallization of the culture's attributes in its natural language.

It is not our purpose, yet, to weigh the merits of the different positions on the scope and nature of philosophical activity, but only to enumerate them. So far, we have identified the view that philosophy is Philosophia, thus not only a specialized activity, but also a distinct tradition that emerges in a particular place and time. We have also identified the view that philosophy is a specialized activity, but one that occurs in all societies. Finally, we may identify the view that philosophy not only occurs in all societies, but that it is coextensive with culture, and therefore that every member of a culture shares equally in it. These different views, presented in this order, move from the most restrictive to the most capacious. In reality, many people are willing to invoke different of these three conceptions of philosophy for different purposes. For example, many who would insist that any expression of a member of a European culture that deserves the name of "philosophy" must be textual, systematic, distinct from mythology or ritual, at the same time hold that elsewhere in the world, as in Africa, we might find philosophy expressed as part of an oral tradition, embedded in mythology or poetry.

Radin's account has the apparent virtue of permitting its defenders to portray the specialized activity of certain members of "primitive" societies as a sort of precursor to the specialized activity of the Greco-European philosopher. The search for such precursors would be a commonplace of nineteenth- and early twentieth-century ethnography: the shaman is depicted as an evolutionary ancestor to the temple priest, and the temple priest to the philosopher. I have explicitly refused to endorse such an evolutionist conception of the history of human thought in this book, but one need not do so in order to appreciate that there is, in fact, a shared activity that unites the people who occupy the social roles, variously, of the shaman, the priest, and the philosopher, in different places and times—namely, that they all purport to have some sort of authority regarding the true order of things beyond the mundane order of appearances. The shaman and the priest typically do not offer arguments to ground their knowledge claims about this reality, any more than, say, the morphology of Bantu words can be said to offer explicit arguments about the nature of the supreme being. Radin and Kagame principally differ, then, in their understanding of the relative ubiquity of philosophy in traditional cultures: the one holds that it is found in a specialized class of experts, the other that it is mixed into the natural language spoken by everyone.

We have already seen some of the early efforts of Greek philosophers to distinguish their activity from that of, say, historians or poets, and we have also seen a great deal of uncertainty (for example, in Heraclitus, or among Socrates's accusers) as to how exactly philosophy is to be marked off from such activities as history, poetry, and myth. Again, whether philosophers have attempted to mark it off or not, in actual practice it has always been thoroughly intermingled with these other activities: the gold of philosophy in the ore of culture. Aristotle often cites Homer as an authority, for example, and Plato frequently switches into the register of myth without giving any indication that he thinks of this switch as a move away from philosophy and into another register of intellectual activity. In medieval Islamic and Christian philosophy, when philosophers often explicitly understood their own activity as subordinate to and an auxiliary of theology, we also often find the authority of scripture playing a crucial role within the context of philosophical arguments. Revelation thus supports arguments from reason as much as these arguments buttress the truth of revealed scripture. Some Eurocentric views of philosophy have maintained that the Orthodox schools of Indian thought, the *darśanas*, could not possibly be considered as philosophy, since these are almost by definition devoted to the task of explicating the Vedas, a collection of texts held to be of divine origin. But it would be hard to consistently maintain this argument for, say, Patañjali's *Yoga Sutras*, without being prepared to extend it, for example, to Augustine's *City of God*.

Even if we are able to conceptually distinguish philosophy from its neighbors in myth and poetry, in most of the actual textual productions categorized as "philosophy" we find that it seldom exists in its pure form. As with gold contained in ore, philosophy can often only be separated from surrounding elements in a historical text by an elaborate, and generally destructive, technical procedure. And if we are prepared to undertake this procedure for Augustine or Patañjali, it is difficult to see why we should decline to do so when we encounter, say, a claim from a Lakota elder about the hidden forces in virtue of which it makes sense, citing Radin's own preferred example, to say that rocks are married to the earth. What all of these cases have in common is that they leverage an individual's social authority to make weight-bearing claims about the nature of reality in a way that ultimately serves to ground or to legitimate or illuminate the cultural tradition that, from the outside, would be considered that culture's "mythology." To extract a philosophy from natural language, as Kagame hopes to do, is a more difficult process still. But what the philosophy blended into everyday natural languages lacks, and the philosophy that the shaman or priest blends together with mythology possesses, and what makes it more difficult for outsiders to recognize as philosophy, is arguably only the authoritative voice of the shaman or priest, which helps to separate his claims out from their cultural embeddedness.

One problem that arises in an evolutionary model of philosophy, which sees shamans and priests as proto-philosophers, is that to some extent it identifies the authority in early societies in the wrong place. For what would later be called "philosophy" concerns itself not just with the transcendent or supernatural beings with whom holy men and women purportedly have closer contact than others do. Philosophy also concerns itself, as has already been suggested, with less easily sacralized abstractions, such as quantity and number—though of course even number can be imbued with sacral importance, as in Pythagorean numerology. Here, it seems that the early authorities would be not the priests but the specialists in weights and measures. Wherever we find abacuses being used, for example, we may infer the presence of a conscious activity of reasoning in which individual rings or beads on the apparatus are understood to represent other entities beyond themselves. Beans in a bowl can stand for individual cows, or for fixed quantities of cattle. Wherever there are such practices, we may be reasonably sure of an awareness of the concept of quantity or number quite independently of quantities or numbers of this or that sort of entity.

Again, bean counting is very close, both conceptually and genealogically, to tabulation, or to list making on clay tablets, which in turn was the principal purpose of the earliest forms of writing.[13] Before there were sacred texts, and long before oral epic poems were committed to writing, markings that represented cattle, jugs, bushels, and so on were being used to record everyday transactions. Anthropologists have long noted that the emergence of practices such as these, even the composition of apparently unstructured lists, played a crucial role in the emergence of an awareness of the possibility of ordering our thought. Placing units of cattle on a list of things bought and sold opens up the possibility of visualizing information in terms of logical oppositions. There has never been writing without at least some awareness of the possibility of formalizing thought into a logical system. Again, the first writing was focused principally on commercial transactions, while many early sacred texts had long prehistories as oral traditions. These include, notably, the Rig Veda, which lies at the beginning of the Orthodox Indian philosophical traditions. In the Indian case, writing was typically seen as an expedient prosthesis for finite human minds, while the "true" text, what the Rig Veda *really* was, was understood to be a spoken work, one that would ideally be memorized by those who claimed knowledge of it. It is thus somewhat surprising to see even recent authors arguing that the abstractions we associate with intellectual communities arose, in Randall Collins's words, "at the same time as public systems of writing." This, for Collins, is not a contingent connection, but indeed results from the fact that "lectures and texts are chained together." He cites, as an example to help make his case, the dialogues depicted in the Upanishads between sages, as well as "lecture-like guidance by masters of disciples."[14] But this misses the important point, again, that within the early Indian context speech and text belonged to very different conceptual spheres, and it was only the former that was seen as crucial to those abstractions that constitute at least one of the important sources for what we now think of as philosophy.

Aristotle would distinguish poetry from other activities by noting that it ranges over the possible, but what interests him in this distinction is the characteristic content of poetry. Parallel to this, however, there are also formal elements that mark poetry off from prose. Poetry is, most importantly, rhythmic and repetitive, and to this extent it overlaps with other domains of human cultural life such as music and ritual. This overlap is not apparent today, when much of our experience of poetry is in its written, textual form. But for the memorizers of the Rig Veda, the experiential qualities of this work, including the ritual and quasi-musical significance of its recitation, would have been constantly present to mind. Again, while logic has its roots in the earliest writing, what we think of as early sacred texts often do not emerge out of writing, but rather out of oral, rhythmic, and ritual traditions. Philosophy thus has a shared genealogy with cultural practices seemingly as far apart as early transactional records and early oral epic poetry.

Another activity that has gone on throughout all human cultures and that feeds into the practice of philosophy in significant ways is classification: the placing of kinds of entities in the natural and social worlds into hierarchical relations with one another. It was in virtue of the elaborate taxonomical schemes of Amazonian groups that Claude Lévi-Strauss determined that all human societies have, at the very least, a "logic of the concrete," even if they do not all have a theory that makes it possible to replace the concrete entities in a given classificatory scheme with abstractions or variables.[15] Yet it is not clear how classification of concrete entities could be carried out without some idea of abstract kind categories into which these entities may be slotted. There is a tremendous literature debating just what might be meant by "logic of the concrete," and there is no need for us to enter into it here. It is sufficient to point out that, as recent scholarly work in ethnotaxonomy has confirmed, the order and intricacy of nature is just as complex in the minds of members of traditional nontextual cultures as it was in Aristotle's or Linnaeus's mind when they wrote their respective pathbreaking works of scientific taxonomy.[16]

Aristotle, more than Linnaeus, is often credited with having a theory of kinds that underlies his description of animal kinds, and thus with having a philosophy of science behind his contributions to taxonomical science. But here as elsewhere, we may ask whether this underlying theory needs to be made explicit by its holder in order for that conceptual scheme to be deemed philosophical, or whether it is enough that the philosophical commitments can be extracted by a diligent researcher. The problem for Amazonian ethnotaxonomy is much the same as for Bantu natural language: there is extra work to be done if we wish to extract an explicit and systematized treatment of concepts. But whether this extra work means that the knowledge-systems at their source are or are not philosophical seems to depend on a stipulative answer to the question as to what philosophy is, which is to say it depends on an answer that has little force beyond simply reporting the relative narrowness or breadth of the conception of philosophy on the part of the person answering the question.

Radin's work and some other noteworthy exceptions aside, philosophy has generally defined itself as an activity that is exclusively to be found in complex institutions, and thus at the heart of urban societies, to the exclusion of different, supposedly more "primitive" forms of life that could otherwise reveal radically different ways of thinking about basic philosophical questions. Thus in the *Scienza Nuova* of 1710, Giambattista Vico states this view as clearly as it could possibly be stated: "First the woods, then cultivated fields and huts, next little houses and villages, thence cities, finally academies and philosophers: this is the order of all progress from the first origins."[17] For Vico, "the order of ideas must follow the order of institutions," and it is only a certain kind of institutions—namely, the crowning institutions of sociocultural development—that can give rise to recognizably philosophical ideas. The rest is myth, superstition, and "the logic of the concrete."

To take an interest in these latter forms of thought is to abandon philosophy and to retreat into anthropology, or cultural studies, or what the Germans call *Folkloristik*. This retreat is typically seen, relative to philosophy, as a sort of irrationalism. The German incarnation of this interest arose out of a rejection of Enlightenment philosophy toward the end of the eighteenth century, which was premised on the idea that any thinking worthy of being called "philosophy" will emanate from metropolitan centers. The reaction in Germany took the forms of a very productive and valuable tradition of human-scientific study of myth, culture, and folklore, but also of a very unproductive and even noxious tradition of philosophy that explicitly prized irrationalism, and that saw this mode of thought as better suited to dark forest paths than to the urban institutions Vico had considered as preconditions of philosophy. But in much German philosophy this tendency remained thoroughly dismissive of forms of thought in, say, the Amazon, as if the Black Forest were able to stimulate reflections that the rain forest cannot, and in this respect it remained just as metropolitan as the Enlightenment rationalism it held itself to be rejecting. Relatedly, it failed to acknowledge that all of

Germany had become, in the modern period, a carefully administered and regimented space. Even the dark forest paths had been rationalized on maps and in paperwork in government offices. There was no wilderness left, and so no real escape from the metropole.

It is perhaps in part the fear of the irrationalism attempted by Heidegger and other *Holzweg*-wanderers that has made the urban and sedentist prejudice in Anglo-American philosophy so solid as to pass unnoticed. It is now very unusual for a member of the mainstream community of philosophy in the Anglophone world to refuse to acknowledge the desirability of greater diversity, in the demographics of the profession as well as in the actual content studied. But the change of content is generally, at most, only an opening up to traditions of thought that are *already* recognizably philosophical by the same broad criteria through which Anglo-American philosophers understand themselves: formalized debate, fixed and unmoving institutions of training in the tradition, textuality, explicit separation of the tradition from the aims of theology, ritual, myth, and so on. This is not so much a rejection of Eurocentrism as it is an expansion of the empire. In most cases, the newly absorbed traditions are recognizable as philosophical because they are as a matter of historical fact cognate with, or offshoots of, the very same metropolitan and lofty-minded institutions in which philosophy is practiced and reproduced. Thus, for example, African American traditions are in a position to be absorbed. But these traditions have grown up, since the very beginning, in direct, fertile contact with Euro-American traditions. How could they fail to do so, given the intimate, complicated, shared history of Americans of (principally) African descent with those of (principally) European descent? Just think, for example, of the life course, the education, and the habitus of a philosopher such as W.E.B. DuBois, who spent some of his most formative years in Berlin.

Now that many are eager to absorb DuBois into the philosophical canon, and we now judge that it is a shame and a scandal that thinkers of his caliber were excluded for so long, we still have to ask the question: what is it we are still excluding, perhaps without even realizing it? Here one might invoke the knowledge traditions of the people of interest to Zora Neale Hurston: the oral lore of nontextual peoples of the US South that she collected, inspired in no small measure by Franz Boas, whose intellectual heritage extends back to that other German tradition that I have already evoked, the one that gave us not irrationalist philosophy but rather folklore studies. Not Heidegger, but the Brothers Grimm.

Vico's demarcation of philosophy from "poetry," which he sees as a mode of thought characteristic of pre-urban archaic cultures, is based on the different valuation in these spheres of activity placed on the universal and the particular. Unlike Aristotle, for whom poetry ranges over possibles and thus is in some sense closer to philosophy than it is to history, for Vico poetry plunges into particulars, while metaphysics rises us up to universals. Whether this distinction has any validity or not, it is obvious, and Vico will even admit, that on his understanding it would be impossible ever to do pure philosophy. Today interdisciplinarity is generally considered a virtue, but the human sciences that are held to be most relevant to contemporary philosophy are the ones that study modern, urbanized minds and societies: empirical psychology (usually focusing on urban Americans, sometimes branching out to foreign cities such as Hong Kong)[18] and empirical sociology. What is left out are recognizable expressions of culture such as the narrative arts and to a lesser extent the visual arts, particularly those of non-Western, nonurban societies. Philosophy remains indifferent to the sort of work done under the banner of ethnography, ethnomusicology, folklore studies, comparative mythology, and so on: everything that might get us mixed up with "the poetic," in Vico's sense.

Vico's distinction tends to inform the way we think about philosophy's special place among disciplines today, and also grounds the dismissal as "unphilosophical" of the study of the expressions of arts and culture that tend to focus on particulars. The recognition of the value of particular things as being of intrinsic interest, a matter treated at length in the first chapter, was arguably one of the most powerful elements of the countertradition I have evoked that emerges at a certain point in German philosophy and that leads eventually to the full efflorescence of the *Geisteswissenschaften*. This countertradition is the one that does not limit the range of worthy ideas to those that are produced within a particular institutional setting, and that therefore cannot index the progress of human thought, as Vico seeks to do, to the growing complexity of human institutions.

To go along with this countertradition, to get serious about inclusiveness by reconceiving philosophy in a maximally capacious way, as including not just institutionally based textual knowledge but also orally transmitted folk knowledge, is something that is unlikely to happen soon. Most would take it to be a self-destructive move, an abandonment of any meaningful distinction between philosophy and the rest of human culture. But one serious problem is that unless this reconception occurs, all of the current efforts at inclusiveness within Anglo-American academic philosophy will remain superficial half-measures. There are forms of difference undreamt of in academic philosophy's current efforts at diversification. Vico has explicitly identified these forms as characteristic of non-urban peoples. We echo the Vichian prejudice today without realizing it, to the extent that all of the forms of otherness that we would like to see included in the philosophical canon, and in the profession of academic philosophy, are forms that are well represented in the city.

The point I am making is one that is largely unfamiliar to Marxists and to social democratic liberals, but that will perhaps be more familiar to anarchists as well as to a certain variety of wistful conservatives. It was made forcefully by the archconservative Australian Catholic poet Les Murray, who complained of "that sanctified anti-rural prejudice that goes right back to classical times and which no antidiscrimination law or postcolonial rhetoric ever protects you from—so to hell with those."[19] But we do not need to go along with Murray's concluding malediction in order to accept that there is such a prejudice. This is a prejudice that philosophy continues to accept without reflection, on the presumption that to give it up would be to lapse into the nonphilosophy of anthropology or folkloristics. But the prejudice excludes a huge section of humanity, and also sustains in particular an artificial bias in favor of the present, as the present is the age of the most intense urbanization, and textualization, in human history. And it occludes from view many extremely valuable insights about the nature and formation of moral commitments to animals, to the environment, to ancestors. It ensures that we will only see a small part of the range of human experience and self-understanding.

I hear Thomas Nagel holding forth on whether death is or is not an objective misfortune, or Hannah Arendt on why it is troubling to see human viscera, or Daniel Dennett on which creatures may be killed with no moral qualms, and which may not be, and I think: why should I listen to *you* in particular? There is a whole world full of people out there, some on farms, some in rain forests, and some in slums, all charged up with beliefs of their own about these and many other things. My philosophy would be the one that would take the broadest possible measure of these beliefs, without concern for the institutional affiliations, the literacy, or the geographical niche of their holders.

A familiar observation has been made in connection with the history of philosophical reflection on the nature of human distinctness, which has it that language has moved in in the past century or so to fill a role that had previously been taken up by belief in a divinely implanted soul. We allow the faculty of language to play a role in defining what is most excellent about human beings in part because appeals to the inherence of an immortal, eternal, immaterial principle that makes us what we are have, so to speak, fallen out of fashion. While the soul has a greatly reduced place in contemporary philosophy, a reduction that was already well under way in the nineteenth century, nonetheless language is often invoked in ways that suggest that it is this faculty that gives us our own share of divinity, as the soul once did. Thus the poet Paul Valéry evocatively describes language as "the god gone astray in the body."[20] Richard Sorabji also describes this process very well in his account of the history of thinking about human uniqueness in relation to the rest of the animal kingdom. It used to be, he explains, that what set us apart was our soul; when that distinction could no longer be supported, the special difference was thought to lie in language; when it was revealed that many animals have complex systems of communication, a further precision was made so that "language" would be understood, along Chomskian lines, as consisting by definition in infinitely recursive syntax. "They don't have syntax, so we can eat them" was meant to be the conclusion about animals, but as Sorabji notes with understatement, this is far from being a valid inference.[21]

This continuity is of interest to us in connection with the work of Alexis Kagame and others, already introduced, on the inherent philosophical character of natural languages, such as those of the Bantu family. As we have seen, Kagame believes that there can be no philosophy without linguistics. Incidentally, he is also a Catholic priest and is working on Bantu philosophy in a respectful and critical relationship to the Belgian missionary Placide Tempels, who in 1945 published the seminal study *La philosophie bantoue*.[22] Tempels was convinced that all truly "primitive" peoples had a clear and distinct concept of the supreme being, and that from this concept flowed a full command of logic and ethics that were a reflection of the divine reason and goodness. "The faith of really primitive peoples in the Supreme Being," Tempels writes, "lies at the root of all the religious conceptions current among semi-primitives: animism, dynamism, fetishism, and magic."[23] The purportedly lowest-grade forms of belief that anthropologists had long associated with "primitive" peoples were in fact only a degradation of a once pristine grasp of a truth that differed little from the one the Christian missionaries had come to share. Thus the work of the missionary was not so much to convert as to remind the native inhabitants of their real ontological commitments.

Tempels is echoing a standard liberal theological approach to Christian missions in the non-Christian world that had begun to emerge already in the seventeenth century, and one of whose most lucid exponents was G. W. Leibniz. In the *Discourse on the Natural Theology of the Chinese* of 1714, for example, Leib-niz argues that the ancient Chinese seem to have had a clear concept of God, but that in the recent era they had allowed themselves to be blindly governed by law and tradition to the extent that they had forgotten the basic truths they had known long ago. Again, proselytizing is thus understood not as conversion, but as inducing a sort of cultural anamnesis that reminds us all, Christians and pagans alike, of our shared commitments.

For Leibniz, too, even those cultures that have forgotten the eternal and divine truths that are the patrimony of all human-ity nonetheless produce abundant traces of these truths, per-haps subconsciously, in their texts, their oral traditions, and their everyday language. It is in this connection that Leibniz imagines, in the *New Essays concerning Human Understanding* of 1704, how the future course of the study of human wisdom will develop. "When the Latins, Greeks, Hebrews and Arabs shall someday be exhausted," he writes,

> the Chinese, supplied also with ancient books, will enter the lists and furnish matter for the curiosity of our crit-ics. Not to speak of some old books of the Persians, Ar-menians, Copts and Brahmins, which will be unearthed in time so as not to neglect any light antiquity may give on doctrines by tradition and on facts by history.[24]

With these textual traditions mastered, Leibniz thinks that the real work will have just begun: "And if there were no longer an ancient book to examine, languages would take the place of books, and they are the most ancient monuments of mankind."[25]

Kagame, like Leibniz, believes that natural languages, in this case Bantu languages, are the most ancient monuments of mankind. And like Tempels, Kagame believes that the ancient monument of Bantu natural language contains markers of ontological commitments that are shared among all speakers of these languages, including commitment to the reality of a supreme being. Kagame summarizes the categorial system of Bantu thought by noting that the most general category is designated by the root -*ntu*, meaning "being" or "existent" or "something."[26] There are in turn four most basic categories of being: *muntu* (existent with intelligence, or "person," also the source of the European corruption "Bantu"); *kintu* (existent without intelligence, or "thing"); *hantu* (localizing existent, or space-time); and *kuntu* (modal existent, or the manner of being of an existent).[27] This is all part of what Kagame describes as Bantu general metaphysics. There is also a special metaphysics of the "Pre-Existent," which is the primary cause of all existents, and which is not included in the categories just outlined.

There is no single term for the preexistent that could directly translate the word "God," though there are many partial synonyms, functioning as proper names, in particular Bantu languages (for example, *Mulungu* in ChiNyanja, *Nzambi* in Ki-Kongo). One may nonetheless make explicit a sort of Bantu theory of the "divine names," in the manner of Dionysius the Areopagite, by analyzing the numerous ways in which diverse aspects of the Pre-Existent are named and discussed in Bantu natural language: *Likatonda* (the Great Creator), *Limdimi* (the Great Guardian), *Limgalizi* (the Great Benefactor), and so on.[28] According to Kagame, the concept of transcendence is logically prior to all the other divine names. One can derive from actual use of natural language a commitment to the view that the Pre-Existent is "not a Being, that is to say an essence."[29] When ethnographers attribute to the Bantu the view that there is a supreme being in the European sense they are committing a heresy from the Bantu point of view, since they affirm "that the Pre-Existent arose from what exists, that it is not Eternal, that it is subject to movement."[30] Thus Kagame interprets the implicit theology of Bantu natural language as comparable to the apophatic theology of Greek figures such as Dionysus the Areopagite, in that God is beyond being and nonbeing, but is nonetheless the ultimate cause of everything that falls within this basic opposition. God is, to the extent that he may be spoken of in human language, *nyamuzinda* or "the beginning and end," *leza* or "all-powerful," *kalaga* or "preeminent," and so on, but all of these predicates, again, rely on the basic, primitive commitment to the view that God cannot be part of the general metaphysics of the category theory.[31] God is not, in sum, an -*ntu*.

We do not need to enter into the details of Kagame's subtle and exhaustive study. What is important is simply to gain an appreciation for his methodology, to grasp the significance of his effort to extract a category theory, and to delineate its boundaries and describe what lies beyond it, simply from the way people talk, from their grammar and vocabulary. In effect, Kagame is doing exactly what Leibniz had anticipated we would someday have to begin doing in order to have a truly exhaustive account of the variety of human wisdom. Ethnophilosophy, on this understanding, is no less philosophy than is the study of canonical texts.

However, it may be that the ontological commitments that Kagame is able to extract from natural language look too much like the commitments he already had at the outset of his study. It would be a remarkable thing if the Bantu had spontaneously converged on the same basic understanding of God as had certain late antique Greek Christians working under the broad influence of a Platonic metaphysics. Like Tempels, Kagame is dismissive of the elements of Bantu thought that had been classified by earlier ethnographers as "primitive," and he sees his denial of the centrality of "fetishes" or of ancestor worship in Bantu culture as a crucial part of his defense of their (and also his own) dignity and equality to all other human beings. Like Leibniz and Tempels both, Kagame thus conceives the difference between Christian tradition and pagan cultures as one simply of clarifying our real ontological commitments and coming to see that we in fact already believe the same things, that we all have an equal share in the truth in virtue of our descent, as children of God, from the same first parents. What is particularly striking is that these old theological ideas should survive so robustly into the plaidoyers of the twentieth century for the integrity and sophistication of traditional, nontextual knowledge systems, not just on the part of European missionaries but also of figures such as Kagame, who are working with the very sophisticated technical apparatus of twentieth-century linguistic philosophy, and who see themselves in effect as mediators between the intellectual traditions of Europe, on the one hand, and indigenous culture on the other.

The view of Leibniz and Kagame, that all cultures express the same philosophical truths from their own perspective, is in the end a variety of cosmopolitanism. This doctrine is most closely associated with figures in Hellenistic philosophy, though its core ideas are very simple and very widespread. Diogenes the Cynic answered the question, "Where are you from?" by saying simply, "I am a *kosmopolites*—a citizen of the world."[32]

Many scholars have noted the broad resemblances between this Cynic gesture, on the one hand, and, on the other, the various universalist, and therefore necessarily transnational, religious movements that appeared in the so-called Axial Age, not least Buddhism and Christianity. Both sought to establish the global validity of their central truth claims, and in so doing to break the historical link to a given culture. When Christ recommends that what is Caesar's be rendered unto Caesar, while what is God's be rendered unto God (Matthew 22:21), he is among other things delimiting two separate spheres of rule, one of which enjoys only local or regional legitimacy, the other of which both entirely overlaps with and extends infinitely beyond the domain of the former.

Christ's commandment is harder to follow however when "Caesar" sets himself up as a representative of the divine order to which Christ had his primary loyalty. Christ was able to distinguish between the two sorts of rendering only because Caesar was not, yet, Christian. But when an earthly ruler claims to be acting in the name of the divine order, then we have a political universalism that translates fairly readily into imperialism: divine truth is universal; I rule in the name of divine truth, therefore, my rule must be extended as widely as possible. This was already the case for the Buddhist emperor Aśoka, who effectively transformed Buddhism into a pan-Asian religion through imperial conquest.

The Maurya Dynasty of the third century BCE, over which Aśoka ruled, would by no means offer the last illustration of the general rule, whereby universalism, when translated into political action, tends to run roughshod over the interests of neighbors and minorities who might have preferred to keep going with their localism. This conflict between the local and the universal extends well beyond the universalist religions that appeared in antiquity, and even as far as the supposedly universal values of secular democracy—liberty, equality, and so on. As scholars such as Michael Mann[33] and, in his own way, Charles Taylor,[34] have noted, there are many respects in which minority groups fared better prior to the emergence of the democratic republics—here France and Turkey are the preferred examples—that sought to wash out the local concerns and values of minorities in favor of overarching values that are expected to be shared and cherished by all human beings equally, qua human beings.

Diogenes's claim to be a citizen of the world, then, is one thing when it is a sort of report on the disposition of a harmless world renouncer; it is quite another thing when world citizenship is understood as the inevitable outcome of the rule of a leader in possession of universal truth. This tension, one might suggest, has always been at the heart of cosmopolitanism. Claims to possession of universal truth, and claims of loyalty only to the global level at which such truths hold, are one thing in the hands of philosophers and mendicant monks, another in the hands of armies. And yet even when there is so to speak an armed wing of the spread of universal truth, we often find a proper cosmopolitan spirit in the philosophers who give voice to the values that are simultaneously being spread by force by their contemporaries in armies, missions, aggressive trade cartels, and in the gray area between all three of these. Nowhere is this clearer, perhaps, than in the history of early modern European cosmopolitanism, particularly as it was expressed in European reflection on the share of universal truth that East Asian civilizations may be thought to enjoy.

With the 1624 expulsion of the Spanish from Tokugawa Japan, and the following Closed Country Edict of 1635, in most of the seventeenth century Japan remains as if blurred out in the European imagination, though much recent scholarship has been focused on the previous century's significant syntheses of Western and Japanese knowledge systems. China by contrast remained an important field on which European thinkers and actors continued to try out their ideas about what commitment to a universal order of truth must be, and about the different ways this truth can be expressed in different cultural settings.

We might helpfully distinguish between two overlapping strains of reflection on universal truth and the way it is expressed differently in different local inflections. One is played out more in the domain of practices and values: are this distant culture's practices on an equal footing to mine, or are my prejudices about my own culture's distinctly superior forms justified? This is principally the sort of prejudice Diogenes was seeking to renounce when he identified himself as a *kosmou polites*. But there is another variety, which is perhaps best expressed in Aristotle's observation in the *Nicomachean Ethics* that "nature is unchangeable and has everywhere the same force (as fire burns both here and in Persia)."[35] From the fact that nature is everywhere the same, it follows that different people in different parts of the world are accounting for the same thing when they offer up descriptions or causal explanations of how the world works. There is then a sort of "scientific cosmopolitanism," to speak anachronistically, that holds that these different explanations are different ways of expressing the same truths, and that insofar as nature is governed by reason, these different explanations are all therefore rational.

Both strains come together in the question of natural theology, the question whether it is possible for a person or a group of people to come to a sufficient knowledge of God—sufficient, that is, for salvation—by means of reflecting on the order and orderliness of God's works alone, or whether by contrast revelation is also needed? Revelation, obviously, happens within a particular culture at a particular historical moment (in the case of Christianity, it is thought to have happened among eastern Mediterranean Jews a few centuries after the reported enlightenment of the Buddha in north India), while reflection on nature can happen anytime and anywhere.

Typically, the different sorts of cosmopolitanism go together: where it is presumed that each culture no matter what its textual sources of knowledge is capable of coming to knowledge about the order of nature and ultimately about this order's divine source, it is also presumed that different cultural expressions are going to be relatively insignificant variations on a single underlying human nature. This is particularly clear in Leibniz's dual interest in China: first, at an urgent, practical level, to take the side of the liberal Jesuits in the so-called rites controversy by defending the cultural practice of ancestor veneration as in no way incompatible with acceptance of Christian dogma,[36] and second, offering a theoretical account of the Chinese distinction between the transcendent and immanent, arguing that this suffices as evidence for an understanding of the fundamental distinction between God and creation, and that such a distinction is already sufficient for purposes of salvation in the next world and piety in this one, and reflecting, finally, on the philosophical-anthropological sources of this understanding.

Since his foreword to the 1699 Jesuit report from China, the so-called *Novissima Sinica*, Leibniz had been preoccupied with the parity between Europe and China, conceiving them as two mutually balancing poles of the Eurasian continent; he writes "that the greatest culture and the greatest technical civilization of humanity are concentrated on the two extreme ends of our continent, in Europe and in China ... which is equally a sort of Europe of the East, which adorns the opposite end of the earth."[37] Leibniz ultimately believes that every culture is equally equipped to express the eternal wisdom written into the natural order, which is an expression of divine reason. But he supposes like many contemporaries that China constitutes a special case among world cultures, as having attained a level of technological and political complexity equal or superior to that of Europe, but as having done so without the help of what, by European standards, would have been recognizable as philosophy.

A common prejudice held that the Chinese are in effect wise automata, or that Chinese technology and statecraft are developed blindly, without reflection on the first principles, of nature or of justice behind these. This prejudice took a different form, yet not categorically different, in early modern European assessments of, say, the herbal-medicinal knowledge of Native Americans living in traditional hunter-gatherer societies; here, it was supposed that the knowledge was a sort of outcropping of nature itself, that it did not fundamentally differ from zoopharmacognosy, or the ability of animals to seek out plant remedies when ill. Thus a typical term for aboriginal people was *les naturels*: the people who are literally not distinct from nature. In China, however, Europeans imagined that a separation from nature had occurred as a result of practices and technologies, but without the reflection on abstract principles that Europeans had tended to suppose must ground these practices and technologies in order for them to exist.

Various implausible theories were contrived to account for this apparent paradox. The Jesuit Athanasius Kircher, to cite one example, maintained that the Chinese had their origins in the ancient Near East, even that the Chinese writing system is a deformation of Hebrew. On this theory, the Chinese wandered long and far, and ultimately forgot the metaphysics and knowledge of first principles that had once underlain their science, ethics, and statecraft. Leibniz would not need to make up such implausible scenarios. For him, it is helpful to recall, absolutely everything is an expression of one and the same rational order, and every substance contains within its complete concept every truth about every other substance. It is for this reason that the study of indigenous languages, for example, strikes Leibniz as worthwhile; again, as he explains in the *Nouveaux essais* of 1704, it is not just the ancient texts of the Chinese and other classical civilizations that need to be studied alongside the sacred scripture, but also the languages of nontextual cultures, since, he argues, reason is embedded in vocabulary itself, in etymologies and in morphemes. So human cultures constitute a living repository of reason and are quite literally the world's greatest library. It follows also, inter alia, that for Leibniz a culture's practices do not need to be given explicit theoretical explanations by members of that culture in order to qualify as rational.

This is exactly what we would expect of the philosopher who gives us *petites perceptions*, the doctrine according to which every substance expresses the entire order of nature, even if most do so in a dim or confused fashion and so never succeed in gaining what could be called "knowledge" in a proper sense. And yet it would be a sort of condescension that Leibniz does not intend to attribute to him the view that Chinese knowledge systems consist in mere *petites perceptions*. On the contrary, by the time of the 1714 *Discourse* he is prepared to argue that at least in antiquity there was knowledge of a separately existing transcendent God. He writes:

It may at first be doubted that the Chinese recognize, or have recognized, spiritual substances. But after having thought about this much, I judge that yes, they do; although perhaps they do not recognize these substances as separate, and entirely beyond matter. There would be no harm here as concerns created substances, for I myself tend to suppose that angels have bodies, which was also the opinion of many of the ancient Church Fathers. I am also of the opinion that the rational soul is never entirely liberated from a body. But as concerns God, it may be that the sentiment of some of the Chinese has been to give him a body, to consider God as the soul of the world, and to join him with matter, as the ancient philosophers of Greece and of Asia did. However, in showing that the most ancient authors of China attribute to Li or to the first principle the very production of Ki or of matter, there is no need to start from scratch, and it will suffice to explain what they meant. [In this way], it will be easier to explain to their disciples that God is the *Intelligentia supramondana*, above all matter.[38]

We may certainly share the concern of those anti-Eurocentric authors who would get stuck on the first lines of this passage, on Leibniz's extreme presumption in granting to himself the authority to judge in this matter, from afar, with a rudimentary knowledge of the Chinese language, and assuming at the outset that *Li* properly understood must come out as a wholly transcendent principle in order to be, not just *like* the Christian God, but indeed correct. But let us try to set that aside in order to see what else is going on here. Leibniz is to some extent echoing Kircher's old *prisca theologia*, an esoteric theory of the hidden unity of all ancient knowledge traditions, but is doing so in a rather more charitable way. He does not suppose that the ancient texts of the Chinese need to come from the same source as those of the ancient Church Fathers in order to arrive at the truth.

For Leibniz, in effect, the Chinese have a concept of God even if they do not know it, or always know it. The concept can be extracted from *Li*, even if historically there is a tendency to regress toward a corporealized *anima mundi*, a regression that has also often occurred in Western history, and that Leibniz is, when he writes in the *Discourse*, actively criticizing English natural theology, in particular Locke and Newton, for having brought about. The Chinese do know God—even Newton knows God—but they all need Leibniz to help them clarify the concept they already possess. This is part and parcel of Leibniz's general method of conciliation; he supposes that everyone agrees, and that disagreement results only from insufficient clarity in the way we understand the terms we are using. Leibniz is famous for having supposed that we could prevent wars by declaring *Calculemus!*—Let us calculate!—as if war ever had, as its deep cause, disagreements about belief.

So Leibniz believes we all share in the same universal rational order, that we all know this order with varying degrees of clarity or confusion, and that we all therefore know, in some way or other, the truth. These beliefs taken together clearly constitute a variety of cosmopolitanism, which Diogenes himself would have recognized. But Leibniz also embodies the tension we have already discerned in the cosmopolitan commitment to universal truth; he thinks we all share in the same truth and therefore thinks we need to send missionaries to other parts of the world in order to convince them of the truth they already implicitly have and subconsciously know. While Leibniz liberally declares that China should be sending missionaries to Europe in matters of ethics, he never doubts the necessity and righteousness of the Christian mission to teach the Chinese, and indeed the entire world, not how to act, but about the first principles that ground right action.

Leibniz tends to side with the Jesuits in their conflicts with Rome; many of his principal informants are Jesuit missionaries such as Nicolò Longobardo. But his concrete purpose is to promote Protestant missionary activity to rival the Catholics, and he is particularly close to the liberal Protestant Orientalists of Halle, such as the scholar of Amharic and Ethiopian studies, Hiob Ludolf.[39] Here, though, it is difficult to separate what Leibniz and his like-minded missionary associates hoped to deliver to the Chinese and other non-Christian cultures, and what by contrast they hoped these groups might deliver to them. Leibniz writes the *Discourse* as a justification for ongoing missionary activity in China, but his main argument is that it is a mistake to suppose that on arrival the missionaries must, so to speak, start from scratch. On the contrary, he supposes that there is already much there to work with. And Leibniz's concern for promoting missionary activity may have more to do with his eager interest in having missionaries bring back information about what there is to work with, so to speak, what the Chinese themselves believe, than with any real interest in changing what they believe.

We see exactly the same hope for a fruitful bidirectionality in Leibniz's parallel campaign to obtain samples of all the non-textual languages of the Russian empire,[40] which would consist in a transcription of the Lord's Prayer. This would serve the dual purpose of rendering this core bit of Christian doctrine for the first time in the pagan languages of the Samoyed and the Kalmyks, but it would also gain, for Leibniz himself, a new bit of linguistic data to add to his ever-expanding database. This project is but one instance of Leibniz's vastly more ambitious "science of singular things," discussed at length in the previous chapter: the amassing of massive amounts of individual bits of data in different fields of knowledge that will enable an eventual mapping of the range of diversity within a given domain, and then, ultimately, will make possible an account of the unity that underlies the diversity.

Other clear examples of this approach are in areas as different as the study of magnetic variation and the collection of public-health statistics. But perhaps the most fruitful of all was the role that this approach played in the foundation of comparative linguistics as a concrete domain of scientific inquiry. The presumption was that each natural language amounts to an expression of the same rational order, even if each will be in its unique way more confused in certain domains than in others: an Amazonian language might be vastly "clearer" (in both the metaphysical and the linguistic senses), for the description of the properties of some medicinal plant; Latin might, for now anyway, be clearer in its ability to express the true nature of God. But there is no reason in principle why any given natural language should not be able to express the same truths about the world as any other. The Lord's Prayer is no less the Lord's Prayer in Samoyed than in Latin.

Cultural practices pose many of the same problems that natural languages do, and send us looking for the unity behind the diversity. They also generate serious epistemological problems for any outside attempt to judge the beliefs that are guiding the practices. The awareness of such problems, and of a consequent need to deploy a principle of charity in cases of intercultural contact, seems to have been what guided the liberal Jesuits, with whom Leibniz agreed, in the rites controversy. It is all very easy to declare, from Rome, that a Catholic service must look exactly the same in China as it does in Saint Peter's Basilica, but the missionaries on the ground will understand that of necessity accommodations need to be made to local realities.

Correlatively, in the direction not of adoption of Christianity but of its rejection or apparent rejection, Shūsaku Endō tells the story, in his 1966 novel *Silence*,[41] of a Portuguese missionary who decides to trample on the *fumie* the Japanese authorities have laid at his feet. This saves him from the fate of being hung upside down and bled to death. But it also comes, in the local context, to seem to him not as an expression of the ultimate sacrilege, but rather of his supreme commitment to and love of Christ. Ritual is perhaps infinitely variable; the meaning of gestures can easily be reversed. What Father Rodrigues believed to stay fixed and unchanging through this reversal was the truth of Christianity, even though his gesture was sure to cut him off forever from the earthly institution for which he worked. Similar stories abound in the ethnographic record: the Danish-Inuit anthropologist Knud Rasmussen tells of the Greenlandic shamans who, in the early twentieth century, converted to Christianity by eating, as their first communion, parts of the internal organs of the walrus that had previously been tabooed to men of their status.[42] There is obviously nothing about walruses in the Bible, but the fact that Christianity could only take root through the body of the walrus shows the inevitability of responding to local exigencies in the expansion of a universal order.

Father Rodrigues was, we might suggest, a true cosmopolitan, of Diogenes's caliber. He did not need to remain attached to Rome, because he was, in fact, a Christian, and the matter of his continued ordination by an earthly institution made no difference one way or the other. This is the purest sense of *kosmopolites*; the difference between the Cynic and the Christian lies in the different ways they understand the *kosmos*—variously as either a nature that gives its own immediate and self-evident dictates, or as a natural order created and directed in accordance with a divine plan. But these are minor variations on the same basic commitment.

Most expressions of cosmopolitanism, by contrast, are marked by the circumstances of their origins, and therefore by a certain paradox that I have been trying to describe here: Leibniz, for example, takes himself as a citizen of the world, believes that we are all citizens of the world, but also takes the civilization in which he happens to have been born to be the one with the clearest understanding of certain basic truths about that world. This in turn legitimates the project of going out into the rest of the world and convincing other people, perhaps aggressively, to appreciate these truths. "I'm here to tell you we're all the same, it says, whether you agree or not."

Plainly, not everyone agrees, and this fact remains, mutatis mutandis, one of the enduring problems of the purported universality of modern liberal-democratic secularism. It is at the heart of debates about everything from wars of intervention on the international level, to minority rights at the national or provincial or local level. Cosmopolitanism as an individual philosophy of life seems a lovely and harmless thing; once it becomes a force for social change, it seems to generate difficulties that no political philosopher, or politician, has been able to resolve.

If cosmopolitanism as a political ideal is heavy with paradox, it is not hard to understand why the idea that philosophy itself, as conceived in the Western tradition, is intrinsically cosmopolitan, and therefore that it is something we ought to find people doing everywhere in more or less the same way. An alternative to philosophical cosmopolitanism, which nonetheless does not lapse into Eurocentrism or into the idea of "philosophy" as a proper noun, takes each culture as having its own irreducible and untranslatable philosophy, embedded in the ore of culture without any possibility of extraction in its pure form. In 1959 the Second Congress of Negro Writers and Artists took place in Rome. This event included a special Commission on Philosophy, which passed an important resolution concerning the distinctive features of African philosophy:

> Considering the dominant part played by philosophic reflection in the elaboration of culture, considering that until now the West has claimed a monopoly of philosophic reflection, so that philosophic enterprise no longer seems conceivable outside the framework of the categories forged by the West, considering that the philosophic effort of traditional Africa has always been reflected in vital attitudes and has never had purely conceptual aims, the Commission declares:

> 1. *that for the African philosopher, philosophy can never consist of reducing the African reality to Western systems;*
> 2. that the African philosopher must base his inquiries upon the fundamental certainty that the Western philosophic approach is not the only possible one; and therefore

>> a) urges that the African philosopher should *learn from the traditions, tales, myths, and proverbs of his people,* so as to draw from them the laws of

a true African wisdom complementary to the other forms of human wisdom to *bring out the specific categories of African thought.*

b) Calls upon the African philosopher, faced by the totalitarian or egocentric philosophers of the West, *to divest himself of a possible inferiority complex,* which might prevent him from starting from his African being to judge the foreign contribution.[43]

One evident problem here is the double standard that such a conception of African philosophy seems to set up; it supposes without reason that the traditions, tales, myths, and proverbs of European popular culture are somehow not suited to such study, that European philosophy is by definition systematic and explicit, while something about African traditions, tales, and so on, makes these especially or uniquely suitable as a source of African philosophy. Yet, again, the idea that a popular philosophy can be extracted from such sources has also been defended in Europe, particularly in Germany, by thinkers such as Leibniz, Herder, Goethe, and the Grimm Brothers. In many respects the emergence of the study of comparative mythology and of *Folkloristik* in the nineteenth century was motivated by the belief that scientific philosophy as represented in particular by French rationalism had reached its limits and failed to adequately capture the lived experience of distinct national cultures. European history has not *just* been about scientific progress, institutions, discoveries, and so on. It has also been about agricultural fertility rites, songs and dances, divination from the flight paths of birds. One might reasonably express a concern that in adopting the methodology described by the 1959 Rome commission for the development of African philosophy, and in implying that this methodology is useful for Africa but not for Europe, the supposed contrast between European forms of rationality and those of other parts of the world is unnecessarily heightened.

In actual practice, much of the philosophical work that would be carried out in the spirit of this resolution was of a distinctively hybrid nature. Perhaps the most well known example of such work is the Ghanaian president Kwame Nkrumah's consciencism, which yielded a book of that name in 1964.[44] For Nkrumah, consciencism is "the map in intellectual terms of the disposition of forces which will enable African society to digest the Western and the Islamic and the Euro-Christian Elements in Africa, and develop them in such a way that they fit into the African personality."[45] Nkrumah describes the personality, in turn, as "defined by the cluster of humanist principles which underlie the traditional African society."[46] Marxist thought is the principal European stream with which Nkrumah seeks to synthesize the humanist principles of traditional African society. He therefore commits himself to materialism as the very basis of consciencism, while understanding materialism to be simply the view that matter exists absolutely and independently.

For Nkrumah, unlike the majority of European materialists, matter exists absolutely and independently. Like other dialectical materialists, Nkrumah stresses against, for example, Locke and Newton, that it is a mistake to suppose that the concept of matter necessarily involves inertness. By contrast, Nkrumah defends a variety of hylozoism: the view that self-motion and even consciousness are properties of matter. It is only on such a picture, he believes, that philosophy can become a "conceptual image of nature,"[47] a conception of philosophy that Nkrumah associates with Spinoza, with his well-known view that "the order and connection of ideas is the same as the order and connection of nature."[48] Nkrumah believes that it follows from the truth of Spinoza's claim that the mind is the idea of that whose body is nature, that "knowledge of the mind can be the direct objective basis of an intervention in nature."[49] Thus the materialism of consciencism is one that issues directly in a practical philosophy: in establishing the correct conception of matter, consciencism then "builds itself" by "becoming a reflection of the objectivity, in conceptual terms, of the unfolding of matter."[50] In this way, as a reflection of the objective unfolding of matter, it also "establishes a direct connection between knowledge and action."[51] By a few more steps, Nkrumah establishes finally that it is nothing other than egalitarianism that is the practical or social correlate of the ontological commitment to materialism.

Much of Nkrumah's version of materialism is familiar from standard Marxist-Leninist formulations of dialectical materialism in the mid-twentieth century. But Nkrumah sees his own consciencist materialism as in agreement with "the traditional African idea of the absolute and independent existence of matter, the idea of its powers of self-motion ... the idea of categorical convertibility, and the idea of the grounding of the cardinal principles of ethics in the nature of man."[52] These are plainly some fairly sweeping claims about the basic philosophical commitments of diverse linguistic and cultural groups across such a broad geographical region as sub-Saharan Africa. One way of interpreting Nkrumah's project charitably might be to suggest that he is simply attributing to the traditional cultures of Africa an implicit understanding of *the truth*, to the extent that he believes his account of materialism is true, and he supposes that a true understanding of nature and of humanity's place in it is something that people can come by in an unmediated way simply by connection to a cultural tradition, and without the need of philosophy made explicit through texts and institutions. Interestingly, to this extent Nkrumah's attempt at constructing a hybrid philosophy suited to Africa ends up in something of the same bind as we have already seen in Kagame's very non-Marxist systematization of Bantu natural-language categories into an explicit Bantu philosophy. Kagame the Rwandan Catholic priest looked at what Bantu-speaking people say about nature and its causes and found apophatic theology with a striking similarity to certain schools of Greek thought in late antiquity. Nkrumah the Ghanaian socialist leader looked at the plight of African people, at what they say and do, and found dialectical materialists.

Anthropologists have long been interested in rendering more precise the very nebulous concept of "culture," and in marking out its semantic overlap with and difference from the concept of "civilization." One familiar point of difference between these two has to do with the opposition between the supposed universality of "civilization," on the one hand, and the irreducible, local specificity of "culture" on the other. Civilization is potentially extensible throughout the entire world, while there is no conceivable global culture (or at least there was not until very recently, with the advent of ultrarapid communications), but rather there are only several distinct local cultures, in the plural. It is significant to note that the word "culture" is etymologically connected to the ideas of growth, planting, and cultivation in the literal sense; originally, agriculture, viticulture, apiculture, and so on were all simply varieties of culture. When the term is adapted to describe human societies, it still carries the sense of organicity, of something that grows up spontaneously from a particular source. Here, culture contrasts with civilization, which can be, it is generally supposed, imposed from above or from without. One is brought up in a culture, but one becomes civilized through inculcation or instruction. Culture is what is distinctive and untransmittable about a particular social group. Interestingly, as Marshall Sahlins has related, the concept of culture is often appropriated by those groups that at an earlier stage were studied by anthropologists interested in culture. Told by the Western researchers that they had a distinctive culture worth traveling great distances to study, some groups took the notion of "custom" (cultural practice) to describe, precisely, that feature of their own group that they had and everyone else lacked. As one Polynesian informant explained to Sahlins: "If we didn't have *kastom*, we would be just like white men."[53]

The concept of culture becomes crucially important within the context of romantic and nationalist reactions to Enlightenment and cosmopolitan ideas about the universality of civilization. The contrast between the connotations of the two terms, "culture" and "civilization," is perhaps at its starkest in certain German Romantic authors of the late eighteenth and early nineteenth centuries, who are reacting to the universalism of French Enlightenment thought. Significantly, the French authors held to embody this thought are often referred to, somewhat disparagingly, as *les philosophes*. Now given what we have already seen, it should not be surprising to learn that the term "philosopher" is coming up, yet again, as a mild pejorative. The *philosophes* are perceived, at least outside the French-speaking world, as not really passing muster as true philosophers, but instead as salon-dwelling poseurs, presumptuously taking their own styles and manners—that is, features of culture par excellence—as worthy of universalization, as something for the rest of the world to aspire to.

Les philosophes, in short, might be said to have committed the error of taking their culture for civilization, of confusing the local with that which is universal or at least potentially universalizable. When les philosophes are mocked in, say, English, the French term is preserved, seemingly to signal that what the Parisians take simply to be their participation in a timeless and transnational activity or mode of thought is in fact, seen from a bit of distance or from an external point of view, something that is distinctively and untranslatably French. Typically, the mockery comes from English speakers who believe themselves to be free of affectations and to be speaking from the point of view of straight-shooting common sense, thus in their own way reproducing the fault they aim to mock. Horace Walpole said of the philosophes in 1779 that they were "solemn, arrogant, dictatorial coxcombs."[54] Although the content of the philosophy has changed dramatically since the Enlightenment, this same basic cultural dynamic arguably continues to characterize the relationship between Anglophone and Francophone philosophers today: both take themselves to be speaking for the universal, and both take the others to represent an entrenched local culture (in the French imagination, this culture is denoted by the curious term "Anglo-Saxon").

In the interplay between the local and the universal, philosophy seems to be positioned uneasily between both civilization and culture. The example of the Polynesian with his *kastom* may be compared with the way philosophy is sometimes invoked in celebration of local cultures. Once I was staffing the philosophy table at Concordia University's "Portes Ouvertes" day in Montreal. A Mohawk man from the nearby Kanesatake reservation came to our table. He said he had failed out of college decades earlier and was looking to make a new start. He

asked me about the kind of philosophy we teach, and then he
added, unexpectedly: "You know, we've got our own philosophy too." This was long before I had thought about such issues.
I was skeptical, and I said, "Oh yeah?" I could immediately tell
that he sensed the condescension and dismissiveness in my
voice. I steered the conversation back to the curriculum, and
he wandered off after a few minutes more of that. He didn't
come to study philosophy with us.

In retrospect it seems to me that I was faithfully and accurately representing the self-understanding of philosophy as a
discipline that day. This is a self-understanding I'm now committed to questioning, in this book and elsewhere. The reason
for bringing this encounter up at this point, however, is that it
seems to draw out something peculiar about the way the concept of philosophy gets taken up as we move away from its
"official" academic representation and into communities that
have no connection to this representation. In these communities, philosophy is not something that is simply universal;
there are, rather, many philosophies, just as there are many
cultures. The conceit of the academic philosophers, then, might
be thought of as similar to that of *les philosophes*: they take
themselves to be the sole embodiment of something universal,
whereas, seen from the outside, they are only one particular
instance of something that takes on many different forms.
They take themselves to represent philosophy as a civilization, whereas there are really only many different cultures of
philosophy.

The Mohawk man, in contrast to the Polynesian with his *kastom*, did not say that what made Mohawks, or perhaps Native
Americans, distinctive, is that they have philosophy whereas,
implicitly or explicitly, no one else does. If he did misunderstand the concept of philosophy, as Sahlins seems to suggest

the Polynesian misunderstood the concept of custom, it is not in as radical a way. The Mohawk man wished only to insist on a sort of parity between his community's philosophical outlook and that of the community I represented. I could not acknowledge this, because I did not take my community as one community among others, but instead took it as, so to speak, the only game in town.

Interestingly, many American and European students will speak not of their own communities' respective philosophies, but rather of their own *individual* philosophies. That is, students will say that they are interested in cultivating their own philosophy; nonstudents, too, people who have not gone to university, will tell you what their "philosophy of life" is. Our conditioned response to such locutions is to laugh, or to groan, but we are missing quite a bit when we dismiss the people who say these things. Arguably, the phrase "my philosophy" coming from a high school senior reading Albert Camus, or coming from a manual laborer who has lived through many things and reflected on them, is the correlate in an individualist society to the Mohawk's invocation of "my community's philosophy" or "the philosophy of my people." These individuals seek out their own philosophies, because the philosophy their community gives them is a philosophy of individualism. But the project is sincere, just like the Mohawk man's sincere invocation of the philosophy of his own people, and in each case there is a refusal to take philosophy on the terms in which its academic representatives wish to cast it: as something without local inflections, as something that is universal in its scope and potential application, but that licenses only particular people, who come up through a formal institutional process of education, to speak in the name of the universal.

The professional conception of "philosopher" in the early twenty-first-century United States, as already suggested, bears an interesting comparison to the conception of "*philosophe*" in eighteenth-century France. As is well known, the *philosophes*, like most current members in good standing of the APA, were often seen from the outside as not really being philosophers in the fullest sense. Walpole called them "coxcombs," and even in the *Encyclopédie*, composed by members in good standing of the *philosophe* community, the authors have trouble taking the label all too seriously. "There is nothing," the entry on "Philosophe" begins, "that costs less to acquire today than the name of *philosophe*. An obscure and retiring life, some outward signs of wisdom, with a bit of reading, suffice to attach this name to people who ennoble themselves with it without merit."[55]

The authors attempt however to win back the label for a more meritorious sort of person, the one who "even in his passions, only acts after reflection," the one who is guided by "a spirit of observation and justice," and so on. Interestingly, there are separate entries in the *Encyclopédie* for "Philosophical," as an adjective, a personal trait that is characterized by the ability "to judge sanely concerning all things," and for "Philosophy" itself, which admits that the term is vague and admits of many meanings, but which does not in general take the term in question as pejorative. The agentive form of the noun bears most of the negative load, while the standard form and the adjective appear fairly neutral. Curiously, also, in the entry on "Philosophe," there is a distinct subentry dealing with the usage of this label for practitioners of alchemy and chemistry: "The Alchemists did not miss an opportunity to decorate themselves with this great name."[56] This usage is mocked as outdated, yet unlike today it remains familiar enough to demand mention; its familiarity stems, not least, from the numerous products of chemical operations that in the late eighteenth century still bore the name of philosophy: "the oil of the philosophers," "philosophical pulverization," "philosophical calcination," and so on.

In ancient Greece, we learn in the entry on "Philosophy," the men who set themselves up as masters of wisdom would gain audiences not because they were able to instruct them "in solid knowledge that is useful for our well-being," but in order to feed their minds "with curious questions." Since the name of "sage" was too much for such people, the article continues, "Pythagoras ... substituted for this luxurious name the modest title of 'philosopher' ... but the sound reasons for this change did not stifle the pride of the *Philosophes*." The authors catalog the various ancient divisions of philosophy into subdomains, as for example the Stoic conception of philosophy as having a moral, a natural, and a rational part, or the Scholastic philosophers dividing it into logic, metaphysics, physics, and morals. But none of these divisions counts as a definition, since they all leave unsettled the question of what exactly is being divided.

The authors indicate their preference for Christian Wolff's definition of philosophy, which they summarize as "the science of possibles insofar as they are able to be [Philosophia est scientia possibilium, quatenus esse possunt],"[57] thus invoking an earlier instance of a definition Bertrand Russell would offer some centuries later. For this reason, though, philosophy remains a very incomplete science, and will always remain so, "for who could take account of all the possibles?"

Much of the *Encyclopédie* entry on "Philosophy" is borrowed from Johann Jakob Brucker's multivolume work, published between 1742 and 1744, the *Historia critica philosophiae.* This work is noteworthy for its description of the study of the history of philosophy as an integral part of philosophy itself. The history of philosophy, Brucker explains, is

> the history of human understanding, clearly shewing the extent of its capacity, the causes of its perversion, and the means by which it may be recalled from its unprofitable wanderings, and successfully employed in subserviency to the happiness of mankind. Whilst it traces the origins and growth of useful knowledge, it also discovers the manner in which errors have arisen and been propagated, and exposes the injury which they have done to science, literature, and religion. It exhibits great and exalted minds as forsaking the path of truth, and adopting opinions at once most absurd and most pernicious: a representation, which cannot fail to shew the folly of placing an implicit confidence in the judgment of celebrated men, or of admitting any system as true, before it has undergone an accurate examination.[58]

Nor is there any concern, for Brucker, that this sort of antihagiographical scrutiny will "produce a contempt of truly wise and learned men," since "an acquaintance with the mistakes and failures of men, who have unsuccessfully employed great ingenuity and industry in the pursuit of truth, suggests a useful lesson of modesty and diffidence in our own enquiries."[59]

Significantly, Brucker's work, the first comprehensive modern survey of the history of philosophy, does not suppose at the outset that philosophy is the exclusive property of members of a particular tradition. Rather, philosophy is something that can belong to any culture, and each culture needs to be investigated separately in order to determine whether it has philosophy or does not. In fact, for Brucker the proper method of writing the history of philosophy is the one that begins with a sort of historical-ethnographical survey of all known peoples based on all available information, and to extract from the cultural beliefs of, for example, the Abyssinians or the Celts, evidence of philosophical reflection. In the end Brucker's judgment as to which cultures exercise such reflection hews fairly closely to the prejudices of his era. Thus looking at the classical Greek sources on the legendarily brutal Scythians, Brucker concludes that "whatever be thought of the manners" of these people, "to give them the appellation of philosophers would be to call a block of marble a statue."[60]

Of the Celts, by contrast, Brucker concludes that "though their wisdom was of a very different character from that of the Greeks and Romans, they were not so destitute of knowledge as not to have their schools of instruction and their philosophers."[61] Remarkably, Brucker denounces the Greek and Roman historians who wrote on the Celts as unreliable, giving us only "idle tales and extravagant fables,"[62] while also conceding that he has no other point of access to the cultural beliefs of the Celts than through this external perspective. Brucker identifies the Druids as the philosophical class among the Celts, comparable to the Magi among the Persians, and follows Julius Caesar in supposing that their primary social function was to "preside in religious concerns, direct the public and private sacrifices, and interpret the will of the gods."[63]

Brucker maintains that the dogmas of the Druids "were clothed in an allegorical dress," and that they were taught in strict secrecy.[64] But the allegorical and esoteric elements do not disqualify the cultural practice of the Druids from the status of philosophy. Their secret teachings are carefully sculpted,

Brucker seems to think, and thus unlike the unchiseled block to which Scythian cultural beliefs might be compared. And this is already enough, for Brucker, to warrant talk of Celtic philosophy.

Less argument has to be given for the "Eastern" traditions of "Barbarian" philosophy—Chaldean, Phoenician, Persian, Egyptian—which of course had all along enjoyed a respected place in the Greek, Latin, and Christian traditions as sources of wisdom. But is wisdom the same thing as philosophy? Brucker acknowledges that "it has long been a subject of dispute, whether philosophy first appeared among the Barbarians, or among the Greeks."[65] He concedes that the Greeks were singular in having "learned an artificial method of philosophising," but also insists that their "philosophical vanity" made them "unwilling to allow that philosophy had any existence in other countries, except where it had been borrowed from them."[66]

But Brucker believes, reasonably, that the controversy could be easily settled if we simply decided on a clear and appropriate definition of philosophy, and for him the only such is a definition that acknowledges the importance of the progress made through the development of "artificial methods," but that still does not withhold the label of "philosophy" from the activity of "simple reflection" that remains unformalized, and even in some cases unwritten. "In this question," Brucker complains, "as it frequently happens in controversy, from a want of distinct ideas and an accurate use of terms, many things foreign to the argument were advanced."[67] He continues:

> If the meaning of the term Philosophy had been correctly settled; if the infant state of knowledge had been distinguished from its more advanced age; and especially, if

due attention had been paid to the essential difference between communicating doctrines by mere authority, and investigating the principles, relations, and causes of things by diligent study, the whole dispute would soon have been found to be nothing more than a logomachy. For no one would assert, that the barbaric nations were wholly inattentive to wisdom, or strangers to every kind of knowledge, human or divine. On the other side, it cannot be questioned, that they became possessed of knowledge rather by simple reflection than by scientific investigation, and that they transmitted it to posterity rather by tradition than by demonstration. Whereas the Greeks, as soon as they began to be civilized, discovered a general propensity to inquiry, and made use of scientific rules and methods of reasoning. Hence it is easy to perceive, that though the improvement of philosophy is to be ascribed to the Greeks, its origin is to be sought for among the barbaric nations.[68]

There is plenty of room for disagreement with Brucker's stark characterization of the novelty of the Greek approach to philosophical inquiry.[69] And yet it is remarkable that in many respects his definition of "philosophy" as including both methodical inquiry and "simple reflection" is rather more capacious than most implicit definitions that have dominated the practice of academic philosophy for roughly the past century. Brucker holds open the possibility of a common ground between ethnography and philosophy, or between the study of the variety of human cultures and their belief systems, on the one hand, and the study of the cultural practice of Philosophia as descended from the Greeks on the other. This possibility appears to have been entirely foreclosed by the twentieth century, to the extent that today any modest suggestion that we might learn something as philosophers by studying, say, ancient Celtic conceptions of nature, or even ancient Scythian ones, has been relegated to the absolute fringes, to the utterly untouchable New Age sections of the bookstores, and as far away from academic philosophy as possible.

Recent developments in the politics of American academic philosophy suggest that many are growing tired of arrogant dictatorial coxcombs deciding for us what counts as philosophy, and what does not, and instead are looking for new ways to conceive the project of philosophy so as to include voices that have traditionally remained unheard. In the current heady moment, in which the scope of the discipline is up for grabs, Brucker's relatively capacious understanding of the practice might deserve some reconsideration.

Once I took part in a conference in a mid-sized provincial city in Transylvania. As part of the opening ceremony, the local Orthodox bishop was invited to hold forth on the value of philosophy. He seized the opportunity to denounce Marxism, existentialism, and even rap music, and praised all in attendance for guarding the flame of spirituality in a corrupt and materialistic world. His *éloge* dragged on. The most distinguished member of our delegation could be heard snoring. I passed the time looking over the paper I was going to present, which as it happened was on eighteenth-century materialism.

The bishop had heard there were some philosophers coming to town, and he assumed he shared a common language with us. I can only guess as to his exact background, but I imagine this man had spent time in a seminary, and that he read there at least some of the authors academic philosophers would recognize as constituting the Western philosophical tradition (or at least "Western" in the broad sense, including Byzantium): Origen, Clement of Alexandria, probably Augustine, maybe even the pagan Plato. This man had probably incorporated what he learned about these authors into his understanding of questions such as: What is the fate of a person after death? Am I essentially or only contingently associated with a physical body? What is infinity? On most reckonings those are philosophical questions, yet the reaction of the visiting party (myself included) was to dismiss the bishop as something of a yokel. I suspect this would be the reaction of the vast majority of professional academic philosophers in the West, and a fortiori if it were not a Transylvanian bishop, but rather, say, a Mongolian shaman, who deigned to hold forth on the questions on which we take ourselves to be experts.

While at the time I went along with this prevailing sentiment, it now seems to me that this encounter was nothing other than a clash of provincialisms. The problem might simply be that the term "philosophy" is used in two very different senses: one to describe a well-defined tradition of systematic and methodical inquiry, which appears to have developed independently in human history only in South Asia and the eastern Mediterranean; the other, which might be called "folk-philosophy" or "ethnophilosophy," on the model of ethno-astronomy, ethnotaxonomy, and such, to describe the set of cultural variations on a range of beliefs about nature, the self, and so on, which humans qua human cannot help but have. But one way of moving beyond provincialism might be to consider the possibility that all philosophy is in a sense ethno-philosophy. After all, the minds of nonliterate pastoral peoples are exactly the same as those of seminarians mastering Thomistic doctrine. The difference is that the pastoral peoples' minds have different prostheses and institutions to support and to mirror their thoughts. A revealing parallel case is law: does law begin with Hammurabi and receive its first mature expression in the Roman period? Or were these milestones simply the explicitization of something that was already there, that cannot not be there wherever there is a society that is organized in some way or other according to a set of—perhaps unspoken—rules and prohibitions? Is a written legal code the coming-into-being of a new way of thinking, or is it the transfer of a familiar way of thinking into a different, external storage medium? If we are prepared to accept the latter possibility, we are thereby enabled to think about, say, Roman law, in fruitful comparison to, say, Hausa law (generally called Hausa "custom"). And similarly with philosophy.

Philosophy in our narrower sense might be more rigorous than folk belief, yet still indebted to folk belief in ways that it ought to be part of the philosophical project to uncover. A revealing uncovering of this sort has been undertaken in recent decades in the cognitive-scientific study of folk taxonomy. It has become clear, in particular, that the modern system of Linnaean biological classification,[70] while more exact and rigorous than prescientific and preliterate systems throughout the world, is not for that so much a rejection of the earlier systems as it is an outgrowth of them. This discovery tells us something not just about the history of science but also about the way that science at present continues its project of carving up the world.

The distinguishing feature of Indian, Chinese, or European philosophy, on this approach, would turn out to be not some greater clarity or depth of thinking. Instead, it would be a by-product of the way certain, principally Asian, technologies, above all writing and the reproduction of written texts, are incorporated into a society. The presuppositions and aims of inquiry might be different for, say, an uncontacted Amazonian people, and the technologies and institutions for pursuing these aims are certainly different. But there are still human minds there puzzling out the nature of reality and of humanity's place in it. This activity ought to be of interest to philosophers not out of some naive celebration of cultural diversity but rather for the hardheaded scientific reason that it gives us a real measure of the full scope and range of humanity's responses to the questions we call "philosophical." Taking this measure is one way of deepening our understanding of these questions.

ARCHIVES OF THE FRENCH ETHNOLOGICAL
ASSOCIATION
Division: Americas, Brazil
Field Recordings, Document No. A-2042

January 28, 1936

(trans. Jean-Pierre Tordu)

I do not know where my ability comes from. We go
to hunt, and I begin the litany. I beseech the animal
to come out and show itself, in the verses of its own
language that I learned from my grandfather. I recite more verses than I have fingers; I plead and
coo, and even like to make the animal laugh a bit. I
show my mastery of its language, for which I am
said to speak with the very *achan* ["rationality"—
J.-P. Tordu] that permeates all of *gana* ["nature"].

But I know also when to stop channeling and to start speaking in my own voice too, my human voice. This confuses the monkeys and the deer, though the jaguar is too smart for it. And so they come out and give themselves, laughing. Then we set about flaying them, and as we do this we apologize according to the custom. But here too I know when to break with custom and to do just the opposite of what is expected—rather than apologize, I berate the carcasses for their stupidity, for confusing my voice with the voice of *gana*. I tell them that I, a man, can be no part of *gana*, and that when I channel the language of animals I only do so as an impostor. I tell them they do not really know what *gana* is. Many of the women say I should not speak like this, that I am denying what we have always known to be true—that a great hunter speaks the true language of the animals because he is himself of the animals, and of *gana*. But the men just nod and smile and beg their wives to put up with my discourses to the carcasses, because they know that no one ever comes back from the hunt with more meat than I. And they ask themselves, and the animals ask themselves: how could he be so successful in hunting if he were not speaking the *llanac* ["truth"]? Who are we to dispute what this wise man says?

It seems to me reasonable to suppose that there was quite likely never an Aristotle of precontact Amazonia: a member of a traditional Amazonian culture who attempted to lay down an exhaustive and systematic account of all domains of human knowledge. It seems to me equally reasonable to suppose that there *was* quite likely a Socrates of Amazonia (or indeed several): a member of a traditional Amazonian culture who has mastered that culture's forms of reasoning, and has exhibited swift intelligence in questioning these forms and in exposing their presuppositions and shortcomings. It seems so likely that it would be eminently worthwhile to begin to work, collectively and diligently, on developing methods of research, at the intersection of philosophy, anthropology, and history, that would enable us to recover something of what such a thinker might have offered up to his or her interlocutors, and of how and why this would have been meaningful within the particular cultural setting. Ordinarily, the way in which traditional oral cultures are excluded from the scope of philosophical interest is by maintaining a sort of double standard for what philosophy ought to be. They cannot be philosophical cultures, it is said, because they do not produce texts, let alone systematic argumentative treatises. But what this conveniently overlooks is that not just *a* philosopher in the Western canon but indeed *the* philosopher par excellence did little more in his life than to hang around and engage in probing dialogues with like-minded people. But surely this is not an activity that required a particular combination of cultural values and technical practices that Greece had but Amazonia lacked. It is rather something people appear to do everywhere.

The person who embodies the social role in question is the one we are calling a Sage. He or she (again, recall the telling term, *sage-femme*) has grown up in a particular culture, with its own particular philosophical commitments embedded and implicit in its natural language and its other expressions of culture. Perhaps *pace* Leibniz and Kagame, simply growing up in a given culture and internalizing its cultural expressions may not be enough in itself to be, within that culture, a philosopher. In addition, one should perhaps suppose, with Radin, that a philosopher will engage critically with these cultural expressions, take distances from them, play with them. In Greece such a display of intellectual nimbleness has been comprehended under the label of irony, but there is no good reason to suppose that it, perhaps more even than common sense, is not equally distributed throughout the world.

3

INSIDE AND OUT

Featuring the Gadfly

Now I am a seer, not a very good one, but, as the bad
writers say, good enough for my own purposes.

—*Phaedrus* 242c

One of the basic grounds for distinction between philosophy
and poetry, besides Aristotle's distinction considered above,
is that philosophy is that activity of the human mind that cannot be implanted by a muse, but must come from oneself. At
a practical level, this is a difference between explainability
and mysterianism. What is channeled through a speaker by a
muse remains inscrutable to the speaker him- or herself, while
philosophy, on one common understanding, requires the examination of all claims. Philosophy is not, or we do not ordinarily think it is, religion or poetry. It derives from reason, not
from revelation or inspiration, and reason is something shared
equally by human beings simply insofar as they are human. Yet
this seemingly sharp distinction has generally been difficult to
maintain. Socrates ironized on the idea that his own exercise
of reason depended on dictation from a muse, yet in order for

this irony to make sense the activity of philosophy had to have at least some evident affinity with revelation or inspiration.

We might think of intuition as a sort of self-contained revelation or inspiration, as appearing suddenly and as if divinely implanted, but nonetheless as flowing from innate faculties of the individual thinker. Absent an external agent, the thinker really only has his or her internal resources to draw on in a moment of inspiration, but it is often unclear in virtue of what these resources might offer a particularly or unusually accurate means for accessing the truth. Often, in the history of philosophy, the invocation of intuition as a step on the path toward the truth, or as a tool for making philosophical progress, is based on the presumption that the thinker is bracketing or abstracting away from all that she has previously learned, and thus is treating learnedness, or the authority of predecessors, as a prejudicing force rather than as an aid in the discovery of truth. The person who intuits is behaving something like Descartes in his *Meditations*,[1] or like Edmund Husserl in his account of the "bracketing" or *epochē* that plays a role in the phenomenological method,[2] by abstracting away from all that one knows and counting as intuition what is left over. This leftover, unprejudiced something to which the mind of the thinker has access through intuition is often held to be a supremely philosophical sort of knowledge, to the extent that it is not based on any particular facts about the world, not having come from any input in the world.

A closely, and perhaps dangerously, related notion is that of "common sense": one might have an intuition by appeal to one's common sense, not in the antiquated sense of *sensus communis* or the posited internal sensory capacity that unites the sensations brought in through sight, hearing, and so on, but rather in the sense of what one knows without need for any reflection, simply because one generally uses one's mind in an unprejudiced, lucid way. Often, when common sense is invoked in this way, there is a presumption that this is a capacity that ordinary people, or nonphilosophers, have to its fullest perfection, and that it is philosophy that prevents us from relying on common sense. For example, George Berkeley supposed that no ordinary person, endowed with common sense, would have ever made the mistake of supposing that there is such a thing as matter that serves as a substratum to our sensory experiences.[3] The philosopher who abandons the complications of philosophy, who cuts away the conceptual clutter and just sees things as they are, is having a sort of intuition that, again, as in the case of Husserl, consists in stripping away rather than in addition of further steps of reasoning, of conceptual tools, and other ornamentation. Yet other people have thought that the concept of matter is simply self-evident, and not at all an invention of philosophical prejudice. Appeal to common sense can quickly appear to be a waste of time, since one philosopher's conceptual clutter is another's self-evident truth.

Unsurprisingly, intuition is a faculty that is prone to abuse, for there is no further path of verification or assessment possible beyond the thinker's insistence that she is having such and such intuition and that it seems, to her, truly incontrovertible. What makes the report of such an intuition convincing to outside observers, all too often, is the social status of the observer. One fears that, too often, to be a philosopher is simply to have maneuvered into a social and institutional role in which one's reports of one's intuitions will be taken seriously. In this respect, too, the analytic philosopher who reports on her intuitions, and finds herself with sufficient status to have these reports taken seriously, is not in such a different position than the early modern gentleman who attests to the veridical nature of a report on some unusual medical anomaly. Both are giving testimony, the strength of which flows from their social status as individuals.

Dear Professor,

I apologize for sending this message unsolicited, but I imagined that you, a philosopher, might be interested in learning about the philosophical system I have developed, based on an insatiable longing for Truth and decades of activity as an inventor and an independent thinker, and after a long and satisfying career in real estate appraisal. My approach combines the latest discoveries of Quantum Mechanics, archeoastronomy of the Chaldaeans, Mayan calendrical science, and critical thinking. It unites the non-binary thinking of the East with the cool-headed problem solving of the West. Humanities Professor Emeritus Tom Kumpe of Two Prairies Technical College has written that my new philosophical system amounts to a bold "attempt to show the unity of human knowledge," and I think you'll agree with Professor Kumpe if you read what I have to say.

I have included as an attachment the first chapter of my e-book, *Quantum Truths for the 21st Century.* To read the entire work, you are invited to make a donation, in whatever amount you see fit, and to download it from my website. I would be

particularly grateful if you could reply with a testi-
monial as to how it helped to transform your own
philosophical outlook.

I truly believe this book will help you to expand
your philosophical horizons ... unless of course you
are already too set in your ways, and you prefer to
go on wearing blinders, sitting in your comfortable
office, staring out the window and enjoying your
free ride as a tenured so-called "philosopher."

Good day,
Bud Korg

One way of displaying independent-mindedness, and rejection of authority, is to write philosophy in the first person. There is a plainly unobtrusive form of first-person writing,
as when the author of a philosophical text opts to write "as I
stated above" rather than using a basically equivalent passive
construction or a now unfashionable "royal we." But there is
another use of the first person that brings the individual author
to center stage *as* an individual, with all of his or her peculiar-
ities. Here, as well, there are degrees. A moderate intrusion of
the self is perhaps represented by Descartes's *Meditations*.
Here, a somewhat fictionalized version of Descartes is made
to use his intuition in order to arrive at a set of certain and
general truths, truths at which any "I" might have arrived by
following the same rational inferences from intuitions. Another
bolder sort of intrusion of the self in philosophical writing is
perhaps best represented by Descartes's countryman, Michel
de Montaigne, nearly a century earlier.[4] Montaigne frequently

takes himself as the very subject of his *Essais*, not insofar as his intuition or inferences can provide access to general truths, but simply as a subject of intrinsic interest. He describes his own tastes and caprices, telling us, for example, of his preferences in sauces and condiments. What, now, could possibly be philosophical about *this*? Plainly, it would not be a contribution to philosophy if I were to speak here of my own preferences in sauces. I might attempt to insert a comment about these into an academic talk, but it would surely be received as lighthearted banter, extraneous to the project of philosophy. Montaigne's intervention by contrast is relevant to philosophy in view of the particular moment in which it occurred: the moment in European history at which the individual came into sharp focus as, it was thought, the irreducible subject and basic atom of social reality. Many scholars have invoked the name of Montaigne as central to a process in modern European history that is sometimes described as the discovery of the self, or, alternatively, as the invention of the self.[5] As Charles Taylor has sensibly observed, this does not mean that when two paleolithic hunters face down an enraged animal, and it lunges at the one of them, the other does not feel a mixture of relief and pity that the beast has gone after his comrade, and not after *me*.[6] And yet the overwhelming evidence from material culture and, later, from textual sources, and also from ethnographic evidence arriving from outside of the European sphere, suggests that until the beginning of the European modern period there was comparably little attention to the individual subject as something irreducibly salient, as inherently worthy of notice. It is this notice that, concomitantly with Montaigne or shortly after, would give rise to new articulations of ideas in the political sphere about human rights and democratic egalitarianism, and in the metaphysical sphere about the individual "thinking thing" as one of the two basic ingredients of a dualistic ontology. In this context, Montaigne's "discovery" of himself as a subject of intrinsic interest, no matter how trivial or unexceptional the details he describes, may be understood as a bellwether of a number of important innovations that all of us would be prepared to recognize as philosophical.

What is more, even in Montaigne's reports of his individual tastes there is a sort of claim to universality. The guiding idea of the value of describing one's intimate preferences is that this will lay bare the vast degree to which all human beings are alike: even if our individual caprices are inevitably our own, we still all have caprices. To talk about your taste in condiments is thus "common" in both senses of the term: in the sense of quotidian or mundane, and in the sense of being shared. This basic humanist appreciation for what is common to all certainly predates Renaissance humanism—it is, after all, perhaps best expressed in Terence's ancient motto, "I am human, nothing human can be foreign to me." It is also to some extent anticipated not only by premodern humanism such as that of Terence, but also by classical theological models of the human being, which supposed that each of us has superficial properties that distinguish us from one another, but when these properties are stripped away, like the layers of an onion, what is left is the soul, conceived as a sort of sliver or reflection of God. On this conception, we are all in some sense identical, while what differentiates us, such as our taste in condiments, is ultimately irrelevant to the profound question of who we as human beings are. Montaigne shifts this old conception without rejecting it altogether. Human beings are in some sense all identical, but we are able to discern that identity by accounting for the diversity of individuals. And where better to start out in this description than with one's own individual distinctness?

Today, in most genres of philosophical writing, there is little place for any Montaignean preoccupation with the individual self of the author. If an example from one's carpooling or dietary habits is invoked in an article in an academic journal, in ethics, say, this is ostensibly only as an example in the service of a general argument about some ethical theory or principle—though we may conjecture, privately, about the author's desire to let readers know about her or his carpooling or dietary habits.

One seeming exception to the general distaste for first-person writing comes from the area of philosophy influenced by standpoint epistemology, and by the various currents that adopt for themselves a variation of the label "critical philosophy of x."[7] Here, the convention is to position one's claims in relation to who one is socially, with respect in particular to race, class, gender, sexual orientation, and so on. But here one is not really saying "who one is" in a sense Montaigne would have recognized. In fact, one is doing just the opposite: reducing one's individuality to the intersection of a handful of socially salient features of one's identity. In this sense a work of philosophy that sets out from one's standpoint as a member of a given group or ensemble of groups is only superficially first person, only superficially about one's own standpoint, while at a more profound level this sort of work amounts to an attempt, conscious or not, to analyze one's own identity from a third-person perspective. It is also a rejection of Terence's motto, for a key commitment of the epistemology defenders of standpoint theory prefer is that you *cannot* know what it is like to be another person, if that person has different social coordinates than you do, and that some things human really are insurmountably foreign to some humans. But this might be giving up far too soon; indeed, the presumption of such a limitation might in the end be a failure of the imagination. As the philosopher Zhuangzi said to his friend Huizi, who had disputed his claim to be able to know the happiness of a fish on the grounds that he, Zhuangzi, is not a fish: "You are not I, so whence do you know I don't know the happiness of a fish?"[8] For him, not only is nothing human alien, but nothing living as well.

Anyhow, whatever the conventions of the discipline, it remains the case that I adore jalapeños and Tabasco sauce, ground chiles and wasabi, in general all those savors and flavors that the Francophile American food writer M.F.K. Fisher associated with cultures still in their culinary infancy.[9] I hate going to the market in Paris and finding that guacamole has been nativized as "tartinade aux avocats," and dealing with continentals who think paprika qualifies as "piquant." I am impatient and voracious; I eat fast, and I like for the experience to bring me to the threshold of pain. I suspect a good deal could be learned about what and how I think by attention to what and how I eat.

These are not the sorts of declarations for which one is given tenure or grant money. Not only does one not speak of one's dietary preferences, but, with the exception of some philosophers following in the Freudian tradition, background aspects of personality and motivation, which might well explain why one does the sort of philosophy one does, or holds the views one does, must be checked at the door before one enters the temple of professional philosophical writing. Again, it is not that information about one's background motivations does not come out in some way or other—often through informal channels and oral lore, less often through end-of-career memoirs[10]—but simply that this information is not considered to be constitutive of a given philosopher's—for lack of a better word—philosophy.

D ifferences in the narrative voice of a text are often determined by the genre of that text, and we tend to believe, today, that not only memoirs but indeed other sorts of literary work can have at best only a partial or equivocal belonging to the corpus of philosophical writing. Philosophy, again, on one common understanding, ranges over the possible, while history focuses on the actual, but philosophy cares nonetheless about respecting the boundary between the possible and the actual, while poetry, and by extension mythology, science fiction, and literature in general, feels free to roam throughout the domain of the possible without needing to keep the boundary of the actual in sight. But this distinction complicates our attempts to isolate philosophy as a distinct human endeavor, since in fact many texts we now classify as philosophical engage with phenomena that we also now associate with mythology or poetry, while many works we now classify as literature engage directly with questions we now consider philosophical. Consider in this connection the following two citations, both from works written in English between 1600 and 1800. One of these works is considered part of the corpus of the history of philosophy and is studied by scholars of the history of philosophy in the present day. The other is not.

1. [The maiden] was so strong in her fits, that six men or more could not hold her; as once as they were holding her, she was caught up from them so high, that her feet touched their breasts. As also at another time about midnight, she being miserably tormented,

and crying out, The Devil wil carry me away, she was pulled from them that held her, and cast from the low bed where she lay, to the top of an high bed, with her Clothes torn off her back, and a piece of her skin torn away: The Candle in the room standing on the Table was thrown down and put out; at which time there being a little Boy that was almost asleep, but with this noise being affrighted, had no power with the rest to go out of the room, stayed there, and saw a Spirit in the likeness of a great black man with no head in the room, scuffling with the Maid, who took her and set her into a Chair, and told her that she must go with him, he was come for her soul, she had given it to him: But the Maid answered, that her soul was none of her own to give, and he had already got her blood, but as for her soul he should never have it; and after a while tumbling and throwing about of the Maid, he vanished away.[11]

2. Pray, Sir, in all the reading which you have ever read, did you ever read such a book as *Locke*'s Essay upon the Human Understanding?—Don't answer me rashly,—because many, I know, quote the book, who have not read it,—and many have read it who understand it not:—If either of these is your case, as I write to instruct, I will tell you in three words what the book is.—It is a history.—A history! of who? what? where? when? Don't hurry yourself.—It is a history-book, Sir, (which may possibly recommend it to the world) of what passes in a man's own mind; and if you will say so much of the book, and no more, believe me, you will cut no contemptible figure in a metaphysic circle.[12]

These are, respectively, Henry More's 1653 *Antidote against Atheism* and Laurence Sterne's novel, *The Life and Opinions of Tristram Shandy*, written as a serial between 1759 and 1767. While I myself have written history-of-philosophy articles on More, and while I certainly never will write history-of-philosophy articles on Sterne, it strikes me on reflection that I have learned vastly more about the history of philosophy from *Tristram Shandy* than I ever did from the Cambridge Platonist's entire opus. But I won't write any history-of-philosophy scholarship about Sterne because this would be to cross a firm disciplinary boundary. Sterne is a *novelist*, and a satirical novelist at that. The people and things he writes about are avowedly made up, and the stance he takes toward them is an unserious one. The people and things More describes, in contrast, are purportedly real, and the stance he takes toward them is only ever inadvertently funny.

Yet one may ask: why is this a distinction that makes a difference? After all, More's headless demon is surely just as unreal as Sterne's Dr. Slop, and is infinitely *more* fictional than Sterne's John Locke, who, like Ambroise Paré, Evangelista Toricelli, the Bernoulli brothers, and a vast company of other historical figures of interest to scholars of modern philosophy, is a recurring character in the novel, whose ideas are treated with humor, but are nonetheless summarized and criticized with real understanding.

Scholars tend not to take Henry More as a first-rate philosopher, but they do acknowledge that he is of interest to the extent that his writing reflects the preoccupations of his contemporaries in philosophical circles, and might even offer occasional insights. Yet the same could certainly be said of Sterne, and so the reason for admitting the one but not the other cannot be that the one is great and influential, but only that the one's work consists in a series of claims to which the author directly assents, while the other's work consists in claims one generally does not know how to take, made by characters other than the author. But there is no obvious reason why the claims of a work must be made by a narrator who is identical with the author; in fact, many philosophical treatises in the early modern period *were* written with at least a minimum of fictional artifice, such as, again, Descartes's *Meditations*, or the many works written as dialogues between two strictly non-existent characters, only one of whom, generally, stands in for the true author.

When we move out of the European sphere, in the modern period we find many examples of hybrid works combining some elements of fictional narration with both straightforward and satirical philosophical discourse. Consider for example Ahmad Faris al-Shidyaq's remarkable "novel," *Leg over Leg; or, the Turtle in the Tree, concerning the Fāriyāq, What Manner of Creature He Might Be*, first published in Arabic in Paris in 1855. The work does not have a typical narrative structure, and in the era it was often described in French and English as a nonfictional travel report of an Arab in Europe. But it consciously draws on Sterne, as well as on classical Arabic poetic forms such as *shukf*, in order to engage with philosophical ideas, among them the ideas taught in the traditional Arabic system of learning, having significant roots, ultimately, in Aristotle. Thus, for example, there is a long discussion of the question whether grammar is a science, and an illustration of how lessons may be drawn from grammar for the resolution of philosophical questions. A tutor explains to his student, for example, that he "had long harboured doubts over the question of the immortality of the soul and inclined toward the dictum of the philosophers to the effect that whatever has a beginning must have an end. But when I found that grammar has an "inchoative" but no "terminative," I drew an analogy between that and the soul and ceased to be confused, praise God."[13] The tutor goes on to give the student a deliriously ornate analysis of the different types of metaphor that one must master in order to be a true grammarian (and thus, in order to have the elements of philosophy). These include "the aeolian, the ornitho-sibilant, the feebly chirping, the tongue-smacking, the faintly tinkling, the bone-snapping, the emptily thunderous, and the phasmic, while the aeolian itself may be subdivided into the stridulaceous, the crepitaceous, and the oropharyngeal, the crepitaceous may be sub-sub-divided into the absquiliferous, the vulgaritissimous, the exquipilifabulous, the seborrhaceous, the squapalidaceous, and the kalipaceous."[14] Is, now, al-Shidyaq doing philosophy? Is Sterne? Whether they are or not, it is certain that we have something to learn, as historians of philosophy, from the dimensions of their respective traditions that they pick out to satirize.

In both cases, the obstacle to full acceptance as philosophical texts would not seem to reside in the person of the narrator (again, even Descartes's *Meditations* uses a fictional protagonist), but in that other defining feature, that one does not quite know how to take their claims. Nietzsche, who thought that Sterne was "the most liberated spirit of all time,"[15] took it as a sign of some deformation of character, insanity, or dogmatism, that one should take any sentence of *Tristram Shandy* at face value. Nor is there any such thing as an absquiliferous metaphor; al-Shidyaq made that up. This then is the problem: even if a sentence of the novel looks like it is telling you something insightful about British empiricism, or Arabic grammatical science, *it can't be trusted.* We historians of philosophy prefer folklore about demonic possession of maidens to a subtle critique of the empiricist theory of knowledge, as long as the folklore is given to us in earnest.

But Sterne, like al-Shidyaq, is often simply so perceptive that it is hard to read him, in one's role as a philosopher, and not suspend one's usual distinction between fiction and philosophy. Sterne treads into a difficult philosophical problem, for example, when he asserts that wit and judgment cannot go together, since they are plainly two different powers with nothing in common. He illustrates this point by maintaining that one might just as well attempt to fart and to hiccup at the same time. But how is it that Sterne's insights, such as this, seem so compellingly *true*, if at the same time we are being cautioned by the author to not take them seriously? The aim is plainly not to plead for his right as an author to play a simple jester, but rather to show a contradiction between the very claim being made by one of the novel's characters, on the one hand, and on the other the overall power of Sterne's literary creation, and thereby to not permit the fart jokes to justify our dismissal of all of the novel's good judgment. Sterne is making a philosophical argument in part through his choice of style.

In the secondary literature there is much discussion of whether *Tristram Shandy* is an anticipation of Thomas Pynchon, William Gaddis, David Foster Wallace, and others, or whether, by contrast, it is an echo of a forgotten Renaissance tradition of learned wit. Readers will generally take it in whichever direction they feel more at home, but in any case for now I am more interested in the history of philosophy than the history of the novel. In general, there is good reason to be wary of claims that anything good from the past is ipso facto "ahead of its time," rather than looking to see whether what looks like groundbreaking formal experimentation is not the vestige of

some extinct convention. Sterne's novel, with its defiant combination of wit and judgment, strongly suggests that the history of philosophy is a history of self-defining not so much in
terms of the possession of judgment, as in terms of its possession of judgment to the exclusion of wit. Philosophy is serious
business, and one needs always to know how to take its claims.
A joke, Kant will suggest in the *Critique of the Faculty of Judgment*, might be understood as "the sudden transformation of a
strained expectation into nothing."[16] Kant's analysis of humor
is also, effectively, a demonstration of why it has no proper
place in philosophy conceived as a positive project: we want
our philosophical expectations to lead somewhere.

Poetry has generally been held, since Aristotle, to be more
open to the sort of violations just described than philosophy is, even if poetry, unlike humor, does not have surprising
transformations as its exclusive purpose. Yet, again, though
Aristotle attempted to bracket this point of difference, poetry
is not only set apart by its content—it is also, obviously, recognized *as* poetry in view of formal properties such as meter
and rhyme. In this respect, it is not surprising that much philosophy has been written as poetry over the past millennia.
In many cases—Lucretius's *De rerum natura* comes to mind—
the poetic elements are principally formal ones: we have an
atomist-materialist text written in verse, which does not at all
rely on allusion, metaphor, or synesthesia to make the case for
the philosophical view it defends.

It is generally supposed today that elements such as meter
and rhyme are irrelevant for our understanding of the content
of a philosophical text. Poetry is today generally considered a
less-than-ideal vehicle for the delivery of philosophical ideas,

since the formal constraints of meter and rhyme needlessly limit one's freedom to express ideas and arguments, and since poetry tends to rely on metaphor and allusion rather than on direct expression (though, again, it need not do so). One of the great impediments European philosophers have faced in recognizing other intellectual traditions as philosophical is that often the reliance on metaphor and on formal genre constraints in these traditions causes them to be judged as "merely" poetic or literary, and thus as nonphilosophical. This judgment extends not just to folk literary traditions such as the Yakut *Olonkho*,[17] but also to the tradition of Upanishadic commentary that is the product of an "advanced" textual culture and that is very plainly engaged with questions that Western thinkers can recognize as philosophical.

It is plain that very often a straightforward double standard is in play, since as a matter of fact we are often prepared to accept metaphors and other un-argued-for literary devices as contributions to philosophy when these devices are used by canonical European philosophers. In other words, if your status as a philosopher is already not in doubt, then utterances of yours, at any register, may be received as philosophy. Take for example Leibniz's well-known claim in the *Monadology* of 1714 that all of nature is akin to "a pond full of fish."[18] This claim appears within the context of the exposition of a broader theory of composite substance, according to which every parcel of the natural world consists in ordered hierarchies of corporeal beings, even if not every given parcel will constitute a single, individual natural being. Some of the aspects of this theory are supported by empirical evidence and by conceptual distinctions and arguments. But the poetic image of the fishpond is meant to be a part of the general battery of tools available to the philosopher to convince his interlocutors of the truth of his metaphysics of composite substance. It is not a throwaway comment or an aside. A corollary claim that Leibniz makes, within the context of his corporeal-substance metaphysics, holds that the parts of any given organic body are constantly in flux, that there is no stable physical constitution of a natural body. In this connection, Leibniz often observes that the body is "like a fountain." What remains constant is the form, even as the particles are constantly moving through it, and ever on into the composition of other organic bodies.

Is it, now, a philosophical claim when one says that the body is "like a fountain"? Jonardon Ganeri draws our attention to an interesting passage in the Persian Muslim philosopher Dara Shukoh's seventeenth-century study of the Upanishads, a set of sacred texts of the Hindu tradition. Ganeri writes:

> The inter-relation between water and its waves is the same as that between body and soul or as that between *sharira* and *atma*. The combination of waves, in their complete aspect, may be likened to *abul-arwah* or *paramatma*; while water only is like the august existence, or *sudh*, or *chitan*.[19]

We need not dwell on the meanings of the Sanskrit and Persian vocabulary Dara Shukoh deploys; what is significant is the evident satisfaction with the simile not just as an explanation of the body-soul relationship but as in effect a grounding claim for a particular theory of the body-soul relationship. Dara Shukoh defends his account of this relationship by pointing out that there is something else in the world that manifests it—namely, the water of the ocean. The idea is that water, like soul, is everywhere the same, while bodies, like waves, take shape and pass, briefly, through the universal medium of soul.

Such a claim could easily be interpreted by an uncharitable external observer as a mere poetic simile, but by parity of reasoning if this is so then we must also banish Leibniz's very similar observation about the fountain-like nature of bodies.

A fine example of such banishment can be discerned in the materialist philosopher François Bernier's discussion with the Sanskrit pandit, at Dara Shukoh's arrangement, in Delhi in the 1660s. This French disciple of Pierre Gassendi finds it ridiculous that Hindus describe the world as issuing from its divine creator in much the same way that a web is spun out by a spider. On his account, this analogy helps to facilitate the Indian conception of the cosmos as going through repeated cycles of generation and destruction, since the latter phase can be conceived as similar to the spider's withdrawal of its filaments back into its body.[20] Bernier is not impressed, and he takes this metaphor as simple proof that "there is no doctrine too strange or too improbable for the soul of man to conceive."[21]

But what is so strange about it? In a moment of remarkable lucidity, David Hume will later comment on the very same idea of the Brahmins, likely having learned of it from Bernier, noting that this "is a species of cosmogony, which appears to us ridiculous, because a spider is a contemptible little animal, whose operations we are never likely to take for a model of the whole universe."[22] The Western philosophical tradition abounds with cosmological models on which the universe as a whole is conceptualized in broadly biological terms as a sort of giant animal or organic being, notably in the Stoic tradition. But as Hume points out, the apparent ridiculousness of the particular animal chosen to model the cosmos in the Upanishadic tradition has only to do with the symbolic role of the chosen animal within European culture. Insects might be thought to be universally repulsive, and thus unworthy of a role in a cosmological model, but then again we might note the case of the bee, which has played a key role in Western political philosophy,[23] if not cosmology, from antiquity to recent discussions of group rationality and distributed cognition, even if, on close inspection, the creature appears no more and no less repulsive than the spider.

What we are seeing is that one culture's "mere metaphors," which from an outsider's perspective are to be excluded by definition from philosophical argumentation, can appear within that culture as a perfectly valid part of an overall package of strategies, also including empirical evidence and logical deduction, for the support of a philosophical theory. But what if these other elements of the package do not appear, and we are left with a text that contains only or primarily poetically expressed declarations about the nature of the world or of humanity's place in the world?

Walt Whitman offers an interesting case study in this regard. There is nothing more off-limits in professional academic philosophy today than the sort of philosophy we might call "wisdom of the ages": the effusions that spill over into the registers of poetry and religion; the approach that is ready to place the Vedas, Zarathustra, and such, next to the canonical, argument-making texts and figures; the approach that supposes that even the most unhinged "Enthusiasts," the Swedenborgs and Ouspenskys and all the others, have something to tell us about the range of human responses to real philosophical problems (Kant also understood this in his engagement with Swedenborg's nebular hypothesis, which turned out to be not just wildly speculative, but also, in large part, correct[24]). Yet the boundary is in large part an artificial one; we accord to the poetic exuberance of certain canonical figures a special and exceptional legitimacy that they do not really deserve, largely in virtue of the rigorous work these figures have done in other domains. To return to a previous example, I really do not know that Leibniz, notwithstanding the infinitesimal calculus and the principle of sufficient reason, deserves to be listened to any more than Whitman on, say, the question whether the body is the unfolding of the soul, or whether every part of nature is contained in every part. And yet historians of philosophy do write books and articles on what Leibniz has had to say about these questions. I've done so myself.

If we accept this broadened conception of philosophy—that is, if we accept that philosophy has always been fueled and shaped at least in part by poetic effusion (something Plato, certainly, would not have denied)—then Whitman, I claim, is a great philosopher. One sees in him traces, as I've suggested, of Leibniz:

> All truths wait in all things,
> They neither hasten their own delivery nor resist it.[25]

One sees Kant (both a trace of the Copernican turn, as well as, in the title of Whitman's masterwork, an expression of the limits of mechanism as applied to nature):

> A child said What is the grass? Fetching it to me with
>   full hands;
> How could I answer the child? I do not know what it is
>   any more than he.
> I guess it must be the flag of my disposition, out of
>   hopeful green stuff woven.[26]

And one sees a sort of anticipation of Nietzsche's attempt to move beyond good and evil:

> I make the poem of evil also—I commemorate that part
>   also;
> I am myself just as much evil as good, and my nation is—
> And I say there is in fact no evil;
> Or if there is, I say it is just as important to you, to the
>   land, or to me, as anything else.[27]

Nietzsche's partisans will insist that there is much more to it than this, that the German thinker has depths of philosophical subtlety to which the American poet does not descend. One might also argue that the principal difference is this: that while both are prophets of the century to come, Nietzsche's prophecy is one of the continent's impending self-destruction, while the discord between his own bedridden solitude and his visions of a coming superman is almost painful to think about. Whitman's prophecy is one of his own country's aggressive global assertion of itself, and it is perfectly epitomized in his robust sexual self-assertion, though twentieth-century American warmongers would not have been prepared to see the roots of their own world domination in his pansexual polymorphous desire. Nietzsche would have liked to move beyond good and evil, but he is miserable; Whitman's transvaluation of all values is full of life and joy, and he is in all but the details absolutely right about the ascendancy of the nation for which he takes himself to stand.

Whitman's superman-to-come is what he calls a "literatus." He believes that only one nation can lead the world at a time, and he maintains that it is the role of the literatus to provide the nation its soul, which is literature. He describes the virtues of the coming literatus both in prose, in the *Democratic Vistas* of 1871:

> A strong-fibred joyousness and faith, and the sense of health al fresco, may well enter into the preparation of future noble American authorship. Part of the test of a great literatus shall be the absence in him of the idea of the covert, the lurid, the maleficent, the devil, the grim estimates inherited from the Puritans, hell, natural depravity, and the like. The great literatus will be known, among the rest, by his cheerful simplicity, his adherence to natural standards, his limitless faith in God, his reverence, and by the absence in him of doubt, ennui, burlesque, persiflage, or any strain'd and temporary fashion;[28]

and in verse, in *Leaves of Grass*:

> Poets to come! orators, singers, musicians to come!
> Not to-day is to justify me and answer what I am for,
> But you, a new brood, native, athletic, continental,
>   greater than before known,
> Arouse! for you must justify me.

He supposes that his work will serve as a sort of seed for the birth of the new literati worthy of the American superpower. Some of the most delirious passages of *Leaves* play on this seed metaphor to suggest, with a joyous personal arrogance no weaker than the arrogance he hopes to bring about in national character, that Whitman himself is fathering the future of America:

On women fit for conception I start bigger and nimbler
babes;
This day I am jetting the stuff of far more arrogant
republics.[29]

Again and again Whitman channels the loftiest political ideals
and metaphysical visions through his own libidinous body. He
takes this body and its receptivity as the answer to ancient
questions, as to the nature of the soul, for example, and he
refuses like no other modern thinker to let the body's essential appetitiveness compromise its value as a philosophical
clavis:

To be in any form, what is that? ...
If nothing lay more develop'd the quahaug in its callous
shell were enough.
Mine is no callous shell,
I have instant conductors all over me whether I pass or
stop,
They seize every object and lead it harmlessly through
me.
I merely stir, press, feel with my fingers, and am happy,
To touch my person to some one else's is about as much
as I can stand.[30]

Often, what ought to be humorous, abrupt shifting from the
lofty to the base, comes across in Whitman as utterly sincere
and utterly valid:

Divine am I inside and out, and I make holy whatever I
touch or am touch'd from,
The scent of these arm-pits aroma finer than prayer.[31]

There is no motion here between the high and low, the exalted and the base. The body is an explication of the soul, for Whitman as for Leibniz, and for both it follows that the bodily self is immortal and coeval with the cosmos itself:

> Before I was born out of my mother generations guided
>   me,
> My embryo has never been torpid, nothing could
>   overlay it.
> For it the nebula cohered to an orb,
> The long slow strata piled to rest it on,
> Vast vegetables gave it sustenance,
> Monstrous sauroids transported it in their mouths and
>   deposited it with care.
> All forces have been steadily employ'd to complete and
>   delight me,
> Now on this spot I stand with my robust soul.[32]

Whitman's cosmism, or, as he would prefer, kosmism, his sensitivity to the relations between the various orders of being, to the simultaneous difference and identity of the astronomical, the geological, the biological, and the spiritual, constitutes the very core of his ontology, and this is because it is here that Whitman is able to spell out his otherwise supremely egotistical vision of himself as the center of the world, but a center that enfolds and expresses everything else:

> I find I incorporate gneiss, coal, long-threaded moss,
>   fruits, grains, esculent roots,
> And am stucco'd with quadrupeds and birds all over,
> And have distanced what is behind me for good reasons,
> But call any thing back again when I desire it.[33]

In fact, a moment's thought will make clear that nothing in Whitman is more Leibnizian than the poet's most famous phrase, *I contain multitudes*.[34] The great difference however is that Whitman offered this as a defiant celebration of the self-contradiction of which he stood accused, while Leibniz spent his life arguing that the world, which is to say multiplicity in unity, does not and cannot involve contradiction.

Whitman's kosmism is central to his understanding of his vocation as a prophet; he believes the American literature to come, and thus the American soul, must engage with nature in a way never before attempted in European thought. As he explains in *Democratic Vistas*:

> In the prophetic literature of these States, ... Nature, true Nature, and the true idea of Nature, long absent, must, above all, become fully restored, enlarged, and must furnish the pervading atmosphere to poems, and the test of all high literary and esthetic compositions. I do not mean the smooth walks, trimm'd hedges, poseys and nightingales of the English poets, but the whole orb, with its geologic history, the kosmos, carrying fire and snow, that rolls through the illimitable areas, light as a feather, though weighing billions of tons.[35]

This is a remarkable twist on, and departure from, German Romantic aesthetics of the sublime. The Germans had wanted to offer up the infinite complexity of nature against the French mania for prim geometric gardening. But the preferred examples were generally just unkempt gardens, patches of moss, and, yes, leaves of grass. Whitman wishes in his idea of nature to go beyond the biological alone, to encompass the magmic, the Earth's crust and mantle and core, planetary and celestial orbits, and to do so in a way that does not make any ontological divisions but sees the self as no less air than gneiss than grass than sauroid. It is this conception of the environmental sublime—which remains attuned to the cycles that move the same stuff through the upper atmosphere, along the earth's surface, and deep beneath it, and that sees these cycles as unfolding through deep time—that informs the best writing about the American West (I am thinking in particular here of Cormac McCarthy and Gary Snyder, to name just a couple).

Unlike for Kant, for Whitman there is nothing *particularly* wonderful about a leaf of grass, and while Whitman would not deny that the leaf of grass could have its own Isaac Newton, he emphatically does not propose himself for this role. "Hurrah for positive science!" Whitman writes in the "Song of Myself." "Long live exact demonstration!" But then he clarifies:

> Gentlemen, to you the first honours always!
> Your facts are useful, and yet they are not my dwelling,
> I but enter by them to an area of my dwelling.[36]

Whitman's dwelling shares with science a preoccupation with the future, and it is as I've indicated in looking toward the future, in particular the coming century of American hegemony, facilitated by steam and electricity and so on, that the poet is most rapturously optimistic. Whitman's distinction as a prophet comes in large part from the fact that he was, broadly speaking, right (though not every great prophet has or needs such a distinction), and if you are not ready to go along with his transvaluation of good and evil, then this accuracy also makes his legacy problematic in the extreme.

Nietzsche's prophecy was vague and delusional, and if it was able to come to seem like an anticipation of German political history in the following century, this is in large part because Nietzsche was unable to keep his manipulable prophecy out of the hands of his manipulative Hitlerite sister. But Whitman was not delusional, and his prophecy involved a holocaust of its own: he explicitly and joyously cheers for the ongoing geno-cide against the Native Americans, which he believes is a sine qua non of the full realization of American greatness. He does not exclude the indigenous people from the poem of America, but he sees them as part of the primordial legacy of the place, as a feature of the landscape on which the future is to be built.

In 1878, Josiah Royce would write from his home state to William James at Harvard: "There is no philosophy in Califor-nia."[37] That place had been rushed into the union, gaining state-hood in 1849, even as the "Indian Wars" raged throughout much of the interior of the continent. There seems to have been an understanding that a stronghold on the Pacific coast of the continent would be crucial for establishing American maritime domination, and not long after California was made part of the union, the United States would begin to take con-trol in Hawai'i, the Philippines, and beyond. And yet Califor-nia had a problem, that Royce, trained at Harvard and sent back home to found the University of California at Berkeley, felt all too sharply. It made little sense to him to attempt to reproduce the staid and refined forms of philosophical inter-action that had long been established in the East, in a place that remained in every sense a frontier, one whose connection to the East was still in the course of being secured with tre-mendous violence. It was at just this time that Whitman came forth with a style of thought and expression suited to the con-tinental expansion that was underway: ecstasy.

Still another interesting example of the subtle relationship between poetry and philosophy is the case of T. S. Eliot. We might easily imagine a nearby possible world in which we would find the following footnote in some obscure scholarly monograph: "There was in the early 20th century a now largely forgotten American-English philosopher named T. S. Eliot. He published some scholarly articles, notably one in *The Monist* of 1916 on 'The Development of Leibniz's Monadism.'"[38] Here he offers a critical review of the various philosophical legacies Leibniz was seeking to unify, and thereby of the problems he was seeking to overcome. Eliot does not commit himself to Leibniz's philosophical program, but he does affirm of his predecessor's system that "no philosophy contains more various possibilities of development, no philosophy unites more various influences."[39] The reason why we never see such a footnote is that Eliot would not go on to develop any of the various possibilities in Leibniz, but would instead become much better known as a poet, in particular of the modernist masterpiece, *The Waste Land*, of 1922. But one discerns nonetheless a continuous concern to work out many of the philosophical problems that had initially motivated Eliot to work through, as a scholar, the philosophical development of his predecessor, Leibniz. Significantly, though, Eliot would develop in a very different direction. In "The Dry Salvages" of 1940, we are given a stunning survey of the boundaries of the knowable, and of the constant and ineradicable will among human beings to navigate and push at these boundaries. To cite the description only in part, Eliot believes that we are, in our desire to know the unknowable, constrained:

To communicate with Mars, converse with spirits,
To report the behaviour of the sea monster,
Describe the horoscope, haruspicate or scry,
Observe disease in signatures, evoke

Biography from the wrinkles of the palm
And tragedy from fingers; release omens
By sortilege, or tea leaves, riddle with the inevitable
With playing cards, fiddle with pentagrams
Or barbituric acids.[40]

All these are, Eliot writes, "but usual activities." In this life most of us will never arrive at more that "hints and guesses / hints followed by guesses," yet we aspire to a sort of knowledge that is "Never here to be realised." And in the end the only succor is reabsorption back into nature:

We, content at the last
If our temporal reversion nourish
(Not too far from the yew-tree)
The life of significant soil.[41]

This is how the poem ends, with a radical quietism and finitism that is a universe away from Leibniz's bold metaphysics. It is a quietism, moreover, that is very contemporary with that of recognized philosophers such as Wittgenstein. But rather than choosing to "remain silent" in the face of the impossibility of metaphysics, Eliot takes another path: he overflows with language, language that through its richness and overabundance confirms the impossibility of the thing the philosophers had sought after, but provides the reader with a vivid aesthetic experience in the course of this confirmation. The aesthetic experience might be held by some to make the philosophical view at stake more compelling. Metaphysics can't but amount to so much "fiddling with pentagrams"; never mind then! From minor Leibniz commentator to destroyer of metaphysics: this is quite a career T. S. Eliot had as a philosopher—

except that he is not credited as a philosopher. Arguably, however, the way he is credited has more to do with the twentieth century's genre conventions—where philosophy is not written in verse, in contrast with other centuries and other cultures—than with the content of his thoughts or with the scope and aims of his work.

Dear Professor,

Not having received a reply to my initial message several weeks ago, I am taking the liberty of writing to you again, in this long sleepless night in the middle of a long Duluth winter, to encourage you to have a look at my book, *Quantum Truths for the 21st Century*, available for download on my website. The book was recently critically discussed by Professor Morton Rabotnik of the International Business Academy of Orlando, Florida, who called it an important "riposte to the academic philosophers with their narrow and irrelevant preoccupations." I hope you will consider freeing yourself from the narrowness and irrelevance your profession imposes on you.

Yours truly,
Bud Korg
Past President
North Central Division,
American Society of Real Estate Appraisers

The highly abstract matter of the definition of philosophy makes itself felt in certain very concrete and practical problems. For some years I struggled to find a viable criterion by which to classify the books in my private library, which numbered at the time in the thousands. My intention had been to keep all of my philosophy books in my office at work, and all of my nonphilosophy books at home. This seemed at the outset like a simple enough division, and I have known many colleagues who are able to implement it unproblematically. When it's a matter of separating the specialized and technical work of John McDowell or Derek Parfit from the plainly recreational entertainments of Tom Clancy, there can be little worry about a gray area. In my case, however, I found that most of the books I had acquired until that point fell into the gray area. For example, I found myself emptying a box of books shortly after I had arrived in Montreal for my new job, hoping to separate the box's content into two piles, one for home and one for office.

The first book I pulled out was a Penguin edition of Edmund Spenser's *The Faerie Queene*. Surely this belongs at home, I thought. The second book was another Penguin paperback, a collection titled *English Metaphysical Poets*. I looked at the table of contents and was reminded that it included work not only by Spenser but also by the Cambridge Platonist and minor metaphysical poet Henry More, to whom we have already been introduced. The next book I pulled out was an edition of More's *Antidote against Atheism*, the text from which we read an excerpt earlier in this chapter. And the one after that? Believe it or not, it was nothing other than an English edition of Descartes's *Meditations,* including the "Objections and Replies" from Thomas Hobbes, Pierre Gassendi, and, indeed, Henry More.

So here we have a proper slippery-slope problem: if any book has ever belonged in a philosophy library, it is Descartes's *Meditations.* No one would deny this, not Jacques Derrida, not John Searle. But the *Meditations* also plainly belong on the same shelf, or at least in the same room, as the philosophical works of Henry More. Yet More's philosophical works cannot be easily separated from his poetical works: much of the philosophy is written in verse (see, for example, the *Democritus Platonissans* of 1646), and even when it is written in prose it covers many of the same arguments and themes as does the poetry. But More's poetry cannot be understood without some knowledge of the conventions and preoccupations of the other poets of his place and era. More belongs with both Spenser and Descartes. Spenser and Descartes, therefore, belong together.

And come to think of it, does not Spenser himself say much about the idea of spirit, soul, body, substance, and such? One might respond here, well, yes, perhaps he does, but to the extent that when he does he is only invoking folk ideas, popular misconceptions of the sort that Descartes's philosophical analysis aims to dissolve. But this response fails to take into account the fact that Descartes himself engages with such folk ideas in the *Meditations,* and in order to understand what he is arguing against one would do well to go back to at least some of the sources. When Descartes insists that he is not a "subtle vapor," for example, he is arguing against a very deep-seated popular conception of the soul that took it as a liminal substance at the boundary between the material and the immaterial, whereas Descartes's dualism is based on the conviction that every entity must be entirely on the one side or on the other. Some of the most vivid expressions of the conception of soul as a sort of subtle matter, not surprisingly, are found among the poets.

The case I have described is not an exception, but rather a single instance of the general difficulty I have had, and have, in bounding philosophy off from the rest of my reading and thinking life, from everything that is "not philosophy." Should I keep Jean Genet's plays at home or in the office? Genet was an important influence on Derrida, particularly his unhinged 1974 work, *Glas*. This was around the same time Derrida was engaging with John Searle, fruitlessly, on the question of the interpretation of J. L. Austin on intentionality. Could it be that somewhere in the work of Genet one might find a hint as to the real significance of some point of misunderstanding in the Derrida-Searle debate? I would not want to exclude the possibility out of hand. And similarly for virtually every other literary author who has worked, broadly speaking, on the plane of ideas, entering into contact with, bumping up against, the people we categorize as philosophers: Aristophanes, Cyrano de Bergerac, Whitman, Eliot, Beckett. I am not prepared to remove these thinkers to their own library, because to do so would be an impoverishment of my private philosophy shelves.

When I was seven or eight years old, the paradoxes of infinity began to trouble me greatly—for me, the dawning of wonder was also the dawning of anxiety. I thought about how the world must go on forever, yet cannot, and I felt that there was something deeply, urgently wrong with the world. The problem did not strike me as a curious puzzle or an exciting challenge. Rather, I sensed that there was some sort of malevolence behind it. My life, which had in its earliest stages seemed to take shape in a world of warmth and comfort and infinite assurance, depended for its continued existence on an arrangement that, I now suspected, was quite literally impossible.

A million other small things happened between these thoughts and the beginning of my formal study of philosophy. In my early teens I began scouring the shelves of local bookstores for answers to "deep" questions. I went to the "philosophy" section and found little there that gave me much hope. Long before I knew much of anything I was making sharp judgments of quality, and I was already certain that I would not be happy with Will and Ariel Durant, let alone the more common selection of titles available under the subheading of "metaphysics": Shirley MacLaine, Aleister Crowley. When I was fifteen I happened across Wittgenstein's *Tractatus*, and while I still did not know anything I knew it was different, and I wanted very desperately to decipher its terse, meaning-packed lines. I took it home and it sat there, uncomprehended, for several years, like a mysterious fetish object.

I dropped out of high school when I was sixteen and began a course of autodidactic reading in radical thought, or at least authors who gave an appearance of radicalism but in some cases were only bloody demagogues: Kropotkin, Lenin, Mao. The *Tractatus* tarried, still uncomprehended. By the time I worked my way through community college and into the state university system, I was well versed in Russian language, history, and literature, and knew about philosophy mostly through this peculiar filter. I first learned about positivism, for example, via Lenin's critique of Mach. I double-majored in Slavic studies and philosophy, and of the latter I studied, in the mere two years I was pursuing my majors at the university, mostly ancient Greek philosophy, with one professor I found particularly odd and inspiring. When I finished I had offers for graduate studies in Slavic linguistics, in Southern California, or in philosophy, in New York. My ultimate decision for New York was in large part geographical; growing up in California had confirmed for me (though I had not yet read it) my fellow Californian Josiah Royce's denial of the possibility of Californian philosophy, which I took at the time to mean that that place is not conducive to serious thought of any sort, that the telegraph wires of history and memory do not reach that far. California, it seemed to me, was the New World's New World, and so, in going to New York, I was going to the Old World where I could finally get some serious thinking done. And all the more so, I thought, since I was deciding for philosophy over what had come to seem to me to be the small parish of "area studies": why focus on a single language, a single geographical domain, when philosophy can give you *everything*?

So I went to New York, to philosophy, believing this meant that I was going to study the world as a whole, and everything in it, and that I was going to do so profoundly. Somehow, the smattering of philosophy courses I had taken as an undergraduate had not disabused me of the idea that this is what philosophy sets itself up as doing. I suppose it was in my first year of graduate school that I was finally woken up to the gap between my conception of philosophy and philosophy's self-conception as an academic discipline in the Anglo-American fin de siècle. By this time, it seemed too late to pull out, and in any case I had no idea what else I might do in this life. By some happy harmony, I soon discovered Leibniz, who became my beacon and my guide and, more importantly, offered to me a model of philosophy that seemed entirely unfamiliar to those around me. For Leibniz, Slavic linguistics *was* philosophy (see, for example, his correspondence with the Swedish Slavist J. G. Sparwenfeld), as were microscopy, paleontology, and mathematics, and indeed poetry, too, which he wrote, if not terribly well, then, still, with love.

I have never been good at respecting the disciplinary boundaries philosophy seeks to hold up for itself, and for this reason have often supposed that I must be a bad philosopher. I have been particularly interested in those figures, like Sterne or Whitman or al-Shidyaq, who look at philosophy as if from the outside and take everything they need of it in order to do something else, or take the measure of its aims and methods and determine they have no need of it.

But are they really outside? Or is philosophy a peculiar discipline to the extent that it is constituted, rather than compromised, by all those who have rejected it or insisted on standing outside of it, mocking, ironizing, deconstructing, defiantly focusing on their favorite sauces, on their first-person idiosyncrasies and fantasies? It is significant, here, again, that one of philosophy's foundational figures, Socrates, stood in a relationship to the activities generally taken as philosophy in his age similar to the one taken up by Sterne and Whitman in their own age. Philosophy is perhaps the only discipline that is able to canonize the figures, or at least some of the figures, who had sought in their lifetime to break it down or to reject it. Antiphilosophy, like philosophy, is the business of the philosophers, as Steven Shapin said. Bernard Williams has rightly noted that "as long as there has been such a subject as philosophy, there have been people who hated and despised it."[42] Shapin is writing from a position external to academic philosophy, and Williams from the position of a consummate insider.

What Shapin sees, and Williams does not, is that many of the "haters" are themselves recalcitrant philosophers.

It is seldom clear, in this messy business, who is to count as Gadfly, and who as a charlatan, a nonphilosopher, or a hater. Nor does there appear to be any neutral way of settling the matter. One person's Gadfly is another's hack. Either way, such determinations seem to have much to do with the way a given thinker deploys modes of discourse, such as the poetic and the satirical, which have had a problematic relationship to the project of philosophy throughout the history of its attempts at self-definition. In these other modes, different rules tend to apply concerning the use of metaphor, the binding force of the law of the excluded middle, and, perhaps most of all, the obtrusion of the individual personality of the author.

Dear Professor,

Judging from your silence, I gather that you are not interested in reading my e-book, *Quantum Truths for the 21st Century*. I gather you prefer to stay in your safe little academic world, swatting away Gadflies like me with a simple click of your "delete" button. If you were to take a look, you would likely judge that my methods and insights are the work of an amateur. The only thing that counts for you as philosophy is mindless commentary upon commentaries upon commentaries, mere beaver-like chipping away at some brittle twig of a question. But remember this: philosophy doesn't just begin in wonder; once the wonder is gone, it is no longer philosophy. Remember that, professor.

Cordially,
Bud Korg
Real Estate Appraiser (Ret.)

4

BODY AND SOUL

Featuring the Ascetic

Recall the naive undergraduate, introduced in chapter 1, who wished for his philosophy class to be held out on the lawn, since, after all, "it's all philosophy"; hacky-sacking, lazing about in the sun, and enjoying the good life are just as much part of philosophy as considering arguments for or against the existence of the external world. In fact, a great many canonical philosophers have shared a vision of philosophy that is very similar to that of the naive undergraduate.

Many of us are familiar with the current of philosophy that is sometimes called "eudaimonistic." As Pierre Hadot writes of the typical aims of ancient philosophy: "One was to renounce the false values of wealth, honors, and pleasures, and turn towards the true value of virtue, contemplation, a simple lifestyle, and the simple happiness of existing."[1] But in truth such an understanding of philosophy continues well after the ancient period. Certainly, this current is generally associated with a handful of traditions in late antiquity, including Stoicism and Epicureanism, which, it is often said, took theoretical philosophy, about cause or motion or body, for example, as of interest only to the extent that proper understanding of nature is a precondition of proper understanding of ourselves and our place in nature, and it is only such proper understanding, finally, that enables us to be truly happy. But happiness, understood as dependent on both moral uprightness and physical health, was equally central to the project of philosophy as understood, for example, by Leibniz or Robert Boyle. Being happy, on this understanding, is the only real goal of philosophical inquiry, and if this goal could be attained simply by gazing at butterflies then this would be all the philosophy we would ever need or want.

A compelling case can be made that more or less everyone, prior to the emergence of professionalized philosophy in the West over the course of the eighteenth century, took happiness to be the exclusive legitimate goal of philosophy. If some philosophical projects in history appear to be more theoretical and others more practical, this can in large part be explained by the fact that they had differing strengths and inclinations among them, but to the extent that there was a shared conception of what philosophy was, from antiquity to the early modern period, it was that philosophy was principally concerned with helping us to be happy. Knowledge was often conceived as a means to this end, rather than as an ultimate end in itself. Some philosophers, such as the Cynics, believed that positive knowledge was completely unnecessary for the project of happiness, indeed a distraction, and here they seemed to be taking their cue from a particular interpretation of the teaching of Socrates.[2]

To take another very different example, Leibniz and Robert Boyle, around the same time as each other, in Germany and England respectively, both supposed that increase in knowledge could only result in greater appreciation of the power and wisdom of God, and for them such appreciation carried a variety of joy directly along with it.³ These diverse thinkers understood that, whatever the path, whether it included knowledge seeking or not, the project of philosophy was one of coming to a certain inner state, a disposition toward the world, and a cultivation of moral character. Boyle, in his tellingly titled work *The Christian Virtuoso* of 1690, offers a stunning account of the connection, as he sees it, between the study of singular things, appreciation of abstract truths, and, finally, the cultivation of moral character and ultimately of happiness:

> He that is addicted to Knowledge Experimental, is accustom'd both to Persue, Esteem, and Relish many Truths, that do not delight his Senses, or gratifie his Passions, or his Interests, but only entertain his Understanding with that Manly and Spiritual Satisfaction, that is naturally afforded it by the attainment of Clear and Noble Truths, which are its genuine Objects and Delights ... [H]e, that is accustomed to prize Truths of an Inferior kind, because they are Truths, will be much more dispos'd to value Divine Truths.⁴

The undergraduate who wished to hold class on the university lawn was still operating under an assumption, somewhat closer to Boyle's, that truths of a lower order and experiences of a mundane sort are not discontinuous with truths of a philosophical nature. But his graduate TA, channeling the norms of the profession he was still uncertain of having mastered, corrected this naive hope before it was too late. To be a graduate student is, in large part, to submit to the authority of advisors and their predecessors, and to come to recognize, as they did in their time, certain forms of authority rather than others. The sort of philosopher one is, in fact, has very much to do with the sort of authority one is prepared to recognize.

Authority is a curious notion. Etymologically, it is connected to authorship, though in the ancient context *auctoritas* already had primarily to do with the amount of influence or social or political clout a person possessed. For philosophers it is not only human beings who are able to have such clout, but also texts, and even one's own intuitions. Every sort of philosopher may be said to recognize some authority or other, even those who are often held to be iconoclastic or antiauthoritarian. Those who work squarely within a tradition, who write commentaries on predecessors, generally take these predecessors to be authorities, though there is a great deal of flexibility in the notion of authority even here; some commentators take the predecessor upon whom the commentary is being written as more or less infallible, and take their own work simply as clarification or development of what was already contained in nuce in the work of the earlier philosopher. It is this sort of submission to authority, whether or not it had ever occurred in its pure form, that early modern experimentalists such as Bacon and Descartes firmly rejected. But these early modern thinkers sometimes preferred to speak of the replacement of one form of authority by another—namely, the authority of the senses. It is not, for them, that the claims of ancient predecessors carried no weight, but only that these claims had to be measured, where possible, against the evidence that one could experience directly.

In this connection, many early modern philosophers expressed a strongly conciliatory attitude toward Aristotle; he, like they, believed in going out into nature and observing for oneself. Their complaint was rather against Aristotelianism, particularly that of the much maligned Scholastics, who were thought to have preferred the claims of Aristotle even when these were contradicted by direct observation. For many early modern philosophers, the authority of the ancients was not totally dismissed, but was rather reclassified or downgraded to something closer to the status of testimony. In the seventeenth century, notably within the collective research program of the Royal Society of London, sophisticated reflections were undertaken on the varying degrees of veracity that one should ascribe to different sorts of testimony, depending on the particular character, or temporal or geographical distance of the person who provides the report. Typically, it was supposed that people of a low social status and people lacking education, not to mention women, were not capable of providing reports as trustworthy as those of people with the social status of "gentleman" provided.

It was in this connection that the notion of "probability" was often understood in the seventeenth century, as having significant semantic overlap with the notion of authority; it was not the claims themselves that were considered probable or improbable, but rather the people who made the claims. To be "probable" was to be worthy of ap*prob*ation, a quasi-moral status that one acquired through the particular institutional and social role one played. How the notion of probability made the transition in the modern period from describing characters of people to describing the likelihood of states of affairs, is well beyond our present concern. But it is important to note that already in the earlier sense of probability as approbation, there is a concern for the measurement, however inexact, of degrees of veracity, whereas in principle in the invocation of authority, such as that of Aristotle, the claim of the predecessor is held to be true simply in virtue of its having come from a supremely authoritative source. With the rise of the experimental method in the early modern period in Europe, and the new challenge posed to ancient authority by the authority of the senses, ancient authority effectively becomes just one more source of testimony, often fairly good and fairly reliable, but still not different in kind from the sort of testimony one might get in a letter from a country doctor, say, sent to the Royal Society from the Isle of Man, concerning the recent birth of a two-headed calf.

One division between approaches to philosophy that is likely deeper than that between the authority-based and the revolutionary, the rational and the imaginative, the scientific and the poetic, is the one between philosophy conceived as an activity of the mind alone, or, rather, as an activity that necessarily implicates the body. There is a very familiar distinction in the European tradition, to which we are not principally referring here, between theoretical and practical philosophy. Often this basic division includes further subdivisions: metaphysics and epistemology fall on the side of the theoretical, while ethics and social and political philosophy are held to be practical. Within the practical division, in turn, there are further possibilities for reverting back to a more or less purely theoretical approach; metaethics, for example, is a theoretical approach to a subdivision of practical philosophy. The same could be said of uses of ideal theory in political philosophy, such as John Rawls's *Theory of Justice*, which approach questions about how to set up the most just society, for example, in abstraction from the real existence of any particular society. Often, throughout the European tradition, there has been a pronounced concern to unite these two branches, for example in G. W. Leibniz's preferred motto, *Theoria cum praxi*—theory with practice.

Some tendencies in European philosophy, notably Marxism, have sought to establish that theory and practice cannot be separated, or that the one is dependent on the other. In the case of Marxism, it is argued that no one is in a position to propose or defend theories that are not rooted in a particular form of life that is characteristic of a particular social class in a particular stage of history. Plato, for example, could not have been expected to be a dialectical materialist, since the very idea of it is something that could only emerge in the era of capitalist exploitation of labor. Recent work in analytic philosophy of language and epistemology has also sought to unite theory and practice by arguing that in the end there can be no meaningful distinction between knowing how and knowing that: to know that something is the case is to be disposed to react in a certain way under certain circumstances.[5]

These examples show that the idea of uniting theory and practice is deep seated, but again it is not exactly this sense of "practical" and "theoretical" that is of interest to us here. In the European tradition there may be very many philosophers who have sought to unite theory and practice, but they have for the most part presumed that a suitable way of going about uniting them is to sit in a chair and to think and, eventually, to write about the importance of this unification. There are virtually never any concrete exercises prescribed in the European tradition as the physical counterparts to the mental exercises we think of as philosophy. There are practices in the sense of "customs": philosophers perambulate, for example, and expatiate on topics of interest while their disciples follow behind; or philosophers stand at a podium and click at a screen with a remote control. The general consensus, however, is that there are no particular movements through which the body *must* go in order for a particular embodied person to be said to be doing philosophy.

There have been a few instances of rigorous, ritualized motions that have been integrated with philosophy in the Western tradition, but the sort of philosophy here is not simply contemplative or speculative; it is, rather, theurgic, and thus overlaps with ritual magic or religion. In the neo-Platonic school, for example, we find Plotinus urging a form of meditation as a way of attaining union with the divine, while subsequently this rather imprecise exhortation to meditation is turned into a fairly elaborate ritual observance by his student Porphyry. There are also the spiritual exercises of Saint Ignatius of Loyola, which in turn one might see as existing on a broad continuum with the spiritual practices that, if we agree with Hadot, characterized much of late antique philosophy and in truth never fully disappeared from the scene.

Kant had to take a walk at the same time every day, and to fastidiously avoid sweating, in order to keep thinking about philosophical questions in a productive way; G.E.M. Anscombe liked to eat a can of baked beans while lecturing;[6] and so on. It is difficult to know where to draw the line between the concrete motions that might be considered the bodily correlate of the mental activity of philosophizing, on the one hand, and on the other individual habits or routines. It is noteworthy in this connection that many people who do yoga in the West will claim that other aspects of their lives become "yoga" by extension. Thus you might hear someone say that they are taking some time off to get into the "yoga of being a parent," but if you, who does not do yoga in the narrower sense, respond that you are doing the "yoga of slouching at your desk and pounding out another book on your laptop," you will be made to understand that this does not count. The difference is presumed to lie in the individualism of your activity, in contrast with the tradition-boundedness, however loose, of the other's.

Plainly, in certain places and times, individual habits do give way to collective rules that impose a regime for the bodies of all those seeking to make progress within a given philosophical tradition. The most obvious example of this is surely Yoga. By capitalizing the term here, I refer to a branching of one of the six schools of *āstika*, or orthodox Indian philosophy, which emerges largely out of the Sāṃkhya tradition and its encounter with Buddhism and Jainism, and which solidifies around the *Yoga Sutras* of Patañjali, composed around 400 CE. There is of course also "yoga," a significant industry throughout the world, which is based largely on the sale of goods and services promoting individual health and well-being, while also bearing some genealogical relationship to the ancient Indian tradition. In fact, lest this description of yoga with a lowercase "y" sound too dismissive, it is interesting to reflect, also, on the vagueness of the boundary between "philosophy as a way of life," which includes the various spiritual exercises we have discussed, and perhaps most exemplarily Yoga, on the one hand, and on the other the idea of a "lifestyle," such as those marketed by advertising agencies, and which seem inescapably unphilosophical, or indeed subphilosophical.

But we will leave that reflection aside in order to focus, briefly, on Yoga in the proper sense. Patañjali's sutras are a compilation of 196 fairly cryptic aphorisms, which give no clear instructions for the conduct of any particular physical exercises. The first of the four chapters of the text contains the closest thing we will find to a definition of "yoga." Yoga, we learn, is "the restraint of mental modifications."[7] But how do we restrain mental modifications? The answer in the remaining chapters will not appear in a specific set of instructions. The physical exercises themselves date back long before Patañjali's work, and may even be pre-Vedic. They are well attested in the Upanishadic tradition in texts dating to between the fifth and the first centuries BCE. But they become united with a specific *darśana*, and thus "yoked," as the very name of the discipline suggests, to a philosophical doctrine, principally as a result of Patañjali's engagement with the metaphysics of the orthodox school of Sāṃkhya.

It is often maintained that Yoga may be appropriately seen as the practical branch of the theoretical project of Sāṃkhya. This latter is a rigidly dualist *darśana*, which distinguishes reality into two basic principles, *puruṣa* and *prakṛti*, roughly, "self" and "nature." The ultimate aim of philosophy is to break the bond between these two principles, thereby becoming free of the realm of matter by way of *mokṣa*, or liberation. Yoga, then, is the practice that will make this liberation possible, now that Sāṃkhya has identified it as the true goal of reflection.

Identifying Yoga as the practical branch of Sāṃkhya tells the truth, perhaps, but not the whole truth, since from the point of view of the practicing yogi this is not a voluntary or quodlibetal unification of two different sorts of activity; there would be no point in philosophizing about *mokṣa* without also undertaking the steps to attain it. This is perhaps like the "necessary" link between theory and practice in, say, Marxism, except that here the connection is tighter. A Marxist philosopher, again, can still just sit at her desk all day, even if what she does there is write about how her thoughts are dependent on our having arrived at the present stage of history; a yogi, by contrast, cannot sit at a desk and think about how to liberate himself from *prakṛti*, but must actually get down on the ground and start going through the motions. No motions, no philosophy. The motions are not an auxiliary or a propaedeutic, but are the thing itself.

Given that there seem to be *some* expectations about what the body must be doing in any given philosophical tradition, we might suggest that Yoga is but the fullest development of an expectation that is always there in some degree in any tradition of philosophy. Yet at present, in academic philosophy, this expectation is minimal. Ironically, today many academic philosophers will, at the end of a workday, go off to a yoga session in order to *not* do philosophy. They contrast the physical exercise of philosophy with the mental labor that is, by definition, their profession. What an impoverishment of both sides! Philosophy as a job is now balanced by yoga as a lifestyle, and the millennia-long history that has united contemplation with a strict discipline of the body is scarcely recalled in either segment of the day.

There is no name for my practice, nor should there be one. A passing Ionian called me a Gymnosophist, by which he meant that I am a philosopher who wears no clothes. But had he looked closer he would have seen my loincloth, and anyhow most of my upper body is hidden by the great locks of my hair and beard. A hirsute Phrynian passing in the opposite direction paused to mock me, to call me a beggar and a dog. He should be the one to talk!

He seemed to think I had ended up where I am by simple misfortune, rather than by my own free choice. He surely could not have known that I come from Sângala, and that my father was favored by King Menander himself. After my twin brother was appointed to lead the king's campaign to Paliputra on the Ganges, father declared a feast and asked him what he would like. I can still hear his voice: partridges, he said, drowned in honey. He ate fourteen of them in one sitting, feathers and all, and passed out from the copious wine he had taken to wash them down. I recall wishing so earnestly that father had asked me, instead, what I would like. Nothing, I would have said. There is absolutely nothing that I would like to have in this world.

The king is more properly speaking an emperor, and has conquered many lands and many peoples to whom he could not speak in a tongue they know. But he can still dump coins on them, with likenesses of his fair face, and then demand that these be returned to him in tribute. For what else is it to rule? And now Menander wishes to be called Milinda, and has accepted the faith of Sakyamuni. He's discoursing with the sages on the Vedas, on Sāṃkhya, Nyāya, Yoga, and Vaiśeṣika, on philosophy, arithmetic, music, astronomy, magic, and so on. And most of all on the art of war.

This is all fine, I suppose, but my understanding of the faith is not wrapped up in discoursing and conquering, but in the renunciation taught to the Mādhyamikas. This is closer to my dog nature. Empires are false and fleeting, like the mist that forms at dawn and is gone before noon. My brother has now been sent to the embassy at Anuradhapura, on the far southern island to which the Lord Rama, so it is said, long ago built a bridge of limestone. But how long will that last? How long will one coin stay in circulation, before it is replaced by another?

Meanwhile I've made my way to Arachosia, to another of the cities named for Alexander (I've lost count). There is a constant traffic of peoples through this Alexandria's old citadel: Parthians, Persians, Sogdians. Every day there's another wise man who shows up, shouting about this or that revelation, the vision he's had, the latest enlightenment and how to get ready for whatever great destruction is right around the corner. There's another kind of wise man who will teach you how to contort your body into impossible positions, or contort your mind to memorize great bodies of knowledge. The bazaar is a good place for them, for they've all got something to sell.

Their customers think they are buying happiness, but they're really only buying bubbles. These will pop, but the happiness that endures is the one that does not depend on externals, and instead comes from virtue. The *darśanas*, too, are externals, as is all knowledge. The only enlightenment, and the only freedom, is in negation. There was an Ionian, of Athens, who understood this, and taught nothing, but only lived his life as an expression of virtue. He did not accept money in exchange for conversation, and when he was wrongly accused of great crimes he did not find it worth his while to defend himself. This is true wisdom, and true power.

I do not recall the last time I ate. There is no reason not to eat, if filling up one's stomach will bring the most equanimity. But the longer I go without nourishment, I find, the better able I am to train my mind upon negation, and upon the irreality of that boundary, of which most men are so afraid, between life and death. A monk from Fusang came through some time ago, claiming to have consumed only air since earliest boyhood, and to be able to go without even that for days on end. He said he was preparing himself for a state that is neither life nor death, where his body, posed in meditation, will cease to pulse and to give off heat, yet nor will it decay. The weak-minded dreamers at the bazaar practically offered to bathe him in their coins. I looked down from my perch—a stork's nest that had been abandoned by that brave bird for the season—and I laughed out loud at the sight of it. This monk is selling nothing, I thought, quite literally nothing!

I have no coins, and when any fall into my hands I throw them right back, or I deface them by filing them down against a hard stone. I do have friends, but if they go away I am not sad. They are just like me, and to know this is to know that I have within myself all the requisites for good company. And what of desire? When I was younger I would satisfy carnal urges by the easiest remedy available, by the use of the very hands which nature in her wisdom has made long enough to deal swiftly and efficiently with this noisome distraction. But in more recent years I have found that, as with abstention from food, holding out against this desire, too, is more conducive to my contemplative ends.

There is a power that builds up inside me by the retention of seed, which seems also, like the state of hunger, to partake of both life and death at once.

I belong to no school, and I do as I please. But I know there is a true path, and there is a path of ignorance. Most of the so-called learned men are only puffed up with words, and they will pop too, and be shown to have been nothing. To embrace nothing already in life, and therefore to conduct one's life as a preparation for death: that is true wisdom. There is a pleasant ache in the body that hungers and that is parched as it lies exposed to the sun in its elevated stork's nest. But it is not *for the sake of* this pleasure that one sets out on the path of *askesis*. These pleasures are incidental, while what one truly aims for is the happiness of virtue, a happiness that comes entirely from within.

There is nothing to do, and nothing to learn. Is this, then, a *darśana*? Is it philosophy? I will let the hawkers in the bazaar answer that question. Here comes one now: a great brawny Scythian, bellowing about his five simple steps to bodhisattva. No thanks, man. I've got it for free.

So far we have discussed authority, and we have discussed practice. What, now, do these two have to do with each other?

Part of the answer to this question is that mastering the teachings of the great authorities within a given tradition is a sort of practice. In China and India, a central part of the philosophical education long consisted in straightforward memorization of large bodies of work. Inevitably, this memorization evolved into highly refined practices that implicated the body in direct ways: witness for example the Chinese practice of "backing," or reciting a text with one's back turned to it.[8]

There seems to be a connection between the centrality of bodily practices, on the one hand, and respect for authority within a given tradition, on the other. Where reverence for past authority is high, rigid practices will be enforced; where philosophy is seen as the practice of questioning everything and thinking for oneself, doing whatever one wishes to do with one's body, and respecting no one's schedule or rhythms but one's own, seems the more appropriate mode of operation. One cannot question everything from a posture of reverence.

Philosophy is often seen as essentially having to do with just this sort of questioning: as the discipline that "questions everything." Thus Graham Priest writes, "I suggest ... that philosophy is precisely that intellectual inquiry in which *anything* is open to critical challenge and scrutiny. This, at least, explains many of its salient features." First, he goes on, "Philosophy is subversive. Time and again, philosophers have shot at religions, political systems, public mores. They do this because they are prepared to challenge things which everybody else takes for granted, or whose rejection most people do not countenance." Second, "Learning philosophy is something that many students find unsettling."[9] Priest seems to recognize principally the way in which philosophy undermines the present order of things, as dictated by religion, politics, and social values. But of course it is also capable of subverting itself, as a tradition constituted by a certain present disposition to past authorities.

One sometimes suspects that those periods of philosophy that reject past authority, in particular, are not so much interested in questioning authority as they are in simply dismissing it. Sometimes, this dismissiveness is expressed in the form of an exaggerated claim of one's own independence from the past. There are real ruptures in the history of philosophy, and there is much to be learned from tracing them out. However artificial the notion of the "medieval" period is, we may nonetheless say with certainty that this notion is more usefully applied to Europe than to, say, South America; there is nothing "medieval" about the tenth century in Peru (nor, strictly speaking, is there any meaningful sense in which Peruvians can be said to have experienced the tenth century). There is also nothing medieval about what we often call "medieval Islamic philosophy." Whether or not we may see the period between the eighth and the twelfth centuries as a "Golden Age," a term that implies a subsequent decline, it is in any case a mistake to see the period of flourishing of ibn Rushd in Iberia, or of ibn Sina in Central Asia, as a relative void between antiquity and modernity. It was certainly not experienced by the people who lived it as "between two ages," and, within the context of Islamic history, there is no interesting sense in which this period was a transitional one.

One must distinguish between harmless forms of periodization, on the one hand, and distorting ones, on the other. There is nothing distorting about calling Leibniz, for example, an "early modern" philosopher. He would not have used this term himself—it would have been particularly strange for him, or for anyone living in any period, to describe himself as an "early" representative of anything, since this would imply some kind of familiarity with things yet to come. But Leibniz did use near synonyms of "modern" to describe the period he was living in and the style of thinking characteristic of it, and as it turns out there was more of it to come in the future. The distorting periodizations, by contrast, seem to arise particularly when they involve the extension of one region's harmless periodizations to a region for which they were not initially developed. Yet we must also not be so cautious to avoid such extensions that we become blinded to broader, transregional patterns in intellectual history.

A good example of such a pattern is the case of early modern India. Recently, Jonardon Ganeri has forcefully argued that, just as in Europe, in South Asia we may identify a cluster of developments that can justly be described as the emergence of a distinctly modern style of thinking. There is no radical break with the past, but part of Ganeri's argument is that recent revisionist scholarship on the early modern period in Europe may help us to gain a more subtle understanding of the complicated blend of continuity and innovation in India in the sixteenth and seventeenth centuries.[10] During this period, Sanskrit thinkers remain in many respects faithful to the earlier authorities in the traditions in which they are writing, and for this reason from the outside it has long been difficult to detect any ruptures of the sort we associate with modernity. In Europe in contrast we find many early modern thinkers boldly, even haughtily, proclaiming their independence from all authority of the past, announcing their status as modern, individual thinkers.

But recent scholarship shows that much of this was bluster; in many respects early modern philosophy might better be understood as a complicated reckoning with certain legacies of the ancient tradition, and not as a radical break from this tradition.[11] Few early modern European philosophers truly believed they could go it alone, and even the ones who proclaimed that this is what they were doing continued to display, in their actual work, an ongoing debt to ancient thinkers.

Thus, for example, the early modern philosopher who perhaps declared his independence from the past most loudly, Descartes, can be shown to have owed a significant debt to Augustine, and this even in the work, the *Meditations*, in which he declares that it is his intention to proceed having forgotten everything he has learned up until this time.

In India, there is no such comparable expression of radical individualism. But Ganeri has compellingly shown that there is nonetheless a complex interplay between innovation and authority that mirrors the conciliatory syntheses going on simultaneously in Europe, even if the rhetoric of innovation is rather more subdued. In the Indian expression of this interplay there is, Ganeri emphasizes, no "quarrel of the ancients and the moderns," that is, no radical rejection of the authority of tradition, nor any bold claim of the superiority of the present age. What there is, however, is a marked decline in deference to the ancients and a parallel rise in calls to readers to think through philosophical problems themselves. Thus Ganeri cites the sixteenth-century Nyāya philosopher Raghunātha Śiromaṇi, who insists that "these matters spoken of should not be cast aside without reflection just because they are contrary to accepted opinion."[12]

One reason why the sort of call for independent thought that Raghunātha expresses here has generally been overlooked, or has not won for Indian philosophy in this period the appellation "modern," is that most Indian philosophers continued to write works of commentary. We tend to associate this genre of writing with Scholasticism, with the names of figures such as Thomas Aquinas or Francisco Suárez who represent a contrast class to the modern thinkers: commentaries are held in the European tradition to express almost by definition a passive acceptance of the general authority of the earlier text being commented upon. But this is a facile supposition, and in both Europe and India commentaries admit of wide degrees of variation with respect to the critical distance or even opposition they express vis-à-vis the original commented text. As Ganeri explains, while early modern Indian philosophers "still ... write commentaries, and still use concepts and categories that might, if looked at from a distance, seem archaic," nonetheless "the mere activity of writing a commentary ... does not by itself tell one very much about the author's attitude to the text being commented on." Fundamentally, he stresses, the role of a commentary "was to mediate a conversation between the past and the present."[13] There is no "quarrel" of the ancients and the moderns, but nor is there a submission of the moderns to the ancients. There is, rather, a dialogue. There is moreover a distinct sense from the fifteenth to the eighteenth centuries, among Indian philosophers as among Europeans, that tradition has entered a new period, with new standards and a new style. A lesson here is that the relationship to tradition is always complex; a radical, go-it-alone thinker such as Descartes is exaggerating when he claims to have forgotten everything he learned. Correlatively, an Indian commentator such as Raghunātha, while positioning himself in relation to his predecessors, is not necessarily for that reason subordinating himself to his predecessors.

One very significant difference between European and Indian modern philosophy is the fact that in the former case the shape that philosophy took, indeed the self-consciousness of philosophy *as* modern, was largely, or nearly entirely, a consequence of the emergence of modern science. There simply is no sense in thinking about modern European philosophy in general without thinking about the way it is shaped by such developments as the decline of geocentrism, the invention of the microscope, the development of key elements of what would later be called the "scientific method," and so on. In India, by contrast, early modern philosophy continued to engage principally with questions of what we would call "epistemology" and "philosophy of language." In this sense, Ganeri even goes so far as to claim that the rise of early modern Indian philosophy might in certain respects be more suitably compared to the rise of analytic philosophy in the West some centuries later.

Western analytic philosophy turns to the analysis of the language and the methodology of science in particular (in contrast with the content of science) as a response to the meteoric success of the investigation of the natural world over the previous centuries, while by contrast the fact that Indian philosophy in the sixteenth and seventeenth centuries is preoccupied with language, meaning, and knowledge is a reflection of tremendous continuity. The very oldest Indian philosophy is philosophy of language, or what is often called "grammatical philosophy," which has its mature, if cryptic expression in Pāṇini's *Aṣṭādhyāyī* of the fourth century BCE. This continuity in turn shows up the remarkable degree to which philosophy in early modern India remained impervious to natural science. As Ganeri points out, in astronomy, mathematics, and other fields, Indian learning in the same period was highly influenced by Persian and Arabic traditions. But the study of the "core" questions of philosophy (here Sanskrit philosophers and Western analytic philosophers are in close agreement as to what constitutes the core) remained sharply bounded off from Islamic influence, closed off within a sort of Sanskritic bubble, in which there was innovation, certainly, but not as a result of pressure from outside traditions.

It is interesting in this connection to consider the possibility of a structural relationship, across different philosophical traditions, between the sharp perception of philosophy as having a core, on the one hand, and, on the other hand, the imperviousness of certain traditions to outside influence. That is, where philosophy is more or less entirely contained within a single linguistic community with a uniform, shared set of canonical references, there may be a tendency to have a sharper sense of what distinguishes it from other varieties of inquiry, particularly the natural sciences; it will, whether in Sanskrit or in English, have a sharper sense of its own purity. In this connection early modern European philosophy provides a marked contrast to the Sanskrit tradition and to Anglophone analytic philosophy, especially when we consider it as having taken shape in large part as a result of the gradual incorporation of experimental traditions and of varieties of natural-scientific inquiry that may be traced back to a cross-Mediterranean cultural and linguistic translation of Islamic traditions of inquiry. A good case in point is the history of what is sometimes called "chemical philosophy," which recent scholars have shown to have been fundamental in the formation of early modern corpuscularianism and the views of paradigmatically modern philosophers such as Robert Boyle, and which may by a few simple steps be traced back through Iberia and Italy to Arabic texts.[14] In this respect, one might say that what marks early modern European philosophy is its openness to influence from the Islamic world, in contrast to Sanskrit philosophy's closedness.

The tradition of Navya Nyāya, or "New Inference," which had been a driving force in Indian early modernity, continued in India after the fall of the Moghul Empire and the rise of the British, but did so as a low-prestige traditional network that carried on under the radar of the "well-funded colonial colleges and universities."[15] Where, we might ask, is the philosophy in nineteenth-century India? Is it in the august stone institutions where British colonial professors lecture on Hume and Kant? Or is it in the dilapidated clay-and-straw structure down the road, where the Naiyayikas continue their centuries-old tradition of commenting on Gaṅgeśa Upādhyāya? The British colonial professor is likely only dimly aware of this other activity, while the Naiyayika cannot but be aware of the subordinate status of his own tradition. We cannot answer the question, "Where is the philosophy in nineteenth-century India?" without considering the further question: "Who gets to decide?"

One of history's most remarkable cross-cultural encounters between representatives of different philosophical traditions, or at least one of the most remarkable such documented encounters, took place in India well before the British colonial period, at the height of the Mughal Empire, between representatives of the Sanskrit Indian, Persian Islamicate, and European traditions. In the mid-1660s the French natural philosopher, physician, and disciple of the materialist Pierre Gassendi, François Bernier, was introduced by his Muslim host in India, Danismand Khan, to a pandit, who remains unnamed in Bernier's report but has been speculatively identified by P. K. Gode as Kavindracharya Sarasvati, a Maharashtrian scholar and manuscript collector, and an important intermediary between Persianate Muslim learning and the Sanskrit tradition.[16] Bernier is there to serve as a court physician to the Moghul rulers, but he has also passed his time, so he claims, translating Descartes and Gassendi into Persian, and he loses no opportunity to communicate with his hosts on philosophical matters. He is well integrated into the Persian Muslim world, even to the extent of being able to undertake significant translation projects in Persian, which is the language of the ruling elite throughout northern India under the Moghuls. At the same time, the Sanskrit tradition remains a mere curiosity to him, and to some extent he is simply reflecting the intellectual attitude of his Muslim hosts.

The very possibility of his encounter with the Sanskrit pandit is a result of the fact that one of his Muslim hosts, Dara Shukoh, was unusually interested in "interfaith dialogue," though of a sort that is premised on the conviction that the Upanishads, properly understood, reflect and confirm the fundamental, revealed truth of the Qu'ran. Bernier himself is far less ecumenical; he tends to understand Sanskrit traditions of learning as crystallizations of Indian folk traditions, which in turn he describes as a collection of "ridiculous Errors and Superstitions."[17] In this harsh judgment, however, Bernier is in part importing battles he has long been fighting in Europe. In effect he is disappointed to see Indian popular tradition unwittingly favoring the worldview of Gassendi's adversaries such as Robert Fludd, particularly in their interpretation of a recent eclipse as a harbinger of supernatural wrath rather than as a natural phenomenon "of the same nature with so many others that had preceded without mischief."[18] Bernier believes that his Muslim interlocutors are better disposed to appreciate the force of his own rigorously naturalistic philosophical views. He describes the great Moghul himself, "though he be a Mahumetan," as "suffer[ing] these Heathens to go on in these old superstitions,"[19] simply for the sake of maintaining social harmony. Plainly, Bernier perceives the educated members of the Persian Muslim elite as his equals, and as following, as members of both an Abrahamic faith and of a broadly Aristotelian philosophical tradition, in the same broad intellectual heritage as European Christians. The Hindus, by contrast, are conceptualized negatively, as heathens, which is to say as people without a proper faith. Bernier does learn more than virtually any known European contemporaries about the Vedic tradition, but he describes it in unrelentingly disparaging terms, and consistently in a way that illustrates the support that the faith lends to superstition. Thus, for example, he relates a description he has heard of the god Krishna, but only in order to report on the erroneous interpretation the Indians give to the causes of the eclipse:

> We have (say they) our four *Beths* [i.e., Vedas], that is, Books of the Law, Sacred and Divine Writings, given us by God through the hands of *Brahma*. These Books do teach us, that a certain *Deuta*, which is a kind of corporeal Divinity, very malign and mischievous, very black and very filthy (these are their own expressions in their language) seizeth on the Sun, blackens it as 'twere with ink, and so darkens it.[20]

Further in the English edition of Bernier's work we find reproduced a letter to Samuel Chapelain written from Shiraz, in Persia, in 1667, in which he describes a group of people in India he calls "Jauguis," which is to say "Yogis," a term he somewhat correctly parses as meaning "United to God."[21] He describes their physical exercises with a mixture of revulsion and admiration, both tempered by the diagnostic disposition of the physician:

> You shall see many of them sit stark naked, or lie days and nights upon Ashes.... Of these I have seen some in divers places, who held one Arm, and sometimes both, lifted up perpetually above their Heads, and that had at the end of their Fingers wreathed Nails, that were longer

by measure than half my little finger. Their Arms were small and lean as of hectical persons, because they took not sufficient nourishment in that forced posture, and they could not let them down to take anything with them, either meat or drink, because the Nerves were retired, and the Joints were filled and dried up: wheretofore also they have young Novices, that serve them as Holy men with very great respect. There is no Megera in Hell so terrible to look on, as those Men are, all naked, with their black Skin, long Hair, dried Arms, and in the posture mention'd, and with crooked Nails.[22]

Not entirely without reason, Bernier remarks that the ascetic practice of the yogis reminds him of "that ancient and infamous Sect of the Cynicks."[23] He is aware of the transcendent aspiration of the yogis, that in particular there are goals beyond the realm of bodily experience that motivate these practices of the body, but he mocks both the aims and methods as misguided. Here, again, his criticism of the practices he observes seems not to be motivated simply by a contempt for all things "heathen," but also by his distinctly naturalistic views as a Gassendian, which compel him to reject any set of beliefs that is motivated by an aspiration to transcend the natural world.

Bernier goes on to describe how he has acquired his knowledge of local "heathen" beliefs, describing for his correspondent Samuel Chapelain the mediated exchanges he has had in Delhi with the unnamed Sarasvati:

Do not be surprised if, although I do not know Sanskrit ... I will nonetheless not neglect to tell you many things that are taken from books written in that language. For you must know, that my Agah Danechmend-hand, partly upon my solicitation, partly out of his own curiosity, took into his service one of the famousest Pendets that was in all the Indies, and that formerly had a Pension of Dara the Eldest son of King Chah-jehan, and that this Pendet, besides that he drew to our House all the most Learned Pendets, was for three years constantly of my conversation.[24]

This sounds like a promising start for dialogue between philosophical traditions, but as Bernier goes on to describe the interactions we see that he hardly brings to the encounters an openness to learning, instead hearing what the pandit has to say as effectively nothing more than "tales":

When I was weary of explaining to my Agah those late discoveries of Harvey and Pecquet in Anatomy, and of discoursing with him of the Philosophy of Gassendi and Des-cartes, which I translated to him into Persian (for that was my chief employment for five or six years) that Pendet was our refuge and then he was obliged to discourse and to relate unto us his stories which he deliver'd seriously and without ever smiling. 'Tis true, that at last we were so much disgusted with his tales and uncouth reasonings, that we scarce had patience left to hear them.[25]

Disgust aside, Bernier listens attentively enough to be able subsequently to recall from memory, and more or less accurately, the six schools of *āstika* philosophy. He also identifies Buddhism as a *nāstika* or unorthodox school, "but this is not so common as the others, the Votaries of it being hated and despised as a company of irreligious and atheistical people."[26]

In short, Bernier is simultaneously attentive and dismissive, curious and contemptuous, and his negative judgments flow from a combination of simple prejudice against "heathens," perceived as the low-status commoners under the rule of his Muslim Persian host, together with concerns that flow from his status as a libertine materialist philosopher in the battle against superstition back home in Europe. Bernier does recognize tendencies that bring certain Indian traditions closer to his view than others, traditions, for example, "which approach the opinions of Democritus and Epicurus." But he finds that these are presented "with so much confusion that one knows not where to fasten."[27]

Bernier appears to believe that many of the shortcomings of Sanskrit philosophy have to do with a lack of what he would consider rigorous methodology. This is particularly clear when we turn not to his interpretation of what the pandit tells him, but to his own account, in the letter to Chapelain, of his efforts to teach his Indian interlocutors about what he knows. He relates a remarkable, indeed absurd, effort he had made at some point to give an impromptu lesson in physiology by cutting open a few live beasts:

> In anatomy, one can say that the gentiles do not understand anything at all ... And it's no wonder that they are so ignorant in this domain: they never open up the bodies of men or animals. They have such a horror of this that when I opened up some living goats and sheep before my agha, in order to make him understand the circulation of the blood and to show him the vessels of Monsieur Pecquet by which the chyle ultimately makes its way to the right ventricle of the heart, all of them ran away, trembling from fear, and nonetheless they do

not miss an occasion to affirm that there are five thousand veins in man, neither more nor less, as if they had counted them.[28]

The image of Bernier eviscerating a goat in front of an audience of horrified pandits could very well serve as an emblem of the difficulties of communication between intellectual traditions. There are not just linguistic boundaries and basic cultural prejudices in play here, though surely these do in large measure determine the limits of mutual understanding. Beyond these, also, there are plainly different standards of what constitutes proper inquiry, and to some extent Bernier is rightly discerning a cultural and methodological difference between

IMAGE 6. Richard Lower's transfusion of blood from sheep to man. From Matthias Gottfried Purmann, *Grosser und gantz neugewundener Lorbeer-Krantz, oder Wund Artzney ...* Frankfurt, 1705. Published by widow and heirs of M. Rorlach, Leignitz, Frankfurt, 1705. Image courtesy of the Wellcome Libryary, London.

his own basic commitment to experimentation and empirical confirmation as the supreme source of knowledge, on the one hand, and on the other a tendency to rely on the authority of tradition. This tendency must not be exaggerated, and as we have seen, some early modern Sanskrit authors were encouraging readers to examine matters for themselves, regardless of what tradition had said to that point.

Bernier is haughty, dismissive, but not in a way that differs fundamentally from his condemnations of what he sees as obscurantist traditionalists back home. In a way his report of the vivisection is a variation on the already mythical encounter between Galileo and the priest who refused to look into the telescope and to see the moons of Jupiter for himself. Meanwhile, Bernier's host, the Muslim Dara Shukoh, is unable to take Sanskrit learning on its own terms for a very different reason: he sees it as distinguished, and values the depth of its history and tradition, but interprets it in a way that confirms the ultimate truth of Islam. We have, in effect, a triangulation of misunderstanding.

Bernier ultimately believed that the more one learned of anatomy, through experimental means, the more one could deepen one's understanding of how living bodies are able to function as they do without the unifying and guiding principle of an immaterial soul. The pandits knew that the world is full of souls, of infinite kinds, ever circulating and taking on new bodily forms, and they did not need to see the inner workings of a sheep's body in order to find this knowledge corroborated. Their knowledge was a knowledge passed down in tradition by the force of authority, self-evident from the inside and completely implausible from without. There are not exactly 5,000 veins in the human body, though for some millennia, in one part of the world, it made sense to maintain that there are. It is no coincidence that around the same time the veins are finally tallied with precision, souls ceased to be counted among the elements, the entities or the principles, that make us what we are.

Bernier and the pandits each had their own sort of practice, which, whether it was conceived as eudaimonia or not, brought its own sort of happiness. The French philosopher valued empirical study above all else, while his Indian interlocutors prized memorization, recitation, ritual. It was the pandits, moreover, who were more aware of the practical dimensions of their distinct philosophical project, the integration of these dimensions with the theoretical ones, and the impossibility of easily replacing them with new practices, such as anatomical study. This integration of the practical and the theoretical struck Bernier as nothing more than obstinacy and superstition. He was not interested in figuring out what made sense to his interlocutors "from the inside," and often accused them of deploying a "circular" sort of reasoning. If circularity is simply internal connectedness, without concern for justification in terms of external standards, then this is indeed the sort of reasoning the pandits deployed. But they did not experience it as inadequate, even if it could not enable them to make sense of their petulant visitor's seemingly gratuitous goat sacrifice.

5

MOUNTAINS AND VALLEYS

Featuring the Mandarin

In the winter of 2014 a very well known figure in the English-language academic-philosophy blogosphere threatened to sue a somewhat lesser known member of that community for having written, on the Internet, that that well-known figure was "not a philosopher."[1] The offended party believed that to say this of him amounted to defamation, insofar as it impugns his professional competence. The case did not go to trial, and the threat to take it that far was likely entirely empty. But it is worth asking, on the occasion of this frivolous scandal, which would shake the American philosophical establishment, how exactly philosophy had come to this point. What exactly does it mean within the broader history of philosophy that as of 2014 one could plausibly conceive of "philosopher" simply as a sort of license or accreditation, and thus, in turn, could think of the claim that someone is "not a philosopher" as a simple denial of something that is factually true. In this particular story, the denial of philosopher status stemmed from the fact that the professor in question was based in a law school, and not in a philosophy department, though he had a PhD in philosophy.

Does his protestation imply that everyone with a PhD in philosophy is a philosopher? There are plenty of people who meet this criterion but do not self-identify in that way. And there are plenty of philosophers, not just in history but also in recent memory (teaching, for example, at Oxford and Cambridge) who do not have PhDs, but have inspired enough confidence in their academic achievements to allow them to stop at the BA. And once we open up the range of our considerations beyond the boundaries of the English-speaking world's academic distinctions, into the remote madrasas and monasteries and union halls, where philosophical ideas are debated and defended, and beyond the short history in which the legitimating factors cited by the blogger in question make any sense, we see that the great majority of people deemed philosophers in history have not had PhDs, have not belonged to a professional philosophical organization, and have not carried out their careers in "departments."

"Philosopher" is said in many ways, and we may just need to come to terms with the fact that one of those ways at present refers, exclusively, to a particular academic discipline with a highly professionalized structure, even if those who use the term by reference to this structure know full well that Plato, Descartes, and others established themselves as philosophers, in the fullest sense of the term, outside of this structure. But one of the dangers of allowing the professionalized sense of "philosopher" to gain too much prominence is that it seems

in an important sense empty, given that there is so much disagreement about what philosophy is—the science of the possible? The creation of concepts? Shewing the fly the way out
of the bottle?—we are left in a situation in which to be a philosopher easily amounts to nothing other than being accred-
ited *as* a philosopher. In such a situation, one need display no
particular ability, nor be engaged in any particular intellectual
project. One need only display one's credentials. Correlatively,
the professional or accreditation-based conception of the philosopher renders impossible the full recognition of contributions to philosophy from people who lack the correct credentials. Exemptions might be made for people who lived a
long time ago, and so may be posthumously granted credentials
within the current structure (Aristotle or Leibniz would be
most welcome, if they were suddenly resuscitated, at a meeting of the APA), while our contemporaries who are far away
in space and culture are granted no such exemption. There are
people alive right now who are engaging with philosophical
ideas in Tibet and Amazonia, perhaps ingeniously, in social
settings no more different from that of an APA attendee than
were the social settings of Aristotle or Leibniz, yet who would
be utterly out of place if they were to show up at some Balti-
more Marriott between Christmas and New Year's and ask for
their nametags. When it comes to recognizing fellow philosophers, time travel presents more plausible scenarios than travel
tout court.

To the extent that it is empty, the accreditation-based conception impedes or at least problematizes the very serious
matter of struggling for the soul of philosophy, of arguing that
philosophy properly understood is thus-and-so and not otherwise. Naturally, to say that someone is not a philosopher, in
view of that person's intellectual aims and methods, is a base

move to make and generally shows an illiberal or uncharitable spirit at work. But we ought not be prevented, on legalistic grounds, from saying that what another person is doing is not philosophy, whatever that person's professional credentials might be. I am not sure what I do is philosophy, for example, and I'm also not sure it would be an insult, let alone defamation in a legal sense, for someone else to argue that it is not. One thing the plethora of definitions of philosophy shows is that none of us really knows what a philosopher is, or what one must do in order to count as a philosopher. The credential-based definition enables us to bracket the question of what a philosopher is in order to focus on questions that have been agreed upon by the professional community as important. But one strongly suspects that, whatever philosophy is, such bracketing cannot be a part of it. The credential-based definition of "philosopher" is unphilosophical, and for a person to resort to it is strong evidence that that person is not one.

Likely most charges of being "not a philosopher" that have occurred over the past few decades have been volleys across the rift, or apparent rift, that separates "analytic" from "continental" philosophy. This rift deserves mention, even if, from the *longue durée* perspective that has been guiding us in this essay, the century or so in which the tension between these two competing views of the nature of philosophy has been highly anomalous.

In a nutshell, the rift between the continental and the analytic traditions is often held to be one between two camps, each of which seeks to assimilate philosophy to a different, related sphere of cultural activity. The analytic philosophers see philosophy as continuous or overlapping with science, while the continentalists see it as rather more like art or literature. As W.V.O. Quine describes his own conception of philosophy:

I see philosophy not as groundwork for science, but as continuous with science. I see philosophy and science as in the same boat—a boat which we can rebuild only at sea while staying afloat in it. There is no external vantage point, no first philosophy. All scientific finds, all scientific conjectures that are at present plausible, are therefore in my view as welcome for use in philosophy as elsewhere.[2]

This characterization is fair enough, as far as it goes, though one must hasten to add that nearly everyone on both sides of the divide supposes that both art and science are perfectly worthwhile things to philosophize about, that both art and science are among philosophy's sources of fuel. One might further add that continental philosophy does not fuel itself from art in general, but rather keeps apace, in its spirit and attitudes, with contemporary art, whose mode of operation is, so to speak, to keep people guessing, to constantly innovate, and to launch away from any innovation of one's contemporaries so as to distinguish oneself from them. Analytic philosophers do not want to keep people guessing; they want to *end* the guessing by clearing things up. This clarificatory activity, throughout much of the twentieth century, proceeds by changing the focus of philosophy from its traditional concern with supposedly timeless metaphysical questions to the matter of how sentences, including sentences about metaphysics, get their meanings. As Hans Reichenbach nicely described this approach in 1938: his philosophical movement had "reduced the question of the existence of external things to a question of the meaning of sentences."[3]

For us here, however, the important distinction is between current analytic philosophy and the long tradition of Western philosophy, and not between analytic philosophy and a contemporary alternative. There are many milestones that are thought to have marked the emergence of an awareness of such parallel, and even competing, traditions—Frege's criticism of Husserl in the 1890s, the famous dispute between Heidegger and Carnap of 1929–31—but it remains the case that analytic philosophy has often been no less intent on marking itself off from a shared past that belonged to Heidegger and Carnap alike, and that included, for example, Aristotle and Descartes, as it has been in marking itself off from another living tradition.

Another aspect of this demarcation is somewhat less frequently emphasized, but is surely more relevant to a number of the considerations here: continental philosophy has generally been preoccupied, however fruitfully or unfruitfully, with human culture and with the diversity of human cultures, while analytic philosophy has generally not been concerned with the study of culture. Continental philosophy, while overlapping with and drawing from art, also overlaps with and draws from anthropology, for example, in the engagement with the work of Lévi-Strauss that stimulated the development of poststructuralism. For a brief moment in the history of analytic philosophy, Wittgenstein did express some interest in E. E. Evans-Pritchard's work on magic among the Azande people of Sudan,[4] and Quine's thought experiment about the native informant who says "gavagai" (to which, surprisingly, no one has yet taken objection as a crude caricature concocted by the colonial imagination) is obviously derivative of the actual interpretive problems ethnologists have faced in the field. But analytic philosophy has supposed that it does not matter what people in radically different cultures believe. Unless what native informants have to say may be plausibly held to be true, there is for analytic philosophers not much reason to take an interest in it. Thus what ethnographers and many continental philosophers might see as "different forms of rationality," expressed in cultural practices such as natural magic or divination, will be bracketed by analytic philosophers as simply "irrational."

What this bracketing misses is that among the true facts about the world is the fact that this or that culture practices a form of natural magic that presupposes causal links in the world that are different from those science recognizes, and therefore to study this natural-magical practice is to increase one's knowledge of the truth, even if the beliefs underlying the practice are false. But these truths are truths generally considered to be beyond the purview of analytic philosophy. It is true, as already mentioned, that in recent years what is being called "experimental philosophy" has taken an interest in what actual people in different cultures believe, without immediate regard for its truth or falsity. But so far this interest has mostly duplicated the methods of empirical psychology, while circumventing altogether the vast, extant literature from various human sciences dealing with the problems of interpretation and comparison of different cultural beliefs. In recent years also, there has been a certain amount of interest among analytic political philosophers in nonideal political theory, coming for example from feminist and critical race theorists, who do not take the individual human being to be an abstract rational agent, in the manner of John Rawls's *Theory of Justice*, but instead to take different kinds of human being to experience their humanity through different forms of social and physical embodiment.

These new developments complicate the distinction between analytic and continental philosophy considerably, but mostly it remains the case, and certainly was the case over most of the past century, that the one tradition took an interest in art and culture and saw itself as continuous with these, and the other tradition preferred to operate at a level of abstraction where the only neighboring human endeavor was science. But there has not been much interest in explicitly accounting for the reasons *why* the different traditions value the different neighboring domains of human social life. The answer has much to do with contingencies of history and shows each approach to be in its own way parochial.

In truth what we think of as "continental" philosophy took shape out of an intense engagement with certain tendencies in German philosophy by their French interpreters, in a way that accelerated in particular after the end of World War II. There are important respects in which the rupture goes back to Husserl and Frege, and others still on which it goes back even further, to Kant and Hegel. Yet it was not until these oppositions were taken up, indeed overtaken, by French thinkers after the near total collapse of a recognizably German intellectual tradition following the defeat of the Nazis, that the particular trait described above—the association with contemporary art and literature above all else—and the corollary drive for constant inventiveness and creativity, became central characteristics of philosophy on the continent.

In twentieth-century France, the valorization of inventiveness was balanced by a very rigid and stable system of education in which philosophers worked and thrived. An artistic and literary avant-garde functioned outside of state institutions, but the function of the philosophers was often to take up their creative output and to transform it from subversion into the official *patrimoine* of the Republic.[5]

French philosophers absorbed otherwise dangerous art into a system responsible for producing elite functionaries, held to

IMAGE 7. Civil service exam under Emperor Jen Tsung (fl. 1022), from a history of Chinese Emperors (color on silk). Chinese School, 17th century. Bibliotheque National de France. Image couresy of Bridgeman Art.

be embodiments of culture. Although they do not always have such a relationship to the avant-garde, these philosophers, embodiments of a state's ideal of culture, might appropriately be described as "Mandarins." It is not only in France that we find them. They derive their name, in fact, from the elite class of men in Imperial China who passed through the rigorous state examination system (image 7). In Imperial China as in twentieth-century France, the content of the examination focused not principally on technical subjects like mathematics or engineering but on the student's ability to interpret a poem, for example, or in some other way to place himself within a cultural tradition by displaying mastery of its poetic and aesthetic norms. Today, many French high school students must take a national standardized exam in philosophy, which determines their ranking in the university entrance system, in which they must write essays about, for example, whether "beauty" is an equivocal term, or whether perception must be trained. The questions are overwhelmingly focused on moral and aesthetic matters, with very little attention to, say, epistemology or logic. In 2015 students were asked to choose from the following topics:[6]

- Does a work of art always have meaning?
- Is politics free of any expectation of truth?
- Is the conscience/consciousness of the individual only a reflection of the society in which he or she lives?
- Does an artist provide something that must be understood?
- Is there a moral duty to respect every living being?
- Am I what my past has made of me?

The previous year, in 2014, when the French rail workers threatened a strike on the day of the national philosophy exam, explicitly in order to obstruct the test, *The Economist* mockingly pounced on this confluence to announce that three French institutions, "trains, strikes and philosophy" had "collided" to give us what is perhaps the most quintessentially French news item imaginable.[7] This is a profound fact about the formation of the philosophical identity in France. The people who manage to pass this test and go on to join the elite ranks of producers and transmitters of French culture are members of the establishment par excellence, and part of their membership involves the display of a fluent ability to talk about artistic and literary currents. By contrast, any American who can speak proficiently about, for example, Dadaism or 'Pataphysics is almost certainly in some way a member of a cultural countercurrent, and almost certainly sets him or herself up against the prevailing cultural grain.

The state's production of elite cultural cadres, fluent in art and philosophy, goes back to the revolution, when philosophy took on in many respects the status of a civic religion of the sort Rousseau described. The philosophy in question was rationalist, universalist, and inflected with the values of the Enlightenment, and thus in certain respects was the mirror opposite of the skeptical counter-Enlightenment thought of the second half of the twentieth century in French thought. But the institutions are the same: they function to produce people who embody the cultural values of the state through their mastery of certain approved expressions of culture, particularly in the arts, philosophy, and literature. The standards of mastery, here, are simply different from those that one expects of a scientifically literate "Anglo Saxon" philosopher. The ontogenesis of the person who later becomes an embodiment of this form of culture comes not from some subversive adolescent discovery of some strange and unfamiliar ideas. Rather, it comes from rote learning in preparation for state examinations, and, in some cases, a desire for advancement into an institutional elite whose norms are established by boards of bureaucrats. By the time the textual products of this system get translated and make their way into the hands of an inquisitive and subversive American teenager, they have been fully decontextualized, transformed into a fully different sort of object than the one discursively produced, with so much virtuosic insider knowledge and sensibility, and so much weight of tradition and institution, by the French philosophers themselves.

I will not rest content, like my father, as a mere county magistrate. I will pass the provincial examination and I will go on to Beijing for the metropolitan examination. And I will pass on my first try. It would be no real honor to have my perseverance rewarded, and to finally pass the examination in old age, alongside my grandsons. No, I will be an optimus before my twenty-fifth birthday. And why not? By the time I turned eight I had memorized the *Thousand Character Text*, and at sixteen I had learned by heart most of the canon of Way Learning: the Four Books, at least one of the Five Classics. I boldly declared I would memorize the remaining Classics before I turned twenty. My mother grew fretful, and said I would collapse from the strenuous recitation exercises. But here I am now, twenty years old, and reputed throughout Shandong for my memory.

Even the Catholic men from Rome insisted on coming to see me. They wrote excited letters back to their priest at home relating my ability to "back the book," turning my back on the text while reciting it as if it were before my very eyes. They told me my talents rivaled those of their own Matteo Ricci, who had practiced their own memorization technique, which they called the *ars memoriae*. They gave me a copy of *The Catholic Four-Character Classic*, a sort of summary of their "catechism" rendered in terms familiar to the Chinese, and just to surprise them I memorized it in the course of an afternoon. The next time they came by I handed it back and told them I would not be needing it. "I have the book inside of me now," I said.

I excel at it, this memorization, but I do not love it. There is so much concern for rote learning that most of us lose sight altogether of what it is that has been written. This indeed makes us indifferent devourers of books, for whom the Catholic catechism and the *Analects* are all the same. But any optimus knows that you cannot simply take the book in and reflect it back, as if the words were held up to a glass. You cannot give the words back untransformed when you enter the examination compound, the words that you have spent your life absorbing. The Eight-Legged Essay must be written by you, and not by the ancients. At each stage in the composition—breaking open the topic, receiving the topic, beginning the discussion, and so on—one must speak in the place of the sages, and not only allow the sages, again, to speak.

In truth mastery is a difficult thing to understand. Whatever I may write in an examination, I am enabled to write because of the Four Books and the Five Classics, but what I write does not come from these, exactly. Where does it come from? What is that other source? Perhaps I should not dwell on these questions too much. They seem presumptuous, at the present moment, when I have not even passed the provincial examination here in Jinan, and I do not know what fate has in store for me. I have not been to any fortune-tellers to find out, either, but I know only that I have always been pious to my parents and ancestors, and I have always lived morally. If the cosmos has failure for me in store, I will protest that there has been an error. But whose? These are questions that seem to have no answer in Confucius, or in the interpretations of Mencius.

Would I consider paying for success? I have gone to the temple of Wenchang, the patron deity of literature, and made propitiations. I was also counseled by a Daoist monk to throw gold coins in the Yellow River. So I did it. Why not?, I thought. I'll pay off the fish, but I would never pay off the examiners. There is so much striving, so much scrambling for status like a swarm of fish after crumbs. Men spend their lives trying and failing, and they break themselves in the process.

And yet there is so much that is left out of the examinations, so much learning even the best men never have a chance to display. We are tested on our mastery of letters and morals. The sages spoke of proper conduct and filial piety, and of the importance of loyalty to the Emperor for the proper functioning of the state. To speak in the place of the sages, to become a literatus, is to speak of the same things and no more. But there are also stars in the night sky, and a thousand different shapes of leaf, and numerical ratios to be reckoned. I discuss these matters sometimes with the Catholics. They also speak with me of the difference between *substantia* and *accidens*, as being of great importance for our understanding of the world and of ourselves. They attribute what they say of these to their sage Aristotle, and they ask me for help in rendering these concepts in Chinese. I tell them not to waste their time. Our sages occupied themselves with different matters.

Their literati are different, too. They are not subordinated to an Emperor, but rather to a high priest. Yet they are not monks; they are engaged in the world, and pleased with life. They must pass a test of sorts in order to serve their high priest, but it is easy to memorize the relevant materials (as I said, I did it in an afternoon), and involves no great attainment of intellect. At the same time, their learning comes from elsewhere, from a sage who lived centuries before the man they call their savior, and to be learned is to master what this sage and his successors taught, not out of piety or morality (for these are accorded rather to their savior), but out of love of learning. Some of their learning appears much like that of the Buddhist monks, who are so preoccupied with the difference between illusion and reality.

I do not have much appreciation for this distinction, but it need not concern me. There are no Buddhists in the examination compound. To be a scholar-bureaucrat is to subordinate yourself to tradition and to the Emperor, and this involves no speculation on the unseen and unknown, but only excellence in the resolution of practical problems, and of course also excellence in literary style. It involves subordination to the ancients, so that they may continue to speak through us.

Who am I to question this system, which has survived through so many dynasties? I will have my place in it, and there is no use in getting sidetracked by the wild speculations of our foreign guests. I have spent my entire life preparing for the examination, and I have a natural aptness that is rare indeed, though I do not know from where it comes. Again, the only thing that might trip me up is fate. Have I done anything that might cause me to fail? I have always spoken piously of my ancestors, and been respectful to my father and mother. There was just that one time, when I was throwing coins to the fish, and I let slip that I believed I was destined to do better than my father, who was not able to pass the provincial exam until almost the age of forty. Yes, I admit it. I mocked my father. I was all alone by the riverside, late at night. Who was there to hear me but the fish? (I know they heard me, for I could tell they took delight in the mockery.)

M any have plausibly identified the difference between analytic and continental philosophy as resulting from the typical orientation of the prephilosophical educations of analytic and continental philosophers-in-the-making, with analytic philosophers frequently coming from a background in the natural sciences (or at least from a background that inculcated

appreciation of the natural sciences) and continental philosophers coming from a background in the more poetic or ex-
pressive corners of the humanities. If this account is correct, it
follows that the rift needs to be understood as a symptom of
a much more general problem, that it is just one instance of
the famous "two-cultures problem," rather than an internal
affair of philosophy departments alone. If the local rift is to be
closed, in turn, perhaps this might best be brought about not
by the definitive triumph of the science-oriented philosophers
over the literature-oriented ones (which is to say, by local
lights, of the good over the bad, or, which amounts to the
same, of the high-status over the low-status) but rather by a
vastly more significant reconciliation of the natural and the
human sciences, one that takes seriously the old conception
of the humanities as sciences (or *Wissenschaften* in the broad
sense), and thus that accepts that the humanities and the natural sciences are two different but often overlapping branches
of the same general project.

If the two sides are ever to be reconciled, it may be useful in
the process of reconciliation to pay close attention to the way
the artificial split between the natural and the human impacts
the organization of the various branches of the study of the
past. As a recent, very compelling book by James Turner has
argued, it is in fact philology—the reconstruction of the past
through its textual traces—that lies at the origin, and guards the
true spirit, of the modern humanities, including philosophy.[8]
If Turner's argument is accepted, then a shared interest in the
past could well serve as the basis for reconciliation between
the two cultures. Typically, reconciliation is sought, and typically in vain, by trying to bring, say, physicists and literary
theorists, or geneticists and ethicists, into dialogue. But what

if instead the common ground were sought between historians of philosophy, classicists, archeologists, and paleontologists?

It has been a long time since Karl Popper sought to bracket evolutionary biology as a "metaphysical research programme" in view of the apparent unfalsifiability of its claims.[9] Since then (and even at that time, to be fair), much work has been done to secure for the study of past, nonrepeatable events the status, more than honorary, of science. Mutatis mutandis, much of what has been argued in the case of evolutionary biology applies equally well to the study of deep human history—prehistoric migration patterns and so on. Foucault spoke metaphorically of an "archeology of knowledge," but one thing this phrase misses is that archeology already was itself the archeology of knowledge, which consisted in the digging up, analyzing, and interpreting of fragments of material cultures past, some of which had writing on them (for example, Greek columns) and some of which did not (for example, Neanderthal burial mounds). Through sophisticated modeling and induction there does not seem to be any reason why from fragments of material culture one should not be able to construct hypotheses about the beliefs, the "epistemologies," of people far removed in time. Writing makes this task a great deal easier, but even there it is often very hard, and much of what might controversially be described as protowriting (Babylonian clay tablets, Mayan pictographs, and such) stands at least as much in need of interpretation as, say, the layout of a village ruin.

No one has done a more thorough job of spelling out the scientific epistemology of archeology than Alison Wylie.[10] She reveals an endeavor that is thoroughly scientific, even if it does not conform to all the standards of paradigmatic scientificity set by laboratory-based experimenters in contrast with field-based collectors, and revered by early analytic philosophers. It studies something nonrepeatable (so do evolutionary biology and big-bang cosmology), though it is nonetheless falsifiable in just the same way the other sciences of the past are (as a fossil rabbit from the pre-Cambrian would have caused J.B.S. Haldane, so he is believed to have said, to abandon his commitment to evolution), and also built upon countless domains of inquiry whose status as science are perfectly secure (for example, the chemical analysis of soil).

In archeology's indifference to the distinction between textuality and nontextuality—it digs things up and "reads" them, whether they have letters written on them or not—this science provides a model of the sort of approach to the human sciences that could greatly help to overcome its estrangement from the natural sciences. Archeology as traditionally conceived—before so-called postprocessualism, as an archeological echo of postmodernism, came in and destroyed its scientific aspirations in exactly the same way that poststructuralism destroyed the aspirations of anthropology, and deconstruction the aspirations of textual studies—cannot fail to see human culture as a particular kind of natural excrescence, one that eventually sinks back into the earth and intermingles again with the stuff of nature against which it set itself up in opposition for a short while. In this sense, unlike the academic discipline of history as currently conceived, archeology cannot set up a buffer zone out of the nontextual human past ("prehistory") that preserves a distance between the proper domain of the humanists, on the one hand, and on the other hand the natural world "scientists" study. If we abandon the prejudice that textual traces are a uniquely special sort of vestige of the human past, then paleography may be conceived in turn as a particular branch of archeology—the kind that deals with inscriptions on paper and in similar media.

In this connection attention is due to the work of Franco Moretti and likeminded human scientists interested in the big picture and the *longue durée*.[11] The study of literature, Moretti has helped to show, can be fruitfully amended by quantitative analysis, by the mapping and graphing of long-term trends. Such an approach—quantitative, cumulative, and evidence-based—might appropriately be seen as related to the aims of archeology, which seeks in the end to place human culture in the natural world. The history of philosophy, in turn, on this approach, would be the archeology of one small subset of one particular kind of material traces left from the past. This branch of study would require special training in order to develop the ability to recognize a certain kind of subtle thought from a certain sort of trace, but it would not be fundamentally different from the study of other such traces, and would be no less neglectful of the holistic and environmental forces that went into shaping them. That would be a real archeology of knowledge, and it would take us a long way toward solving the two-cultures problem (of which the analytic-continental rift is a local symptom).

But what effect would such an approach have on our understanding of the philosophical canon? There are, plainly, certain criteria by which we may deem a given text more or less worthy of inclusion in the philosophical canon, in virtue of the fact that up until now it has had measurably less impact than other texts. A minor commentary that recapitulates familiar points from other commentaries upon another author is one that, we might suppose, is manifestly worth less attention than the original text that serves as the occasion for the composition of the commentary. But even here a number of problems come up at the outset. One is that the importance of the commentary in question cannot be determined in a context-free way, independently of the question as to what it is we are looking for. We might be looking to understand exactly which questions from a given influential text get taken up in the profusion of derivative commentaries that the text inspires, and which by contrast get left out. In this respect, a derivative commentary would become important to the extent that it could help to reveal to us a pattern in the transmission of philosophical questions. Its derivativeness would not be a count against it, but, on the contrary, would confer on it a representative standing. Philosophers, however, even historians of philosophy, are typically averse to asking the sort of question that would enable a derivative text to come forth as important. Working on minor figures, or late representatives of moribund traditions, is typically an unwise strategy for a graduate student. Disciplinary pressure moves us toward the great thinkers.

In this motion, moreover, there is a presumption that the matter of who was great is already settled. But in order to know this we would have had to have read all of the presumed derivative and minor commentaries that have been given an a priori dismissal. Any one of them *could* contain a novel insight, or a new twist on an old problem. The presumption that we know in advance what the major and innovative texts are, and what the minor and derivative ones are, rests on nothing more than faith or indifference. We might have some justified faith in the communal and multigenerational effort of separating the wheat from the chaff. We might with some justification suppose that *someone* has read the texts we'll never get to and has judged for us that we need not worry ourselves. But how do we know this? To adapt a familiar phrase from the second Iraq War, we do not even know what we do not know;

the corpus of potentially relevant texts for any given problem in the history of philosophy is a corpus of unknown unknowns. We have no reliable estimations of the size of the corpus, nor has anyone within philosophy recognized that such a "census" might be worth taking.

This lack of interest arises from what we might call the orthodoxy of close reading: the idea that the sole legitimate way of engaging with philosophy's past is by intensive, long-term engagement with a single text, shutting out consideration of what might have been happening around or before the production of that text that caused it to say what it does. In other disciplines, particularly literary studies, it is now widely recognized that this approach must be complemented by "distant reading," which is not a form of reading that is distracted or unfocused or hasty, but rather a form of reading that, often aided by computers, considers vast corpora at once rather than focusing on a single text and aims to find patterns across these corpora. Thanks to the innovative work of Moretti, we are now in a position to say how many novels, say, were published in English in the eighteenth century. We do not need to suppose that there is anything particularly original or noteworthy about each of the several tens of thousands of such novels in order to agree that it is good to know roughly how many there are, and in order to agree that whatever we are able to learn about the contents of each of these works can help us to learn what, fundamentally, the eighteenth-century English novel was. And this can help us to learn things we might not have otherwise noticed from close readings of the canonical major works.

As it is, philosophers tend to relate to their canon in a quasi-scriptural way. This is not necessarily an approach that guarantees staleness or stagnation of thought. In fact, traditions of hagiography and scriptural commentary often spiral out into forms of reflection that are worthy of being called philosophical. For example, Talmudic and Upanishadic commentary both started out with the relatively narrow purpose of glossing what ostensibly divinely dictated texts had said, texts that were never thought of as philosophical to the extent that they never, in themselves, offered up arguments or demonstrated any self-reflexive scrutiny. While they started out as mere glosses, willy-nilly they developed, at least in part, into full-fledged philosophical examinations of the nature of reality. Arguably, the incorporation of Aristotle into the Islamic *Kalām* tradition, and later its adoption as a "handmaiden" for Christian theology, shows that in these cases as well starting out with little besides revealed texts, commentators are nonetheless able to generate on their own a philosophical tradition out of the seed of revelation. Along this line of thinking, it might be argued that at least implicitly we treat our canonical figures, Plato, Descartes, Kant, and so on, as having furnished us with revelations, and what we do when we do philosophy on their basis is something akin to philosophically inclined Talmudic commentary. Talmudic commentary is a rich tradition indeed, but what distinguishes it most from the history of philosophy is that it owns up to, and is based on, the revealed status of its germinal texts, whereas philosophers typically would not wish to claim that the reason they pay so much attention to the canonical texts, but not to the minor and derivative ones, is because the canonical texts are dictated or inspired from a divine source. But in practice the way philosophers relate to their canon is closer to scriptural commentary than it is to the sort of distant reading that takes all texts as holding some interest for us, and tries to make sense of the profane origins of the masterworks alongside the obscure and neglected ones.

The "two-libraries" problem described in chapter 3, in which I confessed to being unable to discover any compelling reason not to put poetry books on the same bookshelf as philosophy books, is by no means the result of a "continental" approach to philosophy, which sees it as having significant overlap and affinity with the arts and literature and as sharing with these an imperative for constant innovation. I could also have described the problem of where to put the nineteenth-century medical textbooks I had acquired, the botanical guides, and so on. It would be somewhat more accurate to say that the two-libraries problem is the result of a historian's approach. This approach is, like continental philosophy, frequently dismissed as "not philosophy," though for rather different reasons. The nonhistorian wishes to know *what* Descartes's argument about the nature of the soul is, and whether it is true, and if the matter of *why* Descartes held this view is to be addressed, then it will be presumed that an answer to the *why* question can be found within Descartes's internal processes of reasoning. The historian will seek to answer the *why* question by going and looking for further sources, by asking what Descartes was reading, what the people around him were saying, and so on. The thorough historian will ask, in turn, what these other people were reading, what the sum total of background influences was that led Descartes's contemporaries to say the things they did.

It was with respect to Descartes's dualism that English metaphysical poetry came to appear to me as relevant. It is not, I realized, that we want to know the truth from the poems, as nonhistorians expect they might be learning from Descartes. At least, we are not seeking in them true philosophical claims. We are interested in a more mundane sort of truth, yet one that we believe must figure into any mature or rigorous account of what it is a major figure like Descartes is doing when he makes the claims that nonhistorian philosophers today examine in view of their philosophical truth or falsehood. These mundane truths are of the sort: in such-and-such year, Descartes read such-and-such author who had been influenced by such-and-such poem. One need not, in order to take an interest in this sort of truth, have any particular interest in poetry. As a historian, one follows leads, wherever they might take us. This sort of approach, too, would compel a certain sort of philosopher to keep Searle, Derrida, and Genet together on the same shelf. It is not necessarily that by putting them all together—say, on one's office shelves, in a philosophy department—one announces that they are all, equally, philosophers, or that they have all made equal or roughly comparable contributions to humanity. One might well feel the closest intellectual affinity with Searle, but also suppose that part of exhaustively understanding Searle involves understanding his adversaries, and in turn understanding his adversaries' sources.

By rough analogy, it is not hard to see that, here, Searle is our modern-day Descartes, cutting through confusion and mystification with his clear and distinct ideas; Derrida is Henry More, a sharp and witty contemporary immersed in a literary tradition that trades in enigmas; and Genet, finally, is Spenser, an outlying *littérateur* who can help to enrich our picture of why some famous philosophical debates took the shape they did. The historian of philosophy reads, and reads and reads, in order to come to a general understanding of the contours of an era's intellectual life. In this, the historian might or might not have some idea of the eventual desideratum of coming to know the truth, about, say, the relationship between mind and body. But an author such as Descartes is not read, as a nonhistorian might read him, with the straightforward question, "Is this true?" in mind. The historian aspires to live up to the assertion, misattributed to Aristotle yet profound nonetheless, that a learned mind should consider the thoughts of others without an interest in either accepting or rejecting them. And yet, we often hear that historians, too, are "not philosophers." I have even heard, explicitly, at one of those massive hotel conferences in which people with radically different conceptions of the nature of philosophical inquiry are thrown together and compelled to make small talk, that to read Descartes for any other reason than to determine whether his claims are true or false is to abandon the idea of truth as the end of inquiry. As if there were no difference between relativism and philological sensitivity!

It is in the end my own self-identification as a historian of philosophy that gives me such pain when I try to organize my philosophy bookshelves. It is in the very effort to solve practical problems such as this that I sense my distance from the intellectual profile of the core representatives of the discipline of philosophy in which I received my graduate education and in which, for a long time, I hoped to find a place. It is also this self-identification that makes me fairly dismissive of talk of the analytic-continental divide, for this is a divide that excludes any possibility of a third party, from the perspective of which the differences between the analytics and the continentals look very much like what Freud would have called "the narcissism of minor differences." This third party, were it to have a voice, would advocate for another approach, one that is above all interested in the truth, but that does not insist that one can arrive at the truth simply by reading a text in view of its truth or falsehood. This party, moreover, would be interested in philosophy, conceived as the pursuit of answers to fundamental questions, while nonetheless refusing to set up rules at the

outset for where the legitimate sources of these answers might
be found.

There is a familiar distinction in philosophy between contingent and necessary truths. Truths of the latter sort are
those the negation of which implies a contradiction, or those
that are true simply in virtue of the meaning of the words involved. For example, "A triangle has three sides" is true simply
in virtue of the meanings of the words "triangle," "three," and
"side." If you encounter a figure with four sides, then *necessarily* you have not encountered a very unusual triangle, but
rather a nontriangle.

Contingent truths are those the negation of which implies
no contradiction, or, to put this somewhat differently, those
that *could have* been false (whatever that might mean). Some
contingently true statements involve particular cases, for example, "This swan is white." A special class of contingent
truths, in turn, includes those expressed by empirical claims
about how one expects all entities or phenomena of a certain
kind to be. These are the sort of truths established by inductive reasoning, and it is characteristic of them that they can
always turn out to be falsified by any given case. Thus, "All
swans are white" was held to be true for a long time, as the
instances of observed swans grew and grew, and in each case,
each swan observed turned out to be white. This contingent
truth however, turned out to be false, as European travelers to
Australia, home of the *Cygnus atratus*, realized toward the end
of the eighteenth century.

Any member of the genus *Cygnus* is a swan, and there was
a prior fact of the matter, prior that is to Captain Cook's expedition, about the color-independent features of an entity that
determine whether it is a member of this genus or not. This

is what makes "All swans are white" a mere empirical claim rather than an analytic truth, or a truth that can be established simply in virtue of the analysis of a proposition into the meanings of its component parts.

"All triangles are three-sided" is analytic, and so, it is generally supposed, is "All whales are marine mammals." But the grounds for placing the whales with the triangles rather than with the swans are by no means perfectly clear. What if we found a cetacean population uniquely (and implausibly) adapted to a terrestrial environment? Would they be ipso facto non-whales? We suppose, for now, that "All whales are marine mammals" is true by definition, but this could, perhaps, turn out to be a prejudice supported only by the current imperfect state of our empirical knowledge. In the seventeenth century, "All swans are white" no doubt appeared true by definition as well.

In that same century, when all swans were white, at least in Europe, René Descartes argued that existence pertains to God in exactly the same way that three-sidedness pertains to triangles. That is, he thought, you can no more entertain the idea of a nonexistent God than you can the idea of a four-sided triangle. If you are thinking, "This 'God' is a pretty interesting concept, but I'm still wondering whether he exists or not," then you are not *really* entertaining the concept of God. You only think you are. Says Descartes.

But what if "God exists" is more like "Swans are white" than it is like "Triangles are three-sided"? What if Descartes simply hadn't encountered, yet, an inexistent God? It is perhaps more telling than it first appears to note that one of Descartes's preferred examples of a claim that is true by definition, alongside "God exists" and "Triangles are three-sided," is one that he believes to hold of mountains; a mountain, he claims, is something that has, by definition and of necessity, a valley.

A valley is typically defined as a depression that is longer than it is wide, while a depression is any landform that is lower than the area surrounding it. Valleys, it is not hard to see, are therefore typical of mountains that are organized into mountain ranges, such as the Alps. But there are also so-called freestanding mountains, such as Mount Kilimanjaro, which is entirely surrounded by a plain, or El Pico Tenerife, which is an island mountain entirely surrounded by water. The surface surrounding these peaks is lower relative to the peaks, but it is in no sense a "depression" relative to the earth's surface or to sea level, and so neither is it a depression that is wider than it is long.

It was not until 1846 that the German missionary Johann Ludwig Krapf made a journey to the snow-covered mountains of inland East Africa (the other principal peak being Mount Kenya, 200 or so miles away). As E. G. Ravenstein reports sixteen years later, it would only be possible to doubt the implausible report of their existence "if we assume the missionaries capable of deliberately advancing false statements." In his "Precise Account of Geographical Discovery in Eastern Africa," which serves as a preface to the English translation of Krapf's *Travels, Researches, and Missionary Labours, during an Eighteen Years' Residence in Eastern Africa,*[12] Ravenstein disputes some recent claims as to the location of the African mountains that Ptolemy had described as resembling the *Montes Lunae,* the mountains of the moon. Certain explorers had inferred that these must have been the crescent-shaped chain surrounding Lake Tanganyika, separating modern-day Tanzania from the Republic of Congo. But Ptolemy had no knowledge of the Upper Nile and its termination in the African Great Lakes, Ravenstein argues, and so the moonlike mountains to which the Greek geographer refers could only be those freestanding peaks on the inclined plateau to the east, Mounts Kilimanjaro and Kenya.

Krapf himself had complained of a certain Mr. Cooley who, in his *Inner Africa Laid Open* of 1852 had refused to lend credence to native reports of snow-covered peaks in the region. The locals had told Cooley that "white matter" was "visible upon the dome-like summit of the mountain," and that "the silver-like stuff, when brought down in bottles proved to be nothing but water." Cooley finds this detail outlandish, while Krapf blames his fellow explorer for following poor inductive method by failing to recognize the high probability of reports of seemingly insignificant details: "Had Mr. Cooley been accustomed to weigh and sift evidence more closely, he would have argued differently from that very fact; for by its own law evidence is always strengthened by the record of trivial and immaterial circumstances."[13] Here, it is worth pointing out, Krapf is echoing some of the themes, discussed in chapter 1, of the debates held in the Royal Society of London two centuries earlier about the veracity of anecdotal reports.

Krapf's American biographer, Paul Kretzmann, remains stupefied, several decades after the German missionary's journey, that such a thing as Kilimanjaro exists. It seems strange, he writes, "that there should be mountains in Africa, almost beneath the equator, whose foot hills are covered with the palms and the jungles of the tropics, while their summits are covered in everlasting snow."[14] Kretzmann cites the poet Bayard Taylor's evocative 1855 address to the mountain itself, emphasizing among other features its lack of neighbors, which might help it to form a valley:

Hail to thee, monarch of African mountains
Remote, inaccessible, silent and lone—

Who, from the heart of the tropical fervors,
Liftest to heaven thine alien snows.[15]

Strange, unnatural, alien, moonlike, valley-less: Mount Kilimanjaro confounds the Europeans, imports disorder into their
pat scheme of what must go with what. It is also surrounded,
as Kretzmann reminds us immediately after his description of
East African topology, by people who are believed to have no
concept of God:

> The Paganism or Fetishism which is the native religion of
> a large part of Africa is a form of Animism or the worship
> of spirits. It is a religion of almost unbelievably terrible
> darkness. It believes in numerous horrible demons, and
> the Pagan native of Africa thinks of these as surrounding
> him on every side, continually seeking to do him injury
> and to bring about his death. These demons are supposed
> to inhabit every object, whether possessing life or not.[16]

Existence belongs to God, just as valleys belong to mountains.
Except, it appears, in Africa.

Krapf and Ravenstein were writing two centuries after Descartes, and we cannot expect the French philosopher to have
inferred the existence of Kilimanjaro from slight hints in Ptolemy (if that is what they are). But the Canary Islands had been
thoroughly navigated by the fourteenth century, and several
descriptions of the Tenerife peak were available by the time
Descartes was reading and writing and defining mountains.

Descartes, it has often been noted, was programmatically
uninterested in travel reports, in cultural diversity, in the profusion of knowledge about local divergences that might complicate an attempt to model the world as a rational, ordered

whole. He valued geodesy over geography. He had next to nothing to say about the Americas. In all of this he differs radically from the philosophers, such as Bacon or Leibniz, who took the rise in sea travel as the very cause of the birth of modern philosophy, and correlatively took as the principle task of philosophy the laying by of notions in order to harvest as many particular facts ("This swan is white," "So is this one," . . .) about the world as possible. Descartes by contrast wished to construe philosophy entirely by appeal to notions, which have the advantage of being indifferent to complications that might arrive from the field, from the soiled notebooks of half-literate travelers.

We should perhaps not make too much of Descartes's peculiar choice of mountains and valleys as an example of a truth of definition. Perhaps he had a curious understanding of "valley," such that it is simply the area, any area, that surrounds a mountain. But the significance of this example is brought into sharper relief when it is placed in the light of what really interests him: the existence of God. Descartes would never think to survey the globe, and least of all to survey the people Kretzmann later belittled as backward animists, to find out whether one must accept the existence of God or not. But what if Descartes's geographical error reveals a shortcoming in the approach to theology?

Black swans were incorporated into European taxonomy with little crisis—even though Australia has generally played a role comparable to that of Africa, as a place where the ordinary rules governing nature begin to break down, and even though marsupials and monotremes would indeed send a strong signal back to Europe of such Antipodean chaos, the black swan required only a slight modification. This is because, again, it was understood prior to 1790, when John Latham gave the first natural-historical description of the *atratus* species, that *Cygnus* is a genus term that is not based on feather pigmentation. Descartes could have conceived mountains in similar terms: as the sort of things that, in his experience up until now, have always been accompanied by valleys, but that do not necessarily need valleys in order to be mountains. But he did not proceed in this way. Instead, he took valleys as pertaining to mountains by definition, and he was so committed to this definitional inseparability that he used this example to illuminate his understanding of the ontological argument for the existence of God.

His commitment to this procedure by way of definition, rather than survey, foiled him in the case of mountains. It may have foiled him in the case of God too. It may be that philosophy would have been better served by a survey of the full range of human interpretations of the ultimate ground of our existence and experience—even, or especially, of those interpretations that attribute powers to trees and stones—and not a priori arguments: a Baconian approach to supposedly a priori truths, which seeks to better understand the nature of belief by going out and studying all the possible stances one might take to them—belief, disbelief, ignorance, indifference, and so on. Beliefs, too, are singular things, and they can be collected, out in the field, like flowers or butterflies. This is something that certain early modern philosophers, notably Bacon and Leibniz, seem to have understood about the project of truth seeking, and that others, notably Descartes, seem to have missed. And this rift remains a far more profound division between two conceptions of philosophy, or of philosophy on the one hand and what is now called "science" on the other, than the one between analytics and continentals that has absorbed so much attention.

6

MONEY AND LOVE

Featuring the Courtier

Philosophy, we have seen, is not necessarily the contemplation of universal truths as contrasted with singular things; it is not necessarily the exposition of arguments in writing, since indeed many philosophers, including one of the respected founders of the Philosophia tradition, Socrates, did not themselves write anything; it is not necessarily the exposition of ideas in a systematic, rigorous, or deductive form, since many important contributions have been made to philosophy through the vehicle of allusive poetry, myth, and aphorism; it is not necessarily the project of "getting outside of oneself" and attaining a "view from nowhere," since many important figures and traditions of philosophy, from Montaigne to twentieth-century phenomenology, have emphasized the importance of the first-person perspective. It is not, we might also add, the rejection of money as an obstacle to free inquiry, the rejection of sophistry along with the corrupting power of remuneration; nearly everyone who has the social identity of a philosopher today, and very many in the past as well, expects financial reward for this activity.

In 2012, midcareer and looking for a change, I took a position at a French university. This was, to say the least, a decision that could not be justified in financial terms. It was a step up in terms of prestige, but a severe blow in terms of monthly income, and that in one of the most expensive cities in the world. It was difficult, much more difficult than I had anticipated. But I would not be easily defeated. I decided to get creative and to supplement my income by becoming a philosophical free agent, offering one-on-one philosophical conversations with willing clients. I catered mostly to Anglophone tourists who had fantasies of themselves in the role of Simone de Beauvoir or Jean-Paul Sartre, tourists with romantic ideas of what goes on in sidewalk cafés. They had a somewhat exoticist yet not entirely frivolous longing, and I had the training and temperament to help them fulfill it. And so began a small side business of philosophical moonlighting, at a rate of sixty euros per hour. I identified a market niche, and I produced a flyer:

FORGET THERAPY, YOU'RE IN PARIS!

Try a freewheeling one-on-one philosophical dialogue with a Paris-based philosopher in one of the city's legendary sidewalk cafés.

Bringing together elements of the ancient Greek elenchus, existentialist musing, modern talk therapy, and interactive performance art, this is a simultaneously novel, yet very ancient, way of engaging with philosophical ideas.

Here's how it works: You buy the philosopher an espresso, and get ready to explore the ideas of meaning, truth, God, death, fate, paradox, &c.

Rates start at 60 Euros for a two-hour session.

I saw to it that this flyer appeared in places Anglophone tourists frequented. I created a Facebook page. I even took out an ad in the *London Review of Books*, somewhat mischievously under the "Psychotherapy" heading. But then again, what is mischievous about it? Boethius, Cicero, Seneca: they all thought there was no better medicine for the soul than philosophy. Why not open a mobile clinic? For a long time, I thought that I should keep this work secret, but I changed my mind when I realized that going public with it was the only way for me to drum up any business.

Something struck me early on in this work: the conversations were often at least as interesting, philosophically speaking, as what goes on in, say, an undergraduate introductory course in philosophy. Often, in fact, they were far more interesting. The people who sought out the service were generally mature, curious, and ready to engage with unexpected ideas and arguments. (Many of them, for reasons I have not been able to figure out, were Australian.) The open-endedness of the situation, moreover, the fact that we were not sure what the rules were, the fact that we were entering into a socially and institutionally unfamiliar form of philosophical exchange, ensured that in contrast with the university context unexpected insights and conversational twists often arose.

Of course, in both contexts—the university and the Parisian café—money *is* involved. Arguably, the primary difference is that in the first of these we have the institution to launder the money for us, to create some distance between the activity and the remuneration, and therefore to allow us the illusion that we are not "in it for the money." But I have never met a tenured professor who works for free, and in this respect we are all, every one of us, Sophists.

Yet the reaction was nearly unanimous: "Smith has hit rock bottom," it was said. "We had once expected great things, but just look at him now. He is out there hustling for money, instead of doing philosophy. How sad." This judgment may be important, like Montaigne's sauces, for more than just autobiographical reasons. It may get at the very heart of the project of philosophy as it has been understood for the past few millennia. Philosophy, it is often supposed, is the intellectual project that disdains money. Or at least pretends to do so.

Such disdain forms a central part of the founding myth of Western philosophy, as told by Plato in his relation of the trial and execution of his mentor Socrates. Here we learn that Socrates has been wrongly charged by the court at Athens on what may be reduced to two principal counts: that he teaches doctrines, and that he accepts money for this teaching. The denial of the first charge is important to our story here, too, but we will return to it soon enough. As to the second charge, Socrates protests that it has no foundation. He is not a teacher, and has no reason to charge anyone. "Although," he adds, "if a man is able to teach, I honor him for being paid." Socrates tells of a certain teacher named Evenus, that he would admire anyone who "really has this wisdom, and teaches at such a modest charge. Had I the same, I should have been very proud and conceited; but the truth is that I have no knowledge of the kind."[1]

I am also not sure whether I have any wisdom of the sort that can be sold. I do know some things that other people do not, and I have ways of explaining these things to others that can assist them in coming to know these things more effectively than, say, Wikipedia could. But this is all knowledge, and not wisdom, and what people believe they are paying for when they pay for private philosophical conversations is, precisely, wisdom. There is in this respect a sort of ruse, a sort of charlatanism, in selling knowledge about philosophy that has no parallel in, say, the sale of knowledge of Latin verb declensions. Here, if you learn them from a Latin professor, then you get what you pay for, whereas if you pay me to give you philosophical wisdom, and all I give you are factual claims about the views of other people as a historian of philosophy, you might well feel cheated.

It was not easy to go out hustling, mind you. I am a trained philosopher, after all, and I was long attached to the idea that this vocation entails a contempt for filthy lucre. But our career choice does not exempt us from the burdens of living in the world, and if circumstances require it, philosophers are required to jump into the rat race along with everyone else. There are really only two ways they can do this: they can go with Thales, who speculated on olive presses and made a fortune just to show he had a head for business too, or they can peddle their skills as the Sophists did. I don't know anything about olive presses, or their latter day descendants in Silicon Valley or on Wall Street, so I decided to take the Sophist route.

Disdain for the sort of initiative I took could have much more to do with small-minded veneration of institutions than it does with respect for the purity of philosophy. In an era when the institutions that long seemed to be the sole legitimate home for philosophical activity now seem to be in no small crisis, and if not necessarily in decline then certainly in the throes of radical transformation, it is not surprising to find extramural initiatives taking shape, including the sort of free agency that is no more and no less Sophistic than the university career of the philosopher ever was.

I recall trembling with excitement that first day last February, as I ran down the icy sidewalk toward the General Secretary's apartments. It's hard to believe, this sudden turn of events. There I was, a few months ago, the author of a single work on the sources of Klopp's doctoral dissertation on the concept of inertia. And now, here I am, the homeland's most renowned expert on Kloppism-Noginism, called by the GenSek himself to serve as his loyal tutor! After he was humiliated at the Security Council meeting when the ambassador from the United Provinces of C**** dropped that unscripted question about Klopp's debt to Epicurus, the GenSek's councilors decided it was time for a crash course in Kloppist-Noginist philosophy. As if that had anything to do with revolution and state building!

You have to understand, the GenSek is a fine Kloppist-Noginist, but books just aren't his forte; he was too busy making revolution back when others were preparing for their exams. His first exposure to Klopp was in prison, where he wound up in the aftermath of some low-level, hunger-driven chicken thievery. He never got his Klopp from a leather-bound volume in the collected works at the Philosophy Faculty. No, that was a luxury reserved for me, and others of my class. The GenSek got it from poverty, from life, from the dank prison air.

Now it's time for me to give him what I can from my world, so that I may thrive in his world. Because it is his world now.

At our first lesson we talked about Epicurus, and atoms; not the kind you can harness, so the scientists now say, to make apocalyptic weapons, but the kind that exist only as concepts, the kind that must be posited, some thought, so I tell the GenSek, in order to avoid logical pitfalls, such as, that bodies having dimension could be composed out of constituents lacking dimension. The GenSek interrupted, said that whatever only exists as a concept doesn't exist at all, and so there's no use talking about it. He said this with an intentional exaggeration of that folksy southeastern accent of his, and I couldn't help find it endearing, even as it caused me to worry that he was really not catching on to the spirit of our lessons. I will have to try, I thought, to make it more relevant to the GenSek's life and concerns.

At our next meeting the following week I told him to review Klopp's 1857 manifesto, and to learn by heart the basic principles of Kloppist diacritics: that the basis of reality is body, which contains the principles of life and change; that the survival of the self does not depend on memory, and therefore each self is immortal simply in the constant permutations of body; and so on. There are four principles in all, the "Core Four" we're all supposed to know by heart, these days, by the end of primary school. What ten-year-old does not dream of being selected to recite the Core Four, green bandanna around his

little neck, before a committee of local party functionaries, to display his perfect diction and to be
crowned by a fully costumed Madame Elektrika, if
he is lucky, with a wreath of yew leaves? The GenSek
never went to primary school, and even if he had
gone, that was before the revolution, and he would
have heard nothing but stale old doctrine about the
finiteness of the soul, the singular importance of
what happens over the course of our mortal life,
and the ultimate ground of all reality not in body,
nor yet in matter or in spirit, but rather in various
combinations of light and water. Reactionaries!

When we next meet he is beaming with self-
contentment. He tells me he has mastered the Core
Four. "See," he says in an uncharacteristically play-
ful tone, "it's never too late to learn." He recites
them to me a couple of times, One through Four,
and then announces that this will be enough as a
lesson for today. I had intended to introduce some
new material on Chesterville's three laws of inertia, but the GenSek is in charge, of course. He asks
me about my childhood. I tell him the truth. My
political record is solid and I've got nothing to hide.
I tell him all about my French nanny and my disciplinary problems when Mum sent me away to
boarding school at Le Rosey: it was, I explain, my
delinquency in that staid environment that helped
me to convince the nomination commission at the
university of M**** that, in spite of my privileged
background and my bookish habits, I had my share
of revolutionary spirit too. The GenSek was silent,
reflective, and so I kept on talking. I told him of

how I eventually earned my degree in philosophy in the provincial University of G**** way out east of the Y**** Mountains where it's always frozen. I told him my first intellectual love was the work of Rabelais, in which I admired the unabashed celebration of freedom and excess, but that I matured quickly when I took my first course on diacritics under the renowned Academician Korff. The GenSek had never heard of Academician Korff. Enough for today, he said.

When I next see him I come prepared with an elaborate lesson on Nogin's 1907 "Letter from the Corn Exchange," but the GenSek has other ideas. "I will give a speech on philosophy," he announces. "It will be a grand speech, with electronic amplification, and it will be recorded on the best spools. I will speak of the Core Four, and inertia, and atoms. All the men of the Academy will be in attendance, especially this Korff." Korff died some years ago, I tell him. "Well then whoever replaced him," the GenSek continues, "and it will be made known that philosophy is a great priority in the construction of our Kloppist-Noginist society, and there will be much applause."

The lessons continue, officially. Once a week I go to the GenSek's apartments to tutor him in philosophy. But most often I just sit there drinking strong black tea straight from the saucer as he paces back and forth, regaling me with disjointed stories about the revolution, or about the growth of industry in the next five years, all peppered here and there with allusions to atoms, or Chesterville's three laws, or

Klopp's four principles. One gray afternoon as I was sitting on the GenSek's favorite divan, dipping a beignet in clotted cream, he paced back and forth and blurted out to me, suddenly: "You know I've done away with Korg, don't you?" "Done away," Mister Secretary? I squeaked. "That's right. I disassembled the atoms that once constituted that groveling traitor."

I can't complain, I tell myself. I'm still alive.

He really surprises me sometimes. Just this last week he interrupted some tale of derring-do, how he and his comrades dynamited the railroad tracks outside of T**** or some such thing, in order to tell me of his plan to establish, at the end of his upcoming speech, a "philosophy medal," to be handed out annually by the GenSek himself, in honor of philosophical contributions to the glory of our great revolutionary Kloppist-Noginist homeland. And do you know who is going to be the first recipient of said medal? You guessed right.

But there's still more work to be done, if this is not to be a total wash. For one thing, I must see to it that the audience knows when to applaud, and more importantly when to stop applauding. It would be a disaster if the academicians failed to detect a profound philosophical observation the GenSek had just made, especially if this is an observation he associates with the lessons he has had from me. I would therefore like very much to rehearse with him, but he is intent on lecturing me, now, about the boons of automated sheepshearing.

I place a sugar cube between my front teeth and allow the black tea to filter right through it. I really should try to get through to him somehow. There is much more than my philosophy medal on the line. I crunch the cube between my teeth and I replace it with a new one.

Things could be worse, and they may get worse soon. But I've made it this far. I'm being fed sugar cubes by the Basilisk (as he's called in the streets). Hah! "The philosopher is an ass," as that example from my logic textbook had it, so long ago. But what can I do? There is so much that is beyond my power.

In the two centuries, and some, since Kant, philosophy has grown increasingly professionalized, as a result of internal developments in the field as well as the complicated social and institutional history of the modern university. Today, no one could make any sense of the claim that a philosopher, qua philosopher, might enjoy discoursing upon storms and tempests, or delivering the results of her research upon the medical virtues of syrup of ipecac. Still further from our understanding of the social role of the philosopher are models from the deeper past, which come mostly from the church and the temple, a social milieu from which philosophers would like to maintain a very safe distance: the philosopher as priest or monk, as social mediator between the human and the divine, or as isolated, world-renouncing contemplator of the divine. But these are part of the long heritage of the discipline, too, and it behooves us to understand the way this long history continues to impact philosophy's efforts to define itself.

Such an effort at historical self-understanding becomes particularly urgent in periods of dramatic social and institutional change, such as those the current university system is now facing. Whether we like it or not, the future of philosophy, like much of its past, may well unfold outside of the university. J. M. Coetzee has recently compared the situation of humanities professors today to the one faced by dissenting academics under the communist regime in Poland, where those who were not permitted to teach real philosophy let it be known that they "would be running a philosophy seminar in [their] living room, outside office hours, outside the institution." In so doing, Coetzee writes, "the study of philosophy was kept alive. It may be something along the same lines will be needed to keep humanistic studies alive in a world in which universities have redefined themselves out of existence."[2] Unlike Polish communism, however, the changes happening in the world today are global, and it is difficult to imagine how they could possibly be reversed.

Ironically, one of the mechanisms by which universities are destroying themselves, or at least are seeking to remove their own humanistic hearts, is by forcing philosophers to conceptualize their own work on the model of the positive sciences: by forcing philosophers to apply for large grants, for example, with explicit "methodologies" (which can no longer be simply reading several books and thinking about them) leading to concrete research "results" (which can no longer be simply interesting and compelling observations about the world and our place in it). But what the administrators and the faculty alike miss in their mutual misunderstanding is the depth of the historical relationship, indeed the identity, between what is now being called "science" and what has for a much longer time been called "philosophy." It cannot be that philosophers must retain their independence from the sciences, for it is a simple historical fact that this independence is a recent invention, and not necessarily a justified or useful one. Science, too, used to be motivated by impulses other than grant seeking. If there is, then, a new expectation that philosophers justify what they do in terms appropriated from the sciences, the deeper problem with this expectation might be that these terms are equally inadequate for grasping what it is that science does, or might have done in the past and might do once more in the future. But again, in order to see this, we need to reconstruct the history of natural philosophy, to expose the self-conception of the people who in different eras and contexts sought, to speak with the poet James Merrill, to hack through nature's thorns. And we need to do this in a way that does not cordon natural philosophy off from philosophy on the basis of anachronistic divisions.

For Coetzee, the living-room philosophy of the Polish dissidents is noble, and worth replicating, presumably in large part because it is offered freely, just as Socrates offered it so long ago. But again, this is only one conception of what the philosophical endeavor is, and by no means the most prominent one throughout philosophy's history. Philosophers have been cast in many different social roles, with many different job descriptions. They have been brave outsiders and foolish outsiders, and they have been both brave and cowardly servants of power. Cicero, for example, served power, but he was as true to his own moral sense and as open about his real philosophical commitments as Diogenes the Cynic had been. We all need money, at least those of us who decline to rummage in the garbage and otherwise to live like dogs, but most of us hope to preserve a distinction between getting paid and selling out. At present, a danger exists for professional philosophers that they will betray their own moral sense, and adapt their philosophical commitments, in order to preserve a place, any place at all, within a rapidly putrefying university landscape. They will, for example, agree to teach business ethics classes in which they help the up-and-coming minions of global capital to feel better about bilking the poor and despoiling the environment, rather than forcing them to do what philosophy, on one widespread understanding, calls on us to do: question everything, including our own supposed life calling.

To accept this role is superficially different from the role of the Courtier flattering and placating the terrifying and arbitrary dictator, but morally speaking it is the same. In both cases, we may hope, a philosophical underground will continue to thrive that questions everything and placates no one and will emerge to the surface when the official institutions again show themselves deserving of philosophy's infinite gift.

CONCLUSION

Without claiming to have earned a place among the great works of philosophy, we may at least note that, like many of those great works, this one ends in aporia. We have failed to determine what philosophy is, and absent an understanding of this we are hardly in a position to say what the agent of philosophy, the philosopher, must do. The fact that we came up dry does not however cast doubt on our method. We surveyed the history of human activities carried out under the label "philosophy," as well as many activities that have been carried out under other labels but that bear important resemblances to the ones called "philosophy," and we found that there are simply too many different and only partially overlapping activities to warrant any unified and all-purpose definition of "philosophy" that will be of service across different times and places. The a posteriori and comparative approach, in short, leads us to the definitive conclusion that "philosophy" is said in many ways.

Rather than generating a specific set of instructions as to what a person must do in order to be a philosopher, we found it useful to think of "the philosopher" as represented by various types, again, partially overlapping, who in different times and places it will make sense to consider *as* philosophers. This approach brings us fairly close to something like an "institutional theory," to borrow from George Dickie's "institutional theory of art," which says that what it is to be an artwork is nothing more than to "pass" as an artwork within the institutional setting of museums, galleries, and so on.[1] To be a philosopher, on such an understanding, is simply to be held to be a philosopher.

But is this really all we were able to establish? While there was no conscious decision to do things in this way, the reader will have noticed a decreasing fondness, from the Curiosa down to the Courtier, for the different philosophical types sketched out and analyzed in the preceding chapters. After all, a philosopher, unlike an artwork, has interests of his or her own, and is generally able to sense whether or not he or she is "doing it right." Our Curiosa was shut out of the institutions of philosophy, yet she was driven by a deep internal conviction that she was, in the deepest and fullest sense, doing philosophy. Our Courtier was, for the time being, given the highest institutional approval possible, as tutor to the tyrant, yet, we may imagine, he understood he had left philosophy behind in order to save his hide. The one is free; the other is bound. The one is driven on by wonder, the other by a desire for mere survival. He has refused to acknowledge what the Stoics taught, that sometimes there is more freedom in death than in adapting oneself to existing circumstances simply in order to stay alive. Artworks do not have such choices, even if their creators, the artists, do.

Throughout, we have mounted a plaidoyer for the faculty of wonder, as the deep stratum of human comportment toward reality that in turn gives rise to curiosity.[2] We have been sympathetic to, rather than dismissive of, those manifestations of wonder that induce the wonderer to say things about the world that strike the professional philosopher as erroneous, as subphilosophical, as superstitious. We have taken this approach in loyalty to long influential characterizations of philosophy by thinkers, notably Aristotle, who are held to have been there at the beginning, to have set the very parameters of the project of philosophy.

We have, finally, revealed a great deal of ourselves. Or, rather, I have revealed a great deal of myself: a calculated risk, but one that has been central to the aims of this undertaking. *Je parle au papier, comme je parle au premier que je rencontre*, said—or wrote—Montaigne. "I speak to the paper as I speak to the first person I meet." Philosophy, on one understanding of this activity, began in open speaking. Yet the writing of philosophy, which has gradually moved in to occupy much of the space previously held by the speaking of it, has tended to occlude this openness, to bequeath to us mostly treatises rather than essays. But written philosophy can also be, and sometimes has been, a sort of open speaking too, not least about the author him or herself, his or her motivations and limitations. As Montaigne understood, this speaking can open new possibilities for other speaking, freer speaking, about the most important things. *Un parler ouvert ouvre un autre parler, et le tire hors.* "Open speaking opens up other speaking, and pulls it out." Montaigne adds that this pulling is not unlike the effect of wine or of love. Inebriation should perhaps remain a topic for another conversation. And enamoration? It is contained in the very idea of philosophy and should never be allowed to recede too far from our minds when we are, as they say, doing it.

NOTES

INTRODUCTION

1. Gilles Deleuze and Félix Guattari, *Qu'est-ce que la philosophie?* (Paris: Éditions de Minuit, 1991). (*What Is Philosophy?*, trans. Hugh Tomlinson and Graham Burchell [New York: Columbia University Press, 1994]).
2. Ludwig Wittgenstein, *Philosophical Investigations*, trans. G.E.M. Anscombe, 3rd ed. (New York: Macmillan, 1968 [1953]), Aphorism 309.
3. Ibid., Aphorism 109.
4. Randall Collins, *The Sociology of Philosophies: A Global Theory of Intellectual Change* (Cambridge, MA: Harvard University Press, 1998), 20.
5. Aristotle, *Poetics* I, 9.
6. Henry More, *Antidote against Atheism*, in *A Collection of Several Philosophical Writings of Dr. Henry More* (London, 1662), III xii, 125.
7. John Keats, letter to George and Georgiana Keats, April 21, 1819, in *The Letters of John Keats*, vol. 2, *1819–1821* (Cambridge: Cambridge University Press, 1958), no. 159, 101.
8. See Aristotle, *Metaphysics*, 982b12.
9. Thomas Hobbes, "Epistle Dedicatory," *De Corpore*, in *The English Works of Thomas Hobbes of Malmesbury*, vol. 1 (London: John Bohn, 1839 [1655]), ix.
10. See Peter Schmidt, "The Man Who Ranks Philosophy Departments Now Rankles Them, Too," *Chronicle of Higher Education*, September 26, 2014. http://chronicle.com/article/The-Man-Who-Ranks-Philosophy/149007/.
11. Bertrand Russell, *The History of Western Philosophy* (London: George Allen and Unwin, 1945).

12. Karl Jaspers, *Vom Ursprung und Ziel der Geschichte* (Zurich: Artemis Verlag, 1949).

13. Matthew Stewart, *The Courtier and the Heretic: Leibniz, Spinoza, and the Fate of God in the Modern World* (New York: W. W. Norton, 2006).

CHAPTER ONE: THE CURIOSA

1. For a useful discussion of this passage, see Geoffrey Lloyd, " 'Philosophy': What Did the Greeks Invent and Is It Relevant to China?" *Extrême-Orient, Extrême-Occident* 27, no. 27 (2005): 149–59.

2. K. J. Dover, *Aristophanes: Clouds* (Oxford: Clarendon Press, 1970).

3. Laurent Lange, "Journal du voyage de Laurent Lange à la Chine," in *Nouveaux mémoires sur l'état présent de la Grande Russie ou Moscovie*, vol. 2, by Friedrich-Christian Weber (Paris: Pissot, 1725), 110.

4. Friedrich Nietzsche, *Fragmente: 1875–1879*, vol. 2 (Hamburg: Tredition Verlag, 2012), 85.

5. See, e.g., Joshua Knobe and Shaun Nichols, "An Experimental Philosophy Manifesto," in *Experimental Philosophy*, by Joshua Knobe and Shaun Nichols (Oxford: Oxford University Press, 2007), 3–14.

6. D'Arcy Wentworth Thompson, *On Growth and Form* (Cambridge: Cambridge University Press, 1945 [1917]), 8–9.

7. Francis Bacon, *The New Organon; or, True Directions concerning the Interpretation of Nature*, in *Collected Works of Francis Bacon* (London: Routledge/Thoemmes Press, 1995 [1620]), xxxvi, 53.

8. Gottfried Wilhelm Leibniz, *Sbornik pisem i memorialov Leïbnitsa otnosyashchikhsya k Rossii i Petru Velikomu*, ed. V. I. Ger'e (Saint Petersburg, 1873), 38.

9. Ibid., 96.

10. François Bernier, "A Relation of a Voyage, Made in the Year 1664," in *The History of the Late Revolution of the Empire of the Great Mogol*, trans. H. O. (London: Moses Pitt, 1672), 4: 12–13.

11. See Thomas Wright, ed., *A Selection of Latin Stories from Manuscripts of the Thirteenth and Fourteenth Centuries* (London: Percy Society, 1842), 74. "Hoc omnino non faciam, nisi videro signa amoris, ne me tentes: ergo veni ad meam cameram, reptando manibus et pedibus, sicut equus me portando, tunc scio quod non illudes mihi."

12. See Mary Fissell, *Vernacular Bodies: The Politics of Reproduction in Early Modern England* (Oxford: Oxford University Press, 2004).
13. Nietzsche, *Die Genealogie der Moral*, 3.6.104.
14. Johannes Kepler, *Kepler's Somnium: The Dream; or, Posthumous Works on Lunar Astronomy*, trans. and ed. Edward Rosen (Madison: University of Wisconsin Press, 1967).
15. Ibid., 11.
16. Ibid., 12.
17. Ibid., 13.
18. Ibid., 15.
19. See Carolyn Merchant, *The Death of Nature: Women, Ecology, and the Scientific Revolution* (New York: HarperCollins, 1990 [1980]).
20. See, e.g., Lawrence M. Krauss, *A Universe from Nothing: Why There Is Something Rather Than Nothing* (New York: Free Press, 2012).
21. See James G. Lennox, "Putting Philosophy of Science to the Test: The Case of Aristotle's Biology," *PSA: Proceedings of the Biennial Meeting of the Philosophy of Science Association* 2 (1994): 239–47.
22. Gottfried Wilhelm Leibniz, *De novo antidysenterico americano*, in *Gothofredi Guillelmi Leibnitii Opera Omnia*, ed. Louis Dutens (Geneva: De Tournes, 1768 [1695–96]), vol. 2, part 2, 110–19.
23. James Merrill, *The Changing Light at Sandover* (New York: Knopf Doubleday, 2011 [1982]), 55.
24. William R. Newman, *Promethean Ambitions: Alchemy and the Quest to Perfect Nature* (Chicago: University of Chicago Press, 2004).
25. For an excellent account of the emergence of the research university, particularly in the German context, and this development's impact on the division of the academic disciplines, see William Clark, *Academic Charisma and the Origins of the Research University* (Chicago: University of Chicago Press, 2006).
26. Immanuel Kant, *Meditationum quarundam de igne succincta delineatio*, in *Kants gesammelte Schriften*, ed. Königlich Preussische Akademie der Wissenschaften. Vol. 1, *Vorkritische Schriften 1: 1747–1756* (Berlin: Georg Reimer, 1902), 369–84.

CHAPTER TWO: THE SAGE

1. Theophrastus Paracelsus and Valentin Weigel, *Philosophia Mystica, darinn begriffen Eilff unterschidene Theologico-Philosophische doch teutsche Tractätlein* (Neustadt, 1618). In the rare books collection of the library of the University of Helsinki.
2. See Grant K. Goodman, *Japan and the Dutch, 1600–1853* (London: Routledge, 2013).
3. Bernardino de Sahagún, *The Florentine Codex: General History of the Things of New Spain*, trans. Arthur J. O. Anderson and Charles E. Dibble, 12 vols. (Salt Lake City: University of Utah Press, 2002).
4. See in particular Miguel León-Portilla, *La filosofía nahuatl estudiada en sus fuentes* (Mexico City: UNAM, 1993).
5. Saul Bellow, interview in the *New Yorker*, March 7, 1988. "Who is the Tolstoy of the Zulus? The Proust of the Papuans? I'd be glad to read him."
6. See Sharon E. Hutchinson, *Nuer Dilemmas: Coping with Money, War, and the State* (Berkeley: University of California Press, 1996).
7. See Ezra Zubrow and Elizabeth C. Blake, "The Origin of Music and Rhythm," in *Archaeoacoustics*, ed. Chris Scarre and Graeme Lawson (Cambridge: McDonald Institute for Archaeological Research, 2006), 117–26.
8. Michael Friedman, "Extending the Dynamics of Reason: Generalizing a Post-Kuhnian Approach to the History and Philosophy of Science," lecture at the Max-Planck-Institut für Wissenschaftsgeschichte, Berlin, July 25, 2009. See also J. L. Heilbron, *The Sun in the Church: Cathedrals as Solar Observatories* (Cambridge, MA: Harvard University Press, 2001).
9. Paul Radin, *Primitive Man as Philosopher* (New York: D. Appleton, 1927).
10. For a remarkable and compelling argument for the influence of Native American philosophy on the development of Euro-American philosophy, see Bruce Wilshire, *The Primal Roots of American Philosophy: Pragmatism, Phenomenology, and Native American Thought* (University Park: Pennsylvania State University Press, 2000). See also Scott L. Pratt, *Native Pragmatism: Rethinking the Roots of American Philosophy* (Bloomington: Indiana University Press, 2002).
11. Alexis Kagame, *La philosophie Bantu comparée* (Paris: La Présence Africaine, 1976).
12. J. B. Danquah, *The Akan Doctrine of God: A Fragment of Gold Coast Ethics* (London: Lutterworth Press, 1944). For a somewhat similar engagement

with an ethical system from the North American cultural sphere, see Richard B. Brandt, *Hopi Ethics* (Chicago: University of Chicago Press, 1954).

13. See Jack Goody, *The Logic of Writing and the Organization of Society* (Cambridge: Cambridge University Press, 1986). For a subtle discussion of the conceptual difficulties in defining writing, as these relate to cultural practices of tabulation and record keeping, see Frank L. Solomon, *The Cord Keepers: Khipus and Cultural Life in a Peruvian Village* (Durham, NC: Duke University Press, 2004).

14. Collins, *Sociology of Philosophies*, 27.

15. Claude Lévi-Strauss, *La pensée sauvage* (Paris: Plon, 1962).

16. See, e.g., Scott Atran, *The Cognitive Foundations of Natural History: Towards an Anthropology of Science* (Cambridge: Cambridge University Press, 1990).

17. Giambattista Vico, *Principi di Scienza nuova di Giambattista Vico: D'intorno alla comune natura delle nazioni* (Naples: Stamperia Muziana, 1744 [1725]).

18. See Edouard Machery, Ron Mallon, Shaun Nichols, and Stephen P. Stich, "Semantics, Cross-Cultural Style," *Cognition* 92, no. 3 (2004): 1–12.

19. Les Murray, interview with Dennis O'Driscoll, *Paris Review* 173 (Spring 2005).

20. Paul Valéry, "La Pythie," in *Charmes; ou, Poèmes* (Paris: Éditions de la Nouvelle revue française, 1922).

21. Richard Sorabji, *Animal Minds and Human Morals: The Origins of the Western Debate* (Ithaca, NY: Cornell University Press, 1995).

22. Placide Tempels, *La philosophie bantoue* (Elisabethville: Lovania, 1945; translated as *Bantu Philosophy*, Paris: Présence Africaine, 1959).

23. Tempels, *Bantu Philosophy*, 1959, 20.

24. Gottfried Wilhelm Leibniz, *Die philosophischen Schriften von Gottfried Wilhelm Leibniz*, ed. C. I. Gerhardt (Berlin, 1849–60), 5: 318.

25. Ibid.

26. Kagame, *La philosophie Bantu comparée*, 121.

27. Ibid., 122.

28. Ibid., 131.

29. Ibid., 151.

30. Ibid.

31. Ibid., 152.

32. Diogenes Laertius, *Lives of the Eminent Philosophers*, ed. and trans. R. D. Hicks (London: William Heinemann, 1925), 2: 6.63.

33. Michael Mann, *The Dark Side of Democracy: Explaining Ethnic Cleansing* (Cambridge: Cambridge University Press, 2005).
34. Charles Taylor, *Multiculturalism and "The Politics of Recognition"* (Princeton, NJ: Princeton University Press, 1992).
35. Aristotle, *Nicomachean Ethics*, Book 5, chap. 7.
36. See David E. Mungello, *The Chinese Rites Controversy: Its History and Meaning* (Nettetal: Steyler Verlag, 1994).
37. Gottfried Wilhelm Leibniz, *Novissima Sinica historiam nostri temporis illustrata* (Hannover: Förster, 1699).
38. Gottfried Wilhelm Leibniz, *Discours sur la théologie naturelle des Chinois*, in *Gothofredi Guillelmi Leibnitii Opera Omnia*, edited by Louis Dutens (Geneva: De Tournes, 1768), 4: 170.
39. See Hiob Ludolf, *Historia Aethiopica, sive, Brevis et succincta descriptio regni Habessinorum* (Frankfurt: Joh. David Zunner, 1681).
40. See Justin E. H. Smith, "Leibniz on Natural History and National History," *History of Science* 50, no. 4 (2012): 377–401.
41. Shūsaku Endō, *Silence*, trans. William Johnston (New York: Taplinger Publishing, 1969 [1966]).
42. Knud Rasmussen, *Across Arctic America: Narrative of the Fifth Thule Expedition* (Chicago: University of Chicago Press, 1999 [1927]).
43. Cited in Kwame Gyekye, *An Essay on African Philosophical Thought: The Akan Conceptual Scheme* (Cambridge: Cambridge University Press, 1995 [1987]), 33. For a more recent stock-taking of the fruits and limitations of this approach, see Ivan Karp and D. A. Masolo, *African Philosophy as Cultural Inquiry* (Bloomington: Indiana University Press, 2009).
44. Kwame Nkrumah, *Consciencism: Philosophy and Ideology for De-Colonization and Development with Particular Reference to the African Revolution* (New York: Monthly Review Press, 2009 [1964]).
45. Ibid., 79.
46. Ibid.
47. Ibid., 92.
48. Ibid.
49. Ibid., 93.
50. Ibid., 92.
51. Ibid.
52. Ibid., 97.

53. Marshall Sahlins, "Goodbye to Tristes Tropes: Ethnography in the Context of Modern World History," *Journal of Modern History* 65 (1993): 3–4.

54. Horace Walpole to Horace Mann, July 7, 1779, in *The Letters of Horace Walpole, Fourth Earl of Oxford* (Oxford: Clarendon Press, 1903), 7: 222.

55. Gabriel François Venel and César Chesneau Dumarsais, "Philosophe," in *L'Encyclopédie ou Dictionnaire raisonné des sciences, des art et des métiers*, 1st ed. (Paris, 1751), 12: 509.

56. Ibid., 511.

57. See Christian Wolff, *Philosophia rationalis sive Logica: methodo scientifica pertractata et ad usum scientiarum atque vitae aptata* (Frankfurt and Leipzig: Officina Libraria Rengeriana, 1728), para. 29.

58. Johann Jakob Brucker, *The History of Philosophy, from the Earliest Times to the Beginning of the Present Century*, trans. William Enfield (London: W. Baynes, 1791), 7–8.

59. Ibid., 8.

60. Ibid., 102.

61. Ibid., 85.

62. Ibid.

63. Ibid., 85–86.

64. Ibid., 86.

65. Ibid., 15.

66. Ibid.

67. Ibid., 16.

68. Ibid., 16–17.

69. See Walter Burkert, *Babylon, Memphis, Persepolis: Eastern Contexts of Greek Culture* (Cambridge, MA: Harvard University Press, 2004).

70. See Atran, *Cognitive Foundations of Natural History*.

CHAPTER THREE: THE GADFLY

1. René Descartes, *Meditationes de prima philosophia*, in *Oeuvres*, ed. Charles Adam and Paul Tannery, vol. 7 (Paris: L. Cerf, 1897–1913).

2. Edmund Husserl, *Cartesian Meditations*, trans. D. Cairns (Dordrecht: Kluwer, 1960 [1931]).

3. George Berkeley, *Three Dialogues between Hylas and Philonous, in Opposition to Sceptics and Atheists*, in *The Works of George Berkeley, D. D.*, vol. 1 (London: Richard Priestley, 1820).

4. Michel de Montaigne, *Les Essais*, ed. Jean Céard et al. (Paris: Hachette, 2002 [1580]).

5. See Vincent Carraud, *L'invention du moi* (Paris: Presses Universitaires de France, 2010); Richard Sorabji, *Self: Ancient and Modern Insights about Individuality, Life, and Death* (Chicago: University of Chicago Press, 2006).

6. Charles Taylor, *Sources of the Self: The Making of the Modern Identity* (Cambridge, MA: Harvard University Press, 1989).

7. Kimberlé Crenshaw, "Mapping the Margins: Intersectionality, Identity Politics, and Violence against Women of Color," *Stanford Law Review* 43 (1989): 1241–99.

8. Zhuangzi, *The Essential Writings, with Selections from Traditional Commentaries*, trans. Brook Ziporyn (Indianapolis: Hackett Classics, 2009), 76.

9. See M.F.K. Fisher, *Love in a Dish: And Other Culinary Delights* (Berkeley: Counterpoint, 2011), 97.

10. See in particular Richard Wollheim, *Germs: A Memoir of Childhood* (Emeryville, CA: Shoemaker and Hoard, 2006).

11. More, *Antidote against Atheism*, 107–8.

12. Laurence Sterne, *The Life and Opinions of Tristram Shandy*, in *The Works of Laurence Sterne* (London, 1815), 4: 88.

13. Ahmad Faris al-Shidyaq, *Leg over Leg*, vol. 1, ed. and trans. Humphrey Davies (New York: New York University Press, Library of Arabic Literature, 2014), 165.

14. Al-Shidyaq, *Leg over Leg*, 1: 168–69.

15. Friedrich Nietzsche, "Der freieste Schriftsteller," *Menschliches Allzumenschliches II: Nachgelassene Fragmente 1879–1879*, in *Nietzsche—Werke. Kritische Gesamtausgabe*, 4.3, ed. Giorgio Colli and Mazzino Montinari (Berlin: De Gruyter, 1967), 61.

16. Kant, *Kritik der reinen Vernunft* § 54, AA V, 332.

17. See Nyurgun Bootur Stremitel'nyï, *Yakutskiï geroicheskiï epos Olonkho*, trans. V. Derzhavin, general editor S. V. Mikhalkova (Yakutsk: Yakutskoe Knizhnoe Izdatel'stvo, 1982).

18. Gottfried Wilhelm Leibniz, *La Monadologie*, ed. M. T. Desdouits (Paris: Librairie Classiques, 1884 [1714]).

19. Jonardon Ganeri, *The Lost Age of Reason: Philosophy in Early Modern India, 1450–1700* (Oxford: Oxford University Press, 2011), 37–38.

20. Ibid., 15.

21. Ibid.

22. Ibid., 16.

23. Bernard Mandeville, *The Fable of the Bees; or, Private Vices, Publick Benefits* (London: J. Tonson, 1729 [1714]).

24. Immanuel Kant, *Allgemeine Naturgeschichte und Theorie des Himmels*, AA 1, 215–368.

25. Walt Whitman, *Leaves of Grass* (New York, 1855), 33.

26. Ibid., 16.

27. Walt Whitman, *Leaves of Grass—1860*, "Proto-Leaf," *Walt Whitman: Selected Poems, 1855–1892*, ed. Gary Schmidgall (New York: Stonewall Inn Editions, 1999), 181.

28. Walt Whitman, *Democratic Vistas*, in *The Collected Works of Walt Whitman*, vol. 2, *Prose Works 1892*, ed. Gay Wilson Allen and Sculley Bradley (New York: New York University Press, 1964), 414.

29. Whitman, *Leaves of Grass*, 45.

30. Ibid., 32–33.

31. Ibid., 32.

32. Ibid., 50–51.

33. Ibid., 50.

34. Ibid., 55.

35. Whitman, *Democratic Vistas*, 416–17.

36. Whitman, *Leaves of Grass*, 28.

37. Josiah Royce to William James, January 14, 1879, cited in Ralph Barton Perry, *The Thought and Character of William James*, 2 vols. (Boston, 1935), 1: 781.

38. T. S. Eliot, "The Development of Leibniz's Monadism," *The Monist* 26 (December 1916): 534–56.

39. Ibid., 556.

40. T. S. Eliot, "The Dry Salvages," in *Four Quartets* (New York: Houghton Mifflin Harcourt, 2014), 43–44.

41. Ibid., 45.

42. Bernard Williams, "On Hating and Despising Philosophy," *London Review of Books* 18, no. 8 (1996): 17–18.

CHAPTER FOUR: THE ASCETIC

1. Pierre Hadot, *Philosophy as a Way of Life*, trans. Michael Chase (Oxford: Blackwell, 1995), 104.

2. See R. Bracht Branham and Marie-Odile Goulet-Cazé, eds., *The Cynics: The Cynic Movement in Antiquity and Its Legacy* (Berkeley: University of California Press, 2000).

3. See in particular Robert Boyle, *The Christian Virtuoso: Shewing, That by Being Addicted to Experimental Philosophy, a Man Is Rather Assisted, Than Indisposed, to Be a Good Christian* (London: John Taylor, 1690).

4. Ibid., 43–44.

5. See in particular Jason Stanley, *Know How* (Oxford: Oxford University Press, 2011).

6. Sarah Boxer, "G.E.M. Anscombe, British Philosopher, Dies at 81," *New York Times*, January 13, 2001.

7. See David Gordon White, *The Yoga Sutra of Patanjali: A Biography* (Princeton, NJ: Princeton University Press, 2014).

8. See Benjamin A. Elman, *Civil Examinations and Meritocracy in Late Imperial China* (Cambridge, MA: Harvard University Press, 2013).

9. Graham Priest, "What Is Philosophy?" *Philosophy* 81, no. 316 (2006): 189–207, 202.

10. Ganeri, *Lost Age of Reason*.

11. For a good example, see Stephen Menn, *Descartes and Augustine* (Cambridge: Cambridge University Press, 1998).

12. Raghunātha Śiromaṇi, *Inquiry into the True Nature of Things [Padārtha-tattva-nirūpaṇa-vyākhyā]* (Varanasi: Maha Mandalayantralaya, 1915), 79, 1–80, 3; cited in Ganeri, *Lost Age of Reason*, 4.

13. Ganeri, *Lost Age of Reason*, 6.

14. See in particular William R. Newman, *Atoms and Alchemy: Chymistry and the Experimental Origins of the Scientific Revolution* (Chicago: University of Chicago Press, 2006).

15. Ganeri, *Lost Age of Reason*, 10; see also Daya Krishna, *Developments in Indian Philosophy from Eighteenth Century Onwards*, History of Science, Philosophy, and Culture in Indian Civilization, vol. 10, part 1 (New Delhi: Centre for Studies in Civilization, 2001).

16. See P. K. Gode, "Bernier and Kavindracarya Sarasvati at the Moghal Court," in *Studies in Indian Literary History*, vol. 2, by P. K. Gode (Bombay: Baratiya Vidya Bhavan, 1954), 364–79.

17. François Bernier, *The History of the Late Revolution of the Empire of the Great Mogol*, 105. I have preferred a period translation here rather than the orig-

inal French, principally because it helps to convey the international reach of ideas about Asia in general and India in particular in early modern Europe.

18. Ibid., 104.
19. Ibid., 107.
20. Ibid., 108.
21. Ibid., 130.
22. Ibid., 131–32.
23. Ibid., 134.
24. Ibid., 143–44.
25. Ibid., 144.
26. Ibid., 162–63.
27. Ibid., 62.
28. Ibid., 164–65.

CHAPTER FIVE: THE MANDARIN

1. See, again, Schmidt, "The Man Who Ranks Philosophy Departments Now Rankles Them, Too."
2. W.V.O. Quine, *Ontological Relativity and Other Essays* (New York: Columbia University Press, 1969), 126–27.
3. Hans Reichenbach, *Experience and Prediction: An Analysis of the Foundations and the Structure of Knowledge* (Chicago: University of Chicago Press, 1938), 270.
4. E. E. Evans-Pritchard, *Witchcraft, Oracles, and Magic among the Azande* (Oxford: Clarendon Press, 1976 [1937]).
5. See, e.g., Ferdinand Alquié, *Philosophie du surréalisme* (Paris: Flammarion, 1955).
6. See "Bac S, ES et L 2015: Découvrez les sujets de philo," *Le Monde*, June 17, 2015. http://www.lemonde.fr/bac-lycee/article/2015/06/17/bac-s-es-l-et-stmg-2015-decouvrez-les-sujets-de-philo_4655724_4401499.html #Muhu39MsxeiRtcVs.99.
7. S. P., "French Politics: Trains, Strikes, and Philosophy," *The Economist*, June 16, 2014. http://www.economist.com/blogs/charlemagne/2014/06/french-politics.
8. James Turner, *Philology: The Forgotten Origins of the Modern Humanities* (Princeton, NJ: Princeton University Press, 2014).

9. Karl Popper, *Unended Quest: An Intellectual Autobiography* (LaSalle, IL: Open Court, 1976), 168.
10. See Alison Wylie, *Thinking from Things: Essays in the Philosophy of Archaeology* (Berkeley: University of California Press, 2002).
11. Franco Moretti, *Graphs, Maps, Trees: Abstract Models for a Literary History* (London: Verso, 2005).
12. J. Lewis Krapf, *Travels, Researches, and Missionary Labours, during an Eighteen Years' Residence in Eastern Africa, Together with Journeys to Jagga, Usambara, Ukambani, Shoa, Abessinia, and Khartum; and a Coasting Voyage from Mombaz to Cape Delgado ... With an Appendix Respecting the Snow-Capped Mountains of Eastern Africa* (London: Trübner, Paternoster Row, 1860).
13. Ibid., 543–44.
14. Paul Kretzmann, *John Ludwig Krapf: The Explorer-Missionary of Northeastern Africa* (Columbus, OH: The Book Concern, 1909), 7.
15. Ibid., 7.
16. Ibid., 15.

CHAPTER SIX: THE COURTIER

1. Plato, *Apology*, 19e–20c.
2. See J. M. Coetzee, "Universities Head for Extinction," *Mail & Guardian*, November 1, 2013.

CONCLUSION

1. See George Dickie, *Art and the Aesthetic: An Institutional Analysis* (Ithaca, NY: Cornell University Press, 1974).
2. For a similar approach, see Jeanne Hersch, *L'étonnement philosophique: Une histoire de la philosophie* (Paris: Flammarion, 1993).

BIBLIOGRAPHY

The following works were consulted for the parafictional sketches; any historical inaccuracies in these sketches are the result of our own invention.

Cavendish, Margaret. *Observations upon Experimental Philosophy.* London: A. Maxwell, 1666.

Descola, Philippe. *Par delà nature et culture.* Paris: Gallimard, 2005.

Elman, Benjamin A. *Civil Examinations and Meritocracy in Late Imperial China.* Cambridge, MA: Harvard University Press, 2013.

Kumanev, Viktor Aleksandrovich. *30-e gody v sud'bakh otechestvennoï intelligentsii.* Moscow: Nauka, 1991.

Lévi-Strauss, Claude. *Tristes Tropiques.* Paris: Plon, 1955.

Tarn, William Woodthorpe. *The Greeks in Bactria and India.* Cambridge: Cambridge University Press, 2010.

WORKS CITED

Alquié, Ferdinand. *Philosophie du surréalisme.* Paris: Flammarion, 1955.

Atran, Scott. *The Cognitive Foundations of Natural History: Towards an Anthropology of Science.* Cambridge: Cambridge University Press, 1990.

Bacon, Francis. *The New Organon; or, True Directions concerning the Interpretation of Nature.* In *Collected Works of Francis Bacon.* London: Routledge/Thoemmes Press, 1995 [1620].

Bellow, Saul. Interview in the *New Yorker,* March 7, 1988.

Berkeley, George. *The Works of George Berkeley, D. D.* London: Richard Priestley, 1820.

Bernier, François. "A Relation of a Voyage, Made in the Year 1664." In *The History of the Late Revolution of the Empire of the Great Mogol*, translated by H. O. London: Moses Pitt, 1672.

Boxer, Sarah. "G.E.M. Anscombe, British Philosopher, Dies at 81." *New York Times*, January 13, 2001.

Boyle, Robert. *The Christian Virtuoso: Shewing, That by Being Addicted to Experimental Philosophy, a Man Is Rather Assisted, Than Indisposed, to Be a Good Christian*. London: John Taylor, 1690.

Brandt, Richard B. *Hopi Ethics*. Chicago: University of Chicago Press, 1954.

Branham, R. Bracht, and Marie-Odile Goulet-Cazé, eds. *The Cynics: The Cynic Movement in Antiquity and Its Legacy*. Berkeley: University of California Press, 2000.

Brucker, Johann Jakob. *The History of Philosophy, from the Earliest Times to the Beginning of the Present Century*. Translated by William Enfield. London: W. Baynes, 1791.

Burkert, Walter. *Babylon, Memphis, Persepolis: Eastern Contexts of Greek Culture*. Cambridge, MA: Harvard University Press, 2004.

Carraud, Vincent. *L'invention du moi*. Paris: Presses Universitaires de France, 2010.

Clark, William. *Academic Charisma and the Origins of the Research University*. Chicago: University of Chicago Press, 2006.

Coetzee, J. M. "Universities Head for Extinction." *Mail & Guardian*, November 1, 2013.

Collins, Randall. *The Sociology of Philosophies: A Global Theory of Intellectual Change*. Cambridge, MA: Belknap Press of Harvard University Press, 1998.

Crenshaw, Kimberlé. "Mapping the Margins: Intersectionality, Identity Politics, and Violence against Women of Color." *Stanford Law Review* 43 (1989): 1241–99.

Danquah, J. B. *The Akan Doctrine of God: A Fragment of Gold Coast Ethics and Religion*. London: Lutterworth Press, 1944.

Deleuze, Gilles, and Félix Guattari. *Qu'est-ce que la philosophie?* Paris: Éditions de Minuit, 1991.

Descartes, René. *Meditationes de prima philosophia*. In *Oeuvres*, edited by Charles Adam and Paul Tannery. Paris: L. Cerf, 1897–1913.

Dickie, George. *Art and the Aesthetic: An Institutional Analysis*. Ithaca, NY: Cornell University Press, 1974.

Dover, K. J. *Aristophanes: Clouds.* Oxford: Clarendon Press, 1970.

Eliot, T. S. "The Development of Leibniz's Monadism." *The Monist* 26 (December 1916): 534–56.

———. *Four Quartets.* New York: Houghton Mifflin Harcourt, 2014.

Elman, Benjamin A. *Civil Examinations and Meritocracy in Late Imperial China.* Cambridge, MA: Harvard University Press, 2013.

Endō, Shūsaku. *Silence.* Translated by William Johnston. New York: Taplinger Publishing, 1969 [1966].

Evans-Pritchard, E. E. *Witchcraft, Oracles, and Magic among the Azande.* Oxford: Clarendon Press, 1976 [1937].

Fisher, M.F.K. *Love in a Dish: And Other Culinary Delights.* Berkeley: Counterpoint, 2011.

Fissell, Mary. *Vernacular Bodies: The Politics of Reproduction in Early Modern England.* Oxford: Oxford University Press, 2004.

Friedman, Michael. "Extending the Dynamics of Reason: Generalizing a Post-Kuhnian Approach to the History and Philosophy of Science." Lecture given at the Max-Planck-Institut für Wissenschaftsgeschichte, Berlin, July 25, 2009.

Ganeri, Jonardon. *The Lost Age of Reason: Philosophy in Early Modern India, 1450–1700.* Oxford: Oxford University Press, 2011.

Gode, P. K. "Bernier and Kavindracarya Sarasvati at the Moghal Court." In *Studies in Indian Literary History,* vol. 2, by P. K. Gode, 364–79. Bombay: Baratiya Vidya Bhavan, 1954.

Goodman, Grant K. *Japan and the Dutch, 1600–1853.* London: Routledge, 2013.

Goody, Jack. *The Logic of Writing and the Organisation of Society.* Cambridge: Cambridge University Press, 1986.

Gyekye, Kwame. *An Essay on African Philosophical Thought: The Akan Conceptual Scheme.* Cambridge: Cambridge University Press, 1995 [1987].

Hadot, Pierre, *Philosophy as a Way of Life.* Translated by Michael Chase. Oxford: Blackwell, 1995.

Heilbron, J. L. *The Sun in the Church: Cathedrals as Solar Observatories.* Cambridge, MA: Harvard University Press, 2001.

Hersch, Jeanne. *L'étonnement philosophique: Une histoire de la philosophie.* Paris: Flammarion, 1993.

Hobbes, Thomas. *The English Works of Thomas Hobbes of Malmesbury.* Vol. 1. London: John Bohn, 1839 [1655].

Husserl, Edmund. *Cartesian Meditations.* Translated by D. Cairns. Dordrecht: Kluwer, 1960 [1931].

Hutchinson, Sharon E. *Nuer Dilemmas: Coping with Money, War, and the State.* Berkeley: University of California Press, 1996.

Jaspers, Karl. *Vom Ursprung und Ziel der Geschichte.* Zurich: Artemis Verlag, 1949.

Kagame, Alexis. *La philosophie Bantu comparée.* Paris: La Présence Africaine, 1976.

Kant, Immanuel. *Kants gesammelte Schriften.* Edited by Königlich Preussische Akademie der Wissenschaften. Berlin: Georg Reimer, 1902.

Karp, Ivan, and D. A. Masolo. *African Philosophy as Cultural Inquiry.* Bloomington: Indiana University Press, 2009.

Keats, John. *The Letters of John Keats.* Vol. 2, *1819–1821.* Cambridge: Cambridge University Press, 1958.

Kepler, Johannes. *Kepler's Somnium: The Dream; or, Posthumous Works on Lunar Astronomy.* Translated and edited by Edward Rosen. Madison: University of Wisconsin Press, 1967.

Knobe, Joshua, and Shaun Nichols. "An Experimental Philosophy Manifesto." In *Experimental Philosophy,* edited by Joshua Knobe and Shaun Nichols, 3–14. Oxford: Oxford University Press, 2007.

Krapf, J. Lewis. *Travels, Researches, and Missionary Labours, during an Eighteen Years' Residence in Eastern Africa, Together with Journeys to Jagga, Usambara, Ukambani, Shoa, Abessinia, and Khartum; and a Coasting Voyage from Mombaz to Cape Delgado ... With an Appendix Respecting the Snow-Capped Mountains of Eastern Africa.* London: Trübner, Paternoster Row, 1860.

Krauss, Lawrence M. *A Universe from Nothing: Why There Is Something Rather Than Nothing.* New York: Free Press, 2012.

Kretzmann, Paul. *John Ludwig Krapf: The Explorer-Missionary of Northeastern Africa.* Columbus, OH: The Book Concern, 1909.

Krishna, Daya. *Developments in Indian Philosophy from Eighteenth Century Onwards.* History of Science, Philosophy, and Culture in Indian Civilization, vol. 10, part 1. New Delhi: Centre for Studies in Civilization, 2001.

Laertius, Diogenes. *Lives of the Eminent Philosophers.* Edited and translated by R. D. Hicks. London: William Heinemann, 1925.

Lange, Laurent. "Journal du voyage de Laurent Lange à la Chine." In *Nouveaux mémoires sur l'état présent de la Grande Russie ou Moscovie*, vol. 2, by Friedrich-Christian Weber. Paris: Pissot, 1725.

Leibniz, Gottfried Wilhelm. *Discours sur la théologie naturelle des Chinois*. In *Gothofredi Guillelmi Leibnitii Opera Omnia*, vol. 4, edited by Louis Dutens. Geneva: De Tournes, 1768.

———. *La Monadologie*. Edited by M. T. Desdouits. Paris: Librairie Classiques, 1884 [1714].

———. *Novissima Sinica historiam nostri temporis illustrata*. Hannover: Förster, 1699.

———. *De novo antidysenterico americano*. In *Gothofredi Guilelmi Leibnitii Opera Omnia*, edited by Louis Dutens. Geneva: De Tournes, 1768.

———. *Die philosophischen Schriften von Gottfried Wilhelm Leibniz*, 6 vols. Edited by C. I. Gerhardt. Berlin, 1849–60.

———. *Sbornik pisem i memorialov Leïbnitsa otnosyashchikhsya k Rossii i Petru Velikomu*. Edited by V. I. Ger'e. Saint Petersburg, 1873.

Lennox, James G. "Putting Philosophy of Science to the Test: The Case of Aristotle's Biology." *PSA: Proceedings of the Biennial Meeting of the Philosophy of Science Association* 2 (1994): 239–47.

León-Portilla, Miguel. *La filosofía nahuatl estudiada en sus fuentes*. Mexico City: UNAM, 1993.

Lévi-Strauss, Claude. *La pensée sauvage*. Paris: Plon, 1962.

Lloyd, Geoffrey. " 'Philosophy': What Did the Greeks Invent and Is It Relevant to China?" *Extrême-Orient, Extrême-Occident* 27, no. 27 (2005): 149–59.

Lower, Richard. *Tractatus de corde: Item de motu & colore sanguinis et chyli in eum transitu*. London: Typis Jo. Redmayne Impensis Jacobi Allestry, 1669.

Ludolf, Hiob. *Historia Aethiopica, sive, Brevis et succincta descriptio regni Habessinorum*. Frankfurt: Joh. David Zunner, 1681.

Machery, Edouard, Ron Mallon, Shaun Nichols, and Stephen P. Stich. "Semantics, Cross-Cultural Style." *Cognition* 92, no. 3 (2004): 1–12.

Mandeville, Bernard. *The Fable of the Bees; or, Private Vices, Publick Benefits*. London: J. Tonson, 1729 [1714].

Mann, Michael. *The Dark Side of Democracy: Explaining Ethnic Cleansing*. Cambridge: Cambridge University Press, 2005.

Menn, Stephen. *Descartes and Augustine.* Cambridge: Cambridge University Press, 1998.

Merchant, Carolyn. *The Death of Nature: Women, Ecology, and the Scientific Revolution.* New York: HarperCollins, 1990 [1980].

Merrill, James. *The Changing Light at Sandover.* New York: Knopf Doubleday, 2011 [1982].

Montaigne, Michel de. *Les Essais.* Edited by Jean Céard et al. Paris: Hachette, 2002 [1580].

More, Henry. *Antidote against Atheism.* In *A Collection of Several Philosophical Writings of Dr. Henry More.* London, 1662.

Moretti, Franco. *Graphs, Maps, Trees: Abstract Models for a Literary History.* London: Verso, 2005.

Mungello, David E. *The Chinese Rites Controversy: Its History and Meaning.* Nettetal: Steyler Verlag, 1994.

Murray, Les. Interview with Dennis O'Driscoll. *Paris Review* 173 (Spring 2005).

Newman, William R. *Atoms and Alchemy: Chymistry and the Experimental Origins of the Scientific Revolution.* Chicago: University of Chicago Press, 2006.

———. *Promethean Ambitions: Alchemy and the Quest to Perfect Nature.* Chicago: University of Chicago Press, 2004.

Nietzsche, Friedrich. *Fragmente, 1875–1879,* vol. 2. Hamburg: Tredition Verlag, 2012.

———. "Der freieste Schriftsteller." *Menschliches Allzumenschliches II: Nachgelassene Fragmente, 1879–1879.* In *Werke: Kritische Gesamtausgabe,* 4.3. Edited by Giorgio Colli and Mazzino Montinari. Berlin: De Gruyter, 1967.

Nkrumah, Kwame. *Consciencism: Philosophy and Ideology for De-Colonization and Development with Particular Reference to the African Revolution.* New York: Monthly Review Press, 2009 [1970].

P., S. "French Politics: Trains, Strikes and Philosophy." *The Economist,* June 16, 2014. http://www.economist.com/blogs/charlemagne/2014/06/french-politics.

Paracelsus Theophrastus, and Valentin Weigel. *Philosophia Mystica, darinn begriffen Eilff unterschidene Theologico-Philosophische doch teutsche Tractätlein.* Neustadt, 1618.

Perry, Ralph Barton. *The Thought and Character of William James*. 2 vols. Boston: Little, Brown, 1935.

Popper, Karl. *Unended Quest: An Intellectual Autobiography*. LaSalle, IL: Open Court, 1976.

Pratt, Scott L. *Native Pragmatism: Rethinking the Roots of American Philosophy*. Bloomington: Indiana University Press, 2002.

Priest, Graham. "What Is Philosophy?" *Philosophy* 81, no. 316 (2006): 189–207.

Quine, W.V.O. *Ontological Relativity and Other Essays*. New York: Columbia University Press, 1969.

Radin, Paul. *Primitive Man as Philosopher*. Foreword by John Dewey. New York: D. Appleton, 1927.

Rasmussen, Knud. *Across Arctic America: Narrative of the Fifth Thule Expedition*. Chicago: University of Chicago Press, 1999 [1927].

Reichenbach, Hans. *Experience and Prediction: An Analysis of the Foundations and the Structure of Knowledge*. Chicago: University of Chicago Press, 1938.

Russell, Bertrand. *The History of Western Philosophy*. London: George Allen and Unwin, 1945.

Sahagún, Bernardino de. *The Florentine Codex: General History of the Things of New Spain*. Translated by Arthur J. O. Anderson and Charles E. Dibble, 12 vols. Salt Lake City: University of Utah Press, 2002.

Sahlins, Marshall. "Goodbye to Tristes Tropes: Ethnography in the Context of Modern World History." *Journal of Modern History* 65 (1993): 3–4.

Schmidt, Peter. "The Man Who Ranks Philosophy Departments Now Rankles Them, Too." *Chronicle of Higher Education*, September 26, 2014. http://chronicle.com/article/The-Man-Who-Ranks-Philosophy/149007/.

Shapin, Steven. *A Social History of Truth: Civility and Science in Seventeenth-Century England*. Chicago: University of Chicago Press, 1994.

Śiromaṇi, Raghunātha. *Inquiry into the True Nature of Things [Padārtha-tattva-nirūpaṇa-vyākhyā]*. Varanasi: Maha Mandalayantralaya, 1915.

Smith, Justin E. H. "Leibniz on Natural History and National History." *History of Science* 50, no. 4 (2012): 377–401.

Solomon, Frank L. *The Cord Keepers: Khipus and Cultural Life in a Peruvian Village*. Durham, NC: Duke University Press, 2004.

Sorabji, Richard. *Animal Minds and Human Morals: The Origins of the Western Debate.* Ithaca, NY: Cornell University Press, 1995.

———. *Self: Ancient and Modern Insights about Individuality, Life, and Death.* Chicago: University of Chicago Press, 2006.

Stanley, Jason. *Know How.* Oxford: Oxford University Press, 2011.

Sterne, Laurence. *The Life and Opinions of Tristram Shandy.* In *The Works of Laurence Sterne,* vol. 4. London, 1815.

Stewart, Matthew. *The Courtier and the Heretic: Leibniz, Spinoza, and the Fate of God in the Modern World.* New York: W. W. Norton, 2006.

Stremitel'nyï, Nyurgun Bootur. *Yakutskiï geroicheskiï epos Olonkho.* Translated by V. Derzhavin, general editor S. V. Mikhalkova. Yakutsk: Yakutskoe Knizhnoe Izdatel'stvo, 1982.

Taylor, Charles. *Multiculturalism and "The Politics of Recognition."* Princeton, NJ: Princeton University Press, 1992.

———. *Sources of the Self: The Making of the Modern Identity.* Cambridge, MA: Harvard University Press, 1989.

Tempels, Placide. *La philosophie bantoue.* Elisabethville: Lovania, 1945; translated as *Bantu Philosophy,* Paris: Présence Africaine, 1959.

Thompson, D'Arcy Wentworth. *On Growth and Form.* Cambridge: Cambridge University Press, 1945 [1917].

Turner, James. *Philology: The Forgotten Origins of the Modern Humanities.* Princeton, NJ: Princeton University Press, 2014.

Valéry, Paul. *Charmes; ou, Poèmes.* Paris: Éditions de la Nouvelle revue française, 1922.

Venel, Gabriel François, and César Chesneau Dumarsais. "Philosophe." In *L'Encyclopédie ou Dictionnaire raisonné des sciences, des arts et des métiers.* 1st ed., vol. 12. Paris, 1751.

Vico, Giambattista. *Principi di Scienza nuova di Giambattista Vico: D'intorno alla comune natura delle nazioni.* Naples: Stamperia Muziana, 1744 [1725].

Walpole, Horace. *The Letters of Horace Walpole, Fourth Earl of Oxford.* Oxford: Clarendon Press, 1903.

White, David Gordon. *The Yoga Sutra of Patanjali: A Biography.* Princeton, NJ: Princeton University Press, 2014.

Whitman, Walt. *The Collected Works of Walt Whitman.* Vol. 2, *Prose Works 1892.* Edited by Gay Wilson Allen and Sculley Bradley. New York: New York University Press, 1964.

———. *Leaves of Grass*. New York, 1855.

———. *Walt Whitman: Selected Poems, 1855–1892*. Edited by Gary Schmidgall. New York: Stonewall Inn Editions, 1999.

Williams, Bernard. "On Hating and Despising Philosophy." *London Review of Books* 18, no. 8 (1996): 17–18.

Wilshire, Bruce. *The Primal Roots of American Philosophy: Pragmatism, Phenomenology, and Native American Thought*. University Park: Pennsylvania State University Press, 2000.

Wittgenstein, Ludwig. *Philosophical Investigations*. Translated by G.E.M. Anscombe. 3rd ed. New York: Macmillan, 1968 [1953].

Wolff, Christian. *Philosophia rationalis sive Logica: Methodo scientifica pertractata et ad usum scientiarum atque vitae aptata*. Frankfurt and Leipzig: Officina Libraria Rengeriana, 1728.

Wollheim, Richard. *Germs: A Memoir of Childhood*. Emeryville, CA: Shoemaker and Hoard, 2006.

Wright, Thomas, ed. *A Selection of Latin Stories from Manuscripts of the Thirteenth and Fourteenth Centuries*. London: Percy Society, 1842.

Wylie, Alison. *Thinking from Things: Essays in the Philosophy of Archaeology*. Berkeley: University of California Press, 2002.

Zhuangzi. *The Essential Writings, with Selections from Traditional Commentaries*. Translated by Brook Ziporyn. Indianapolis: Hackett Classics, 2009.

Zubrow, Ezra, and Elizabeth C. Blake. "The Origin of Music and Rhythm." In *Archaeoacoustics*, edited by Chris Scarre and Graeme Lawson, 117–26. Cambridge: McDonald Institute for Archaeological Research, 2006.

INDEX

academic philosophy, 53, 105, 155, 169, 190–92

actuality, 5–6

African American traditions, 76–77

African philosophy, 98–100

Albertus Magnus, 31, 40

alchemists, 107–8

Alexander the Great, 39

Amane, Nishi, 56–57

Amazonia, precontact, 116–18

analytic philosophy: continental compared to, 19, 193–201, 205–6, 215, 222; language as concern of, 179; science in relation to, 26. *See also* Anglo-American philosophy

analytic political philosophy, 196

ancient Greece, philosophy grounded in, 2–3

Anglo-American philosophy, 7, 76, 78–79. *See also* analytic philosophy

animals, 40

Anscombe, G.E.M., 166

anthropology, 72, 75, 79, 102, 195, 208

Aquinas, Thomas, 40, 177

archeology, 207–9

Arendt, Hannah, 79

Aristophanes, 22, 153

Aristotle, vii, 215; accomplishments of, 11; Arabic thought and, 132; and cosmopolitanism, 88; and Homer as authority, 69; and life sciences, 14, 50; marriage of, 40, 42; and nature as authority, 162–63; on nature of philosophy, 7–8, 238; on philosophers, 66–67; and Phyllis, 38–42; on poetry and history, 5–6, 22; religious traditions' incorporation of, 212; and science, 31, 33, 50; and sexuality, 39–43

art, 193–94, 197–200

Ascetic, 159–89; characterization of, 15–16, 183–84; narrative of, 169–73; philosophers as, 42–43

Aśoka, 86

astronomy, 44–47

Lower, Richard, 187
Lucian of Samosata, *True History*, 44
Lucretius, *De rerum natura*, 135
Ludolf, Hiob, 94

MacLaine, Shirley, 154
magic, 44–47, 52, 196
magnetism, 35
Mandarin, 190–222; characterization of, 16–17, 198–99
Mann, Michael, 87
Mao Zedong, 154
Marxism, 100, 165, 168
materialism, 100–102
McCarthy, Cormac, 146
McDowell, John, 151
mechanism, 26
meditation, 166
Merchant, Carolyn, 47–48
Merrill, James, 52, 235
metaphors, 136–39
metaphysical poetry, 213
metaphysics, Bantu, 83
missionaries, Christian, 81–82, 93–96
money, 17, 20, 223, 225–26, 235–36
Montaigne, Michel de, 124–27, 223, 239
More, Henry, 7, 151–52, 214; *Antidote against Atheism*, 129–31, 151
Moretti, Franco, 209, 211
mountain, definition of, 217–22
Mount Kilimanjaro, 218–20
Murray, Les, 79
mystery, 4
myth, 4

Nagel, Thomas, 79
Nahuatl, 59
narrative voice, 124–35, 157
Native Americans, 147
natural history, 6, 30
natural philosophy, 6, 50–52; Bacon and, 27–28; history of, 235; Kepler and, 46–48; negative view of, 23–24; Socrates and, 30; Whitman's notion of, 145–46
natural theology, 88–89, 93
nature: hylozoic view of, 100–101; mystery of, 35; philosophical investigation of, 14, 22–23; universality of, 88. *See also* natural philosophy
Navya Nyāya (New Inference), 180–81
necessary truths, 216–22
neo-Platonism, 166
Netherlands, 55
Newman, William R., 52
Newton, Isaac, 93, 100
Nicomachus (Aristotle's son), 40
Nietzsche, Friedrich: as Ascetic, 15–16; on good and evil, 141, 147; on marital status of philosophers, 42–43; on science, 25; on Sterne's *Tristram Shandy*, 133
Nkrumah, Kwame, 100–102
nonideal political theory, 196
normal science, 16

Olonkho (Yakut epic), 136